WITHDRAWN

THE COTTON REGENCY

The Northern Merchants and Reconstruction, 1865-1880

The Cotton Regency

*The Northern Merchants and
Reconstruction, 1865-1880*

by

George Ruble Woolfolk
Prairie View A. & M. College

BOOKMAN ASSOCIATES

New York

To
Theodosia
and
Douglass Geraldyne,
The Women of Conception and Fulfillment,
This Writing Is Humbly Dedicated

Preface

Students of the history of the Civil War in America have long known that the conflict marked the dividing line between an agrarian era and an industrial age. Charles A. Beard saw the war producing a "Second American Revolution". Yet exactly how the "revolution" was accomplished and who accomplished it has been only partially documented. This study is an attempt to document in part the first stage of the rising business civilization after the Civil War.

The problem of answering critically "who" and "how" for the Second American Revolution involves a critical interpretation of contemporary regional theories and the application of them to historical analysis. The study proceeds upon the hypothesis that the dominant groups in contiguous regions might combine with one another to control other regions. This is the essence of sectionalism as a force in American history.

The problem of sources has been a difficult one. Bits of evidence to be correlated and winnowed may be found in the manuscripts of hundreds of businessmen involved in the movement. The relating of such data to the traditional sources of historical evidence was a task for patient research. I have found one solution to the problem of the evidence in the local and national Chamber of Commerce and Board of Trade records. These provided a central thread around which the traditional sources might be grouped to build a continuous narrative.

With a regional hypothesis and a consistent central thread of evidence this study seeks to demonstrate that the Civil War introduced group democracy as a new pattern in American politics. Formerly considering themselves out of politics as a group, their war experiences rapidly matured the nascent collective political consciousness of American merchant-capitalists. Having successfully put down the masters of the agrarian era, the American bourgeoisie emerged with both the skills and collective experience necessary to begin a new economic national-

7

ism and fit the disorganized American pattern into the bourgeois mould.

At first northeastern business looked upon "King Cotton" as the means by which the new economic orientation might be underwritten. Failing in this, a new idea of national and local pressure politics, springing from the ranks of western urban businessmen, was accepted by the business interests of the nation as a means of controlling the new order. The problem of fitting the staple economy of the South into the national pattern, while no longer of first importance, provided the excuse for expanding communications and general business facilities. Upon these, in part, the wealth of both the northeastern and middle western cities—in fierce competition with each other—was built. The fifteen years covered by this study marked the period of purely commercial exploitation of the South in the interest of the regions to which it was tributary. After 1880 industrial exploitation matured, and thus opened another story.

To present this thesis the writer has divided the study into seven chapters. Chapter I, entitled "Who Is this New Man?", is designed to present the urban regionalist basis of the study and to examine the group of men who make up the organized masters of capital—especially their socio-economic origins, stages of development, time and place of "arrival", and the probable implications of their philanthropic and other extra occupational interest. This chapter deals primarily with the capitalists in the North-eastern Atlantic seaboard; and the same is attempted for those in the mid-west in Chapter VI, "Iron Sluice Gates."

Chapter II, "The Boston, Philadelphia, North-western Alliance", attempts to relate the interest of the organized masters of capital to the traditional political story of Reconstruction. Here is presented an east-west capitalists' alliance along the same lines as that of the radical republicans, and the economic ideas and interest that undergirded that alliance. The Legislative program underlying that alliance, called "The Cotton Policy", is set forth; and the reasons for its eventual failure, after a precarious interlude of doubtful harmony among members of the alliance, are pointed out.

Chapter III, "The Famine Year and After", sets forth the immediate Southern conditions that contributed to the failure of the Cotton Policy. The Issue of "Protection" as a step toward economic nationalism is elaborated here; and the reaction of the English financial community to its defeat, hinted at in Chapter II above, is set forth. The meaning of the struggle for "Protection" to the future of the American economy is explained.

Chapter IV, "Creating the Sellers' Market", is designed to show the futile efforts of the Southerners to solve their post-war problems of land use, population and fluid capital. Thus the stage is set for the efforts of the north-eastern and mid-western capitalists to begin the exploitation of the region, once they had disavowed their own blunders in the vicious politics of the immediate post-war Reconstruction. Here is set forth the idea that the cumulative effects of post-war Southern socio-economic problems was to fasten a diabolical system of credit upon the region which made the South open territory for the commercial ambitions of North and West.

Chapter V, "Westward the Star of Empire", is designed to show how the miscalculations of radical capitalists in the "Cotton Policy", though bringing misunderstanding among them which seemed at one point fatal, served to align the nationalists against the internationalists of New York City in an attempt to break the hold of foreign merchants in the empire city upon the American economy. The capitalists around Philadelphia found the instrument in "Direct Importations". Forced to favor other cities to get this program of local vengeance translated into national policy, nationalists on the Atlantic seaboard called in the aid of the western urban capitalists, who themselves had ambitions for recognition through the creation of a national organization. By making the western commercial centers original ports of entry through federal legislation, eastern capitalists gave the western capitalists equality of bargaining power for the cotton staple.

Chapters VI, "Iron Sluice Gates" and VII, "Knights of the Bag", tell the story of the efforts of the Mid-western capitalists to exploit the Southern territory, especially after their centers had become ports of entry. Their instruments in this fight for commercial hegemony were railroads and traveling salesmen. The factors favoring the winning of that fight are set forth, and the incidents accompanying this successful struggle with the older commercial centers of the north-eastern seaboard are elaborated. They indeed became co-regents of the "Cotton Kingdom".

I wish here to express my appreciation of assistance given to me by Professor William B. Hesseltine and the Department of History in the University of Wisconsin. I am also indebted to the Historical Society of Wisconsin; the Ohio State Archaeological and Historical Society; the Historical and Philosophical Society of Ohio; the Baker Library of Harvard University; the Filson Club of Louisville, Kentucky; the Library of the University of Louisville; the Louisville and Nashville Railroad; the Cincinnati Southern Railroad; the Library of Congress; the National Archives; the Library of the Bureau of Railroad Economics; the Library of the Chamber of Commerce of the United States; and the National Gallery of Art, Smithsonian Institute. I finally wish to thank my wife for her inspiration in the writing of this study and for help in compiling the bibliography. The writer wishes to take full responsibility for any errors that may appear in this work.

G. R. W.

Table of Contents

List of Illustrations

Lorin Blodget
Philadelphia

John A. Stevens
New York

*Courtesy of New York
Chamber of Commerce*

Lorenzo Sabine
Boston

John A. Gano
Cincinnati

Hamilton Hill
Boston

George H. Morgan
St. Louis

1. Who Is This New Man?

There are in every war seeds of revolution.[1] The Civil War was no exception to this rule. The agrarian atom of American life, smashed under the white heat of civil conflict, released the dynamic forces of a group democracy. The Republican Party, conceived in political disaffection and dedicated to the principle of expediency and opportunism in political maneuver, was the agent of the new revolution. Sobered by the fact that theirs was a sectional party on taking the reins of national administration in 1860, Republicans openly sought the advice and support of the budding business power. Much was at stake in the decision to throw the iron dice of war and the fledgling radicalism was in need of friends.

Whatever misgivings Lincoln might have had relative to the ability of this administration to present a united northern front was certainly colored by the neutrality—nay, often thinly veiled hostility—of the three great commercial centers of the northeast, Boston, Philadelphia, and New York.[2] In these three commercial centers, businessmen not only had vast interests at stake in the South, but also had made a fetish of abstaining as a group from political participation. In January of 1861, while the Southern states were actually seceding and the politicians were searching heaven and earth for formulae, representative organizations of businessmen, whatever the opinion of their individual members, held with the Boston Board of Trade:[3]

> But well enough do we know, and rigidly enough shall we observe, the rule which forbids the discussion of political topics in these rooms.

Indeed, while the secession issue was in the valley of decision, masters of capital calmly discussed tariffs, reciprocity treaties, boots and shoes, the iron and coal trade, the international general average and other such neutral subjects.

Early in the morning of April 12, the aged Edmund Ruffin, who had asked for the honor in recognition of his long agitation for Southern independence, touched the match to the first cannon shot of the Civil War. On April 15, 1861, President Lincoln, with an unfailing sense of the dramatic, called for seventy-five thousand volunteers. The "out-of-politics" position of the masters of capital vanished in an upsurge of patriotic fervor. For five days after the fall of Sumter, Boston had been in excitement; and on the 18th, with their rooms in the Merchants Exchange on State Street decked with flags, the Boston Board of Trade met in special session to express an opinion. Branding Sumter "The most cowardly act recorded of 'gentlemen' in all history," Boston's capitalists thought:

> That in the present crisis of our national affairs, it behooves all good citizens to express their devotion to the cause of the country

and that it was

> peculiarly incumbent upon all associated bodies, and especially those connected with commercial affairs, in the most public manner to let their views be known to the government.

Boston's capitalists expressed "entire sympathy" with Lincoln's acts in suppressing the rebellion and recommended the most "vigorous measures" in putting down the Confederacy. Their interests were seriously endangered by Mr. Davis' use of Privateers; but they took comfort both in the ready response of the "Citizen soldiery" to the call for volunteers and in the bankers' consent to make state and federal loans. Ere long, organized Boston merchants asked protection from the Secretary of the Navy for ships which the outbreak of hostilities caught on the way South. Though Secretary Welles promised everything, many of the cargoes were lost. With New England's shipbuilding interest in mind, Boston's capitalists suggested to the President the immediate purchase of ten or twenty armed clippers and ocean steamers to protect the Northern Coast and blockade the Southern coast.

The first few weeks of the war found Boston's masters of capital no longer "out of politics". They were in it and learning fast. Soon Boston's Board of Trade opened its unsuccessful warlong fight with the quartermaster-general for a large slice of government uniform contracts. Moreover, throughout the war New England capitalists continuously clamored for the defense of Boston harbor, especially as the reports of the depredations of the *Alabama* rolled in, and for the protection of merchant shipping. Many of them too, like Edward Silas Tobey, went to Washington to serve on special commissions connected with the executive departments.

Like Boston, America's first port city, long in doubt as to its allegiance, was brought up sharply by the boom of the guns at Sumter. Members of the New York Chamber of Commerce repaired to their rooms at William and Cedar streets after lunch on Friday April 19, 1861.[4] President Pelatiah Perit opened this special meeting, which was so well attended that all of the rooms had to be thrown into one, by declaring a special dispensation for political discussion. He pointed out that the secession crisis had forced Lincoln to call for volunteers, and "as an influential body of men in this commercial centre we are bound to respond heartily to the call."

In the discussion of issues, President Perit hoped that men of the counting houses would forget party distinctions and all unite to defend the Constitution. "All which has been ours in time past, and which constitutes our hope for time to come, is at stake", declared the Chamber's aging President.

> Under the specious name of secession, traitors have seized the public property, have attacked the national forts, and are now threatening the national capitol. The prime of our young men are marching to its defense. Let us

meet the crisis like patriots and men. There can be no
neutrality now—we are either for the country or for its
enemies.

George Opdyke, mayor of New York, claimed that secession
presented only the alternatives of "Anarchy and Depotism"
against "Liberty, Order, and Law", and asked the Chamber
to endorse Mr. Lincoln's action and lend financial support to
the government. The Chamber accepted these ideas with rous-
ing cheers, and, in the face of contrary predictions by European
capitalists,[5] appointed P. Perit, M. Taylor, G.S. Coe, F.A.
Palmer, John J. Astor, W.H. Aspenwall, Stewart Brown, A.
Belmont a committee to secure subscriptions for the balance
of an $8,000,000 federal loan. William E. Dodge presented a
scheme to raise funds to aid volunteers and their families. On
the very day Lincoln took action, the Chamber suggested, for
the defense of American commerce against Davis' "Privateers",
the blockade of all the ports of the states "claiming to have
seceded . . ." Secretary of State Seward—with never a glance
at the profits hidden under patriotism—hastened to express
Lincoln's gratitude to the Chamber for its prompt and willing
support.

As the crisis progressed toward war, the rooms at William
and Cedar Streets became the clearing house for much of the
high politics of the war. At the meeting of July 3, 1861, the
Chamber, like Boston's Board, began a clamor for the defense
of New York's harbor, which was to grow more insistent as
Davis' privateers raided with more boldness.[6] While New York's
organized capitalists again and again renewed their pledge of
faith in and aid to Lincoln's administration, they did not fail,
over the years, to give the most detailed advice to Cabinet
members, the President, and Congress. The Lincoln administration had gained an ally whose fund of knowledge and economic
powers were boundless.

In still a third commercial center, Philadelphia, the opening
of the "brothers war" shook capitalists from their "out-of-

politics" position.[7] Men of the business community promptly laid aside party differences and united before the growing fear for the existence of the government. The Philadelphia Board of Trade, "as the organ of a great commercial community deemed it a duty" to declare in solemn manner their purpose to "sustain the government of the Union against all enemies and at all hazards." A meeting was called for the purpose to which all citizens were invited. Patriotic resolutions and memorials, similar to those passed in the other two commercial centers of the Northeast, were forwarded to the Secretary of State. Philadelphia's Board Secretary, Lorin Blodget, was highly satisfied with Seward's answer. Philadelphia capitalists early took pride in the number of soldiers the city sent to the field, and bore its business and financial sacrifices with a becoming modesty, touched with a slight sense of pique at standing second to New York.

On the question of privateering, the Philadelphia capitalists refused to act with the New York capitalists in their memorial to Congress. The Philadelphia Board did ask the Secretary of the Navy for the protection of the exposed entrance of Delaware Bay and the port of Philadelphia. Gideon Welles answered that, at the moment, the Treasury department would take the responsibility for defending the ports. The capitalists of the city of "Brotherly Love" had to draw what sense of security they could from the presence of a Revenue cutter, appropriately named "Dobbin", which cruised the bay armed only with a rifle gun.

War had indeed brought revolution. For better or worse, organized capitalists threw off their pre-war reticence and soon exhibited a remarkable political precociousness. It soon became clear that here was a new estate in the political scheme which must be seriously reckoned with. The Republican Party, faced with the greatest crisis in the history of the nation, had the good sense to give that estate a position of first rank. This alliance of convenience beween political opportunists and organized business "on-the-make", as later events were to prove, was not an unmixed blessing. Yet the recognition by organized businessmen of their latent power was inevitable and was a symbol of the nation in transition.

The change in the status of organized businessmen served to reemphasize—the protestations of unity behind the government to the contrary notwithstanding—the cleavages already existing in the political complexion of the Northeast. It was only natural that, with the introduction of a new estate into politics, the hidden differences within that estate would become the bone of political contention. These issues were not new. They had been fought over since the era of Jackson and Clay. The only change brought by the new estate in politics was a change in the frame of reference, a new point of departure. Theretofore, the basic issues of protection to nascent industries, free trade, and the distribution of Western trade among the Eastern centers either had been subordinated to agrarian issues or given a peculiar agrarian twist. Now businessmen simply restated these basic issues in business terms, and raised them to categorical imperatives in high politics. The real tragedy of Reconstruction was that the South and the social experiment of adjusting a slave population to freedom were caught in the middle of—nay, often became the weapon in—the battles of the giants of the new order.

The men of capital, who determined the basic issues that ran through the war and emerged to full status at its close, were the products of a growing urban dynamic.[8] Associated in the great cities, these sons of the countinghouse already thought of their cities as centers of commercial empires. Their cities were rapidly becoming national rather than sectional institutions. The flowering of their greatness was coeval with the maturing issues of the sectional conflict. On the morrow of the war, these clusters of countinghouses called cities would found their development upon the occupation of the great West, the rehabilitation of the postwar South, and in all sections, on an application of business enterprise to the exploitation of natural resources such as the world had never known. Transportation facilities, industrial combinations, financial power, legislative favors—these were the weapons for supremacy in the hands of the rival urban Regionalists for the building of a new society.

The relation of the urban dynamic to regional exploitation was apparent long before the sectional conflict reached crisis stage. Pennsylvania's Philadelphia was the nation's first commercial city during the Revolutionary era. But, by the coming of the Civil War, New York City held undisputed sway as America's leading commercial city.[9] Pennsylvanians, on the other hand, turned within to find wealth underground—iron, coal, and eventually, petroleum. Before the Civil War, though textiles continued a significant industrial interest, iron and anthracite coal were Pennsylvania's great staples.

The first great impulse to the production of crude iron on a large scale came in the United States with the successful use of anthracite coal as fuel.[10] Since the site of the industry and its growth were governed by anthracite, the two decades before the Civil War found eastern Pennsylvania the main producing locality and Philadelphia the central market. Proximity to the seaboard made foreign competition easy, except so far as it was hampered by the tariff duties; and the very existence of the iron industry was felt to depend on the maintenance of protection. Out at Chicago, Pennsylvania politicos had demanded this iron pound of flesh as the sine quo non of supporting Lincoln in 1860,[11] and the Morill Act quickly followed the victory at the polls. Masters of capital associated in the Philadelphia Board of Trade nailed the banner of "protection" to their mast, and it became the basic motif of their economic and political regionalism in the critical postwar years.[12]

Boston capitalists, finding themselves outdistanced by New Yorkers in the race for commercial supremacy, had sought con-

solation in a positive attempt to control the economic life of
New England.[13] Merchants in the Athens of America, like
Philadelphia capitalists, had not, for this reason, completely
abandoned the middleman function, neither had they lost interest in trade with the South.[14] Confronted with the superior
facilities of, and the capital available within the region of the
port of New York,[15] associated Boston capitalists buttressed
their waning commercial fortunes by becoming "the seat of
ownership and management" of the diverse industry and communication facilities of New England.[16]

The great staple of New England was the product of her
looms. From the War of 1812 to 1860 the textile industry,
especially cotton cloth, had grown apace under the protective
system which prevailed from 1816 to 1842; nor did it break
stride under the moderate duties from 1846 to 1860.[17] Indeed
production reached such levels that exports of cheap cottons,
the strongest branch of the industry, remained considerable long
after the Civil War.[18] When, therefore, during the Civil War
the price of raw and manufactured cotton soared and the
industry was stimulated, New England politico-economic regionalists began to view all issues through the spindles and
shuttles of their looms. The ideological cloak behind which
New England capitalists hid their pragmatic regionalism placed
them in a position to become the make weight in the growing
rivalry between Philadelphians and New Yorkers. The attempt
of New York capitalists to use the Federal government in an
effort to corner the Western trade in 1863, forced Boston
merchants to join hands with those of Philadelphia and the
River cities, Cincinnati and St. Louis.

New York City, the seat of the Chamber of Commerce
of the State of New York, was the chief trading center of the
United States.[19] From the completion of the Erie Canal to
1860, New York capitalists had forged ahead of their rivals
to place the Empire City in the first position in the middleman
function for both the West and the South.[20] The city became

the center of great wealth, and, by the same token the banking capital of the nation.[21]

However, the city's position depended to a great extent upon the connections of its merchants with England and Western Europe. England, by the grace of Sir Robert Peel and Gladstone, had turned toward free trade. New York capitalists must of necessity pay court to the same idea if their contacts with English capitalists, especially in the disposal of cotton, were to be maintained. By the same token, New York capitalists in their capacity as middlemen were sympathetic with the interest of the Southern states wing of their cotton triangle.[22] After the Civil War broke the hold of the Southern politicos on the Federal government, the attempt of New York capitalists to restore their economic control of the South under the conditions of the pre-war political formula placed them across the path of the economic nationalist of Philadelphia and Boston, who in turn joined the radical republicans to gain their ends through control of the Federal government.

The new urban impulse had already created an inter-regional imperialism out of the Northeast.[23] The South and the West paid before the Civil War $50,000,000 in tribute to the countinghouses of the Northeast for the privilege of purchasing their protected manufactures. West and South also paid an untold sum in making possible the far flung commercial activities of the Northeast. The agrarian character of the Southern economy made it impossible for them to do otherwise. But as the sectional conflict waxed, the political and economic complexion of the West took on special importance.[24] There the activity of the "New" native capitalists was raising the section rapidly in relative power in the Union. The section already possessed a balance of power, and was expected in no short time to become the dominant political influence in the nation. Once established it would be so.

The basis for an East-West community of interest was early apparent. As early as 1850 Ohio stood next to Pennsylvania in the production of pig iron. The state's mines were situated east of the Scioto. Metal deposits in Missouri also were beginning to be exploited and ore deposits in northern Michigan were known to have possibilities by the mid-century.[25] Besides this, the West was the scene of development of considerable manufacturing by the opening of the Civil War. These factors, accompanied by the growth of East-West canal and railroad facilities, tended to create a positive community of interest between capitalists of the Northeast and those in the lake and river country beyond the Allegheny Mountains.[26]

The nature of western agrarian staples also served to develop a trans-Allegheny regionalism. The production of breadstuffs was supplemented by the production of wool. As late as the early forties, wool growing was still an important part of the economy of New England.[27] However, changes in the protective tariff during the forties and the advantages of cheaper land in the West destroyed the profits of sheep raising and transferred the area of concentration of the industry from western New England and New York to western Pennsylvania, Ohio, and Michigan. Northeastern Ohio and adjacent districts of Michigan and Pennsylvania quickly became the center for raising that most difficult of all sheep, the Merino. Ohio, where considerable parts of the state are hilly and easily eroded, was especially adapted to sheep raising. In Ohio, under frontier conditions and greatly intensified by the demand for wool during the Civil War, wool growing was clung to tenaciously and became the basis of an intense and uncompromising demand for protection.

The urban dynamic found its regional expression in the lives of as hardy a group of resourceful, aggressive new men as the American scene has produced. From every walk of life, and usually from obscure origins, came these new men. Educated for the most part in the school of experience, these men evidenced a surprising versatility not only in their chosen field of trade, but also in all of the arts of city building and refinement. They had all of the passion of the bourgeoisie the world over for order, education, philanthropy, the encouragement of the useful arts, religion, and social responsibility. This sense of social responsibility, confined at first to the cities, burst forth under the impact of the sectional crisis into its post-war pattern of inter-regional control.[28]

Associated capitalists in old Philadelphia, James C. and Thomas C. Hand, Christian J. Hoffman, and John H. Michener were typical of the group of men of the new order.[29] However, the Quaker city had no greater son than Frederick Fraley.[30] Financier, founder of Franklin Institute and Gerard College, trustee of the University of Pennsylvania, Fraley was educated in the city schools and read law for his own gratification. He served as city councilman and was instrumental in solving Philadelphia's debt and consolidation problem in 1837 and 1854, respectively. This member of the American Philosophical Society was in the forefront of the rising politics of business. One of the incorporators of the Philadelphia Board of Trade in 1838, he also served in the State Senate as a Whig. When the hour of revolution came, Fraley was on hand to help found both the Union Club and Union League in Philadelphia. He went up to Boston in 1868 to help with the organization of the National Board of Trade, and remained its President from that date to 1898.

Israel W. Morris combined success in the anthracite industry with success as a historian.[31] Liberally educated, Morris devoted his talents as engineer to anthracite mining in Schuylkill County and was recognized as a leader in the industry before the Civil War. Associated with Robert Hare Powel in anthracite and bituminous trade, Morris spent much time in Washington, in connection with the preparation of tariff bills bearing upon the industry. Combining interest in coal and the Lehigh Valley Railroad after the War, Morris retired in 1905 to indulge his taste for rare books and membership in the Pennsylvania Historical Society, American Philosophical Society,

Society of Mining Engineers, and various others. Morris continued his directorship of Gerard Trust of which his son, Effingham, was president.

However, Samual Vaughn Merrick, grandson of a London merchant, was more closely associated with the imperialism of the Quaker city. Educated in common schools, he reached the eminence of the Southwork Iron Foundry by way of apprenticeship to a wine merchant and the manufacture of fire engines. This leading American Iron monger produced steam hammers, sugar refining apparatus, and machinery for ships long before the Civil War.[32]

John Price Wetherill, Philadelphia's great representative to the national businessmen's conclaves, showed all of the interest in the nation's industrial progress as his great ancestor, Samuel Wetherill, four generations removed.[33] Ejected by the "Friends" for his enthusiasm for the Patriot cause Samuel helped organize the nationalistic "United Company of Philadelphia for the Establishment of American Manufactures" in 1775; and the need for dye for his textiles led this Wetherill, by accident, to found the family interest in Drugs and Chemicals. John Price's father, a Whig and personal friend of Henry Clay, was a member of many of America's leading scientific societies and some foreign. John Wetherill faced the era of the new politics of business as the inheritor of a great tradition.

At a crossroads of the world, the international capitalists of New York City were advantageously situated for an aggressive regionalism. The acknowledged first city of commerce and finance of the nation, New York's bustling countinghouses attracted as irresistibly vigorous, enterprising men as they did the trade of America's West and South, and the mundane and exotic of Europe and Asia. It was the goods laid down on the wharves of this magic city that created these new men and made possible the impenetrable web of commerce, finance, manufacturing, communication, and philanthropy concentrated in the ranks of the associated capitalists. Preceded by the generation of John Jacob Astors, John Alsops, and Peter Coopers, the new men, thrown so suddenly into the open arena of national politics, were the inheritors of the best traditions of self-made men.[34] They were typical Americans. Hard work and trading instincts, sharpened in a market where no one need fail, gave them their wealth; which in time prepared them for the politics of the new nation.

From the ranks of the grocery trade came some of the New York's capitalist-politicians. Peer of them all was the millionaire merchant-statesmen Edwin Denison Morgan.[35] Sprung from poor New England parents and self-educated, Morgan rose from a clerkship in his uncle's Hartford grocery and retired in 1849 from the presidency of the giant E. B. Morgan and Company. Whig State Senator, Commissioner of Immigration, manager of Frémont's and Lincoln's presidential campaign, Morgan was by the time of the crisis Republican Governor of New York. Lincoln made him Major General for the Department of New York for recruiting. Though offered the Secretaryship of the Treasury in 1865 by Lincoln and later by Chester A. Arthur, Morgan declined and terminated his governmental services after serving in the Senate from 1863 to 1869.

George Opdyke overshadows Morgan. Sprung from a New Jersey farming family, Opdyke's apprenticeship took him to Cleveland, New Orleans, and back to New York where he became a wholesale clothing manufacturer and retailer with branches in Memphis and Charleston.[36] Adding imported dry goods to his interest, Opdyke was a millionaire by 1853. Contrary to the family Whiggery, Opdyke came to his support of Lincoln out at Chicago through Anti-Slavery Jacksonianism, and the Free Soil Party. This "lay" economist not only made uniforms for the Union Army, but as New York City's War Mayor, stood inflexible during the riots of those who did not wish to put them on. George Opdyke's postwar career was divided between interest in municipal reform, his bank established in 1869, and the new politics of business.

But William H. Vanderbilt was more closely connected with the city's aggressive regionalism.[37] Finishing his education in Daniel Drew's banking house, this eldest son of the fabulous "Commodore" survived a health setback to build a giant chain of railways westward. From the combination of the Hudson River and New York Central, this projector of Grand Central Station soon assumed control of the Chicago and Northwestern, the Chicago, St. Paul, Minneapolis and Omaha, and in a bold stroke, the West Shore and Nickleplate roads. Surviving the strikes of '77 and the Granger agitation, Vanderbilt could retire and indulge his interest in the College of Physicians and Surgeons of his city, his father's interest in Nashville's Vanderbilt University, and other philanthropic pursuits.

The rank and file of lifelong merchants proved just as versatile in combining interest in banking, insurance, communications, and pious philanthropy with their broad-based national and international mercantile pursuits. Peer of them all was William Earl Dodge.[38] Serving an apprenticeship as drygoods clerk and New York buyer for his father's cotton factory, Dodge moved to New York City in 1825. He combined a family and business interest with Anson Phelps with lumber interests in Pennsylvania, Michigan, Georgia, Texas, and Canada. Dodge also helped create the great Scranton, Pennsylvania, Iron Works, and Brass and Copper Works in Ansonia, Connecticut. Director of the Erie, the New Jersey Central, Delaware-Lackawanna and Western, and Texas railroads, Dodge helped with the Atlantic Cable and sat on the boards of Mutual Life, United States Trust, and Western Union. Dodge went as a delegate to the "peace conference" in 1860 and entered the 39th Congress as a "Protection-restorationist". Dodge's philanthropic interest included Temperance, American Bible and Tract Societies, Y. M. C. A., Presbyterian Foreign Missions Board, the Sunday School Union, and theological training for young ministers in the West. Dodge also shared President Grant's interest in the Indian; he not only aided Negro education by endowing Lincoln

University, but left considerable sums for the training of Negro teachers.

Boston, the Athens of America, drew like a magnet aspiring capitalists in the New England hinterlands. Here the Yankee capitalist might bask in the fading glory of two old traditions. There was the great and glorious annals of merchants who went down to sea in fabled ships to the far corners of the Orient and Occident. And then there was the tradition of moral and cultural dominance over the nation by that inner Boston which began at the Athenaeum on Beacon Hill and ended at the Historical Society's building in the Fenway. From the school of hard-knocks in Maine, New Hampshire, Vermont, and Massachusetts, these new men came to make their mark in the countinghouses and then retire to the Valhalla of the Historical Society; for in Boston it was possible to participate in a rather aggressive politico-economic and cultural regionalism.

Among no group of associated capitalists in the nation was the tradition of great secretary stronger than in Boston.[39] Lorenzo Sabine and Hamilton Andrews Hill dominated the new politics of business in a statesmanlike way from the seat of Secretary of Boston's Board of Trade. Sprung from the family of a new Hampshire minister, Sabine was entirely self-educated. He rose swiftly from the bankruptcy of his first business to fifteen years of successful trading on the Maine frontier and preference in local, state, and Federal office of his adopted state. Moving to Massachusetts in 1849, Sabine was appointed confidential agent of the Treasury to study the fisheries "with reference to the operation of the Ashburton Treaty as connected with our commerce with the British colonies", and served the unfinished term of the deceased Benjamin Thomas in the Thirty-Second Congress. Pioneering for ten years following 1857 in the development of the politics of business, Sabine retired to the seclusion of his beautiful library at Roxbury to write *The American Loyalist* and enough other scholarship to fill eight octavo volumes.

Hamilton Hill's father had such strong anti-slavery convictions that he abandoned a successful mercantile establishment in London to take the position of Treasurer at Oberlin College. He remained for twenty-five years prime mover in every movement for political and social reform in that region. This worthy successor to Sabine did not finish Oberlin but entered the shipping and commission merchant ranks and married the daughter of Samuel Walley. From the seat of the secretary of both the Boston and National Board of Trade, Hill served the politics of business well. He served the force of expansion by acting as European emigration agent for the Chicago, Burlington, and Quincy Railroad. Hill went to Congress from Boston and headed some of the key committees. Honored by degrees from Oberlin and Pennsylvania, Hill was either officer or member of the American Philosophical Society, American Statistical Society, American Social Science Association, the Bostonian Society and the Massachusetts Historical Society. Hill shared with Sabine an interest in New England colonial history, but his contribution was in religious history and biography.

Self-taught save for common schooling, Benjamin Franklin Nourse went to Florida at 19 to engage in the cotton business. The house of Nourse and Brooks eventually became one of the leaders in the Southern Cotton Trade. Even though Nourse removed to Boston in 1857, Jefferson Davis and other Southern leaders asked him in vain to join them in secession. This vestryman of Boston's old Trinity Church was a world known cotton specialist, lay economist, and hard money advocate.

In the same tradition was the career of Edward Silas Tobey. Connected with "Phineas and Seth Sprague", shipowners and shipping merchants, Tobey made government connections pay in the crisis by selling the Government ships for commerce and the blockade. Director of Banks and Insurance companies in Boston, mill treasurer, Tobey was confidential adviser to cabinet officers, founder of the Boston Board of Trade and Massachusetts Institute of Technology. Interested in religious extension and social uplift, Tobey remains one of the most representative of Boston capitalists.[40]

Out of the hustle and bustle of the marketplace there gradually arose some ideas which became characteristic of the men of the New Order. A new group, pushing for recognition, has only time for the casual expression of an idea. When that idea, by constant occasional repetition, becames crystallized into an attitude, the idea might be said to be typical of the class or group which gave it voice.

Men of the New Order early took an attitude on politics. There was nothing unique about the "out-of-politics" stand of businessmen; because every new group that entered the arena of pressure politics after the Civil War made the same claim. The businessman's attitude passed through three ill-defined stages. Before the Civil War the prevailing notion ran that the merchant-capitalist was the "forgotten man" of American politics.[41] While realizing that diversity of political views argued against associated capitalists taking a united political position, the notion was current that politics and business existed in two separate categories. Contact with politicians during the war served a double purpose. The masters of capital discovered that their kind of knowledge was the prime requisite in running the modern state. Coeval with the emergence of this new prestige in businessmen was their veiled contempt for the politician and things political.

Joseph Aspinwall set the tone of the postwar attitude of businessmen out at the Detroit commercial convention. His admonition to businessmen to take a deeper interest in governmental affairs arose from the general conviction that,[42]

> It is the great body of workingmen, the merchants, the traders, and the mechanics, that gives the tone to a country. The learned and the rich by their eloquence or their wealth, are the shining lights which glitter and dazzle the eye of the beholder; but it is the energetic, active working portion of the community that stamps its character, pushes forward its enterprises and develops its energies . . .

Businessmen came to feel that politicians were talking and legislating about things which to them were abstractions. Associated with the wealth, material resources, foreign and domestic commerce, industry, and sustaining the taxation of the nation, businessmen felt they were more "practical" and much better fitted to advise on the legislation of the new era.

No longer overawed by the Lions on Capitol Hill and still clinging to the empty fetish of being "out-of-politics" locally and nationally, the postwar politics of business rested its case upon a successful local and national pressure politics; and a continued agitation for the creation of a Federal Department of Commerce with Cabinet rank.[43] The pressure idea gave rise to the national organization of businessmen which sought to extend the influence already enjoyed by powerful businessmen's organization in the Northeastern cities. The very habit of the executive council of nationally organized businessmen sitting in Washington made the step to the next thought in the '70's easy. "Every leading class in the community", thought the masters of capital, "should be fairly represented in the halls of Congress; and surely it is not asking too much to insist that merchants as such, and not as partisans should be sent thither, in numbers somewhat proportionate to the greatness of interest which they are identified." [44] Indeed there were those who held that "commercial" men should participate fully in all politics to help purify it, and national and local examples were not wanting.

Though opinion was divided among businessmen as to the nature and extent of their legitimate participation in politics, there was a general agreement that the federal government was not doing what it could to aid business.[45] A Federal department of Commerce, handling all matters relating to trade and commerce, became the universal demand of organized businessmen. By the middle '70's, masters of capital were sure that panics were due to inadequate information on manufacturing, mining, agriculture, railroads, and shipping. The diversified sources of this information needed to be centralized in one department under "a merchant who knows and appreciates the value of commerce to a great nation, instead of a lawyer or a political demagogue who neither knows nor cares for much outside his own gratification for place and power." [46] Masters of capital wanted "more practical commercial legislation and less political trickery in our business relations with the several states and with foreign nations."

It soon became clear that the pressure group phase of the politics of business along non-political lines was to yield the greatest immediate results. Businessmen came to understand that the issues in government in the postwar era were different. "Henceforward", thought nationally associated capitalists: [47]

> from the very nature of the case, both the national administration and Congress must devote themselves more exclusively to industrial and commercial questions than they have done for many years past, perhaps than ever before.

These so-called "rugged individualists" banded themselves together in the spirit of a third "Urban" chamber of national government,[48] and every effort was made to see to it that the best business brains of the bustling cities the nation over attended the annual gatherings. Nor did the nationally associated capitalists see anything unusual in the fact that Chambers of Commerce all over the world officially accredited representatives to their local and national commercial organizations.

But this new man was a product of the city. He was proud of his city and sought some pungent phrase that best summed up its virtues. Cincinnati was "the Workshop of the interior"; New York, "the chief commercial emporium of the Western World"; Boston, "the centre of the Whole North"; and St. Louis, the "Queen City of the Mississippi Valley", "the largest city west of the Alleghenies and the fourth in the United States", "The Great central city of the continent." [49] Businessmen also expressed their pride by establishing museums, societies for social uplift, boards and commissions for every aspect of urban improvement.

This new man also thought about his city in terms of a destiny. He felt that every citizen in the city and state should bend every effort to help the chief city realize its destiny. Indeed the citizens should adopt the "enlightened principle" that

> neither municipal nor state lines should ever limit their exertions to obtain the freest and amplest communication with external sources of commerce, since it is through such communications with external sources of commerce that a city may most effectually exercise influence outside its own borders, and draw from springs thousands of miles beyond them, the material of wealth and progress.[50]

Urban imperialists understood full well that the "ultimate rank" of their cities depended upon "the extent, the speed, the cheapness, and the safety of the lines of transportation of persons and of things". The early development of the railroad system of the nation owes more perhaps to this theory of the new Urban imperialist than to any other factor. These new men naturally could abide state's rights in no form.

This new man was not only the exponent of an urban regionalism, but he was also clannish and jealous of encroachments upon his domain. He wanted his organization "to represent at least a majority of those who impersonate the wealth, intelligence, and commercial enterprise of the city." [51] The new man also wanted autonomy for his city. He wanted no state politician dictating to him; and resented the civilities that perforce must be lavished upon these bumpkins to keep them from restricting his city's development.[52] Masters of capital resented being bound to political geography which bore no relation either to the economic realities or their ambitions for commercial empires. The urban capitalist found it difficult to understand why state politicians were so slow to grasp a principle like "limited liability." [53]

Perhaps masters of capital resented localism most because the scope of their interest was so broad. Immigration from Europe to fill the labor needs their ingenuity and capital made necessary; the decline of American shipping on the seven seas; international coinage; the international general average; international expositions; international conferences on international law; and interest in uniformity of international postal rates—these subjects occupied a good deal of masters of capital attention wherever they were located.[54] But they had national attitudes as well as international interest. Capitalists were against federal sponsored "internal improvements",[55] convinced that the necessary private capital would be forthcoming if the locally desired projects had merit. Masters of capital were in favor of sound money to a man, and turned a jaundiced eye to bimetalism or any other scheme that sounded tricky.[56] Businessmen had, along with the foregoing, many other ideas that have gone in to make up the intellectual framework of our business culture.

This, then, was the new man in his native habitat. Armed for the most part with a practical education, he faced a post Civil War America with a telescoped political maturity and social conscience. This man was seldom greater than the cash-nexus that lay at the base of the attitudes and prejudices of the bourgeoisie the world over. But the ethics and the humanitarian impulses which his great wealth allowed him to indulge; the pattern of social rectitude which his struggle up from humble origins imposed; the technological and material advancement which the bold strokes which he and his fellows made possible—all of these are inextricably woven into the pattern of what we call modern America.

"Radical Doxology"

I

From Africa the Negro came
Arise, Oh Congress, bless his name.
Stand up, good Stevens, bless the day
The Negro came from Africa.

II

He is the object of our love
In him we live, in him we move
For him we preach, for him we pray
For him we meet from day to day,
That colored cuss from Africa.

Brudder Stevens pitches the tune; after which all retire to pray upon the vitals of the country.

NOTE: This was taken from the *Georgia Enterprise* of May 11, 1866, and is supposed to have been used to close all Radical caucuses.

George Opdyke
New York

John Price Wetherill
Philadelphia

Edward Atkinson
Boston

2.   The Boston, Philadelphia, Northwestern Alliance

Five days after Robert E. Lee surrendered his sword to Grant at Appomattox courthouse, a shot rang out in Ford's theater, and the man who, by the call for volunteers, swept the organized masters of capital into the mill-race of national politics was no more. For four years business associations had handled fumblingly the bright bauble of power, thrust so suddenly into their hands by the national crisis; and for the same period, they had stood, according to their own lights, staunchly behind the man from Springfield. Merchant capitalists paused in the midst of their busy cares to pay, along with a grief-stricken nation, their respects to a fallen leader.

Three days after the tragedy, members of Boston's Board of Trade met in their State street rooms to eulogize the departed chief of state.[1]

Feeling that "now treason has done his worst", the Richardsons, Tobeys, and Bouts moved appropriate, sombre worded resolutions. At the insistence of Benjamin E. Bates, the Boston Board joined in with the mourning city, draping their rooms in funereal black, and on Solomon R. Spaulding's suggestion, the president appointed a seven man delegation to represent the Board at Lincoln's Washington funeral.

Members of the Philadelphia Board of Trade met on the 17th at high noon.[2] All business was suspended so that full attention could be given to appropriate action in view of the "tragical" event. Members of the Board were in a temper and heartily endorsed Stoke's vindictive resolution to the effect that:

> "The crimes of official perjury, of sedition, privy conspiracy, and rebellion, ought not to go unpunished, and that the leaders of this most wicked rebellion should not escape the full penalties of the law."

Masters of capital of the Quaker City promised Andrew Johnson,

35

> "the loyal support of the manufacturing and commercial
> community of Philadelphia, in all wise counsels, in all
> just measures, in defense of the integrity of our country,
> and against all enemies, wheresoever they may be found."

Resolutions bearing these sentiments were dispatched to Andrew Johnson.

The International Merchants of New York's Chamber of Commerce joined their brothers in the Northeast in expressions of grief over the assassination of Lincoln.[3] They agreed to join the Common Council of New York City in the "obsequies" to be held on the 25th at 10:00 A.M. New York capitalists also sent a delegation of thirteen to Washington to attend Lincoln's funeral. The delegation, on arriving in Washington, put up at Willard's. Hugh McCulloch saw to it that the New Yorkers had an "appropriate" place amid the glittering diplomatic corps, politicians, and the milling throng attending the rites. After the ceremony, the delegation visited Andrew Johnson to assure him the same hearty support the New York merchant community had given his departed chief, and was treated to an impromptu speech on government policy. Returning to Willard's Hotel, the delegation received Grant in their parlor, where they told the General they had hoped his life would be spared to complete his work. The delegation sent the stricken Seward a condolence, and a part of the delegation remaining in Washington called on Johnson, Chief Justice Chase, and other department heads. "They had everywhere" said R. H. McCurdy smugly, "met with the consideration and kindness which is due to the representatives of your body".

On the 25th of April at the appointed hour, New York merchants joined the citizens of the city at 14th and Union Square for the city's ceremony honoring the dead President. A long civic procession concluded the ceremony. Thus, the merchants had joined the nation in mourning for the man who, in the greatest crisis of our national development, had stood for union and had won.

During the mourning the British ministry at Washington informed Earl Russell:

> "The late President at the time of his murder, was pursuing a humane and moderate policy towards the Southern States and these atrocious acts, by the indignation they can not fail to arouse in the North, will increase the influence of the party which was already criticizing Mr. Lincoln's leniency as inopportune." [4]

The machinations, if not the influence, of the Radical party waxed with the passing months. On the approach of the first anniversary of Lincoln's assassination, the tussle of his successor with the men of the new persuasion was beginning to reach the critical point. Johnson struck, and on that sunny Washington's birthday in 1866, the angered Tennesseean strode to the portico of the White House in a mood to speak plainly:

> "The gentlemen call for three names. I am talking to my friends and fellow citizens here. Suppose I should name to you those whom I look upon as being opposed to the fundamental principles of the government, and as now laboring to destroy them. I say Thaddeus Stevens, of Pennsylvania; I say Charles Sumner of Massachusetts; I say Wendell Phillips of Massachusetts." [5]

Johnson's detractors were willing to call this hurling of defiance at the powerful coalition in the seats of the mighty at the other end of Pennsylvania Avenue either another instance of his drinking or the want of dignity which this "political accident" brought to the chief magistry of the United States. But there was more than fight in that performance;[6] there was an overtone of disillusion, of despair. Johnson had believed in Union and the highest goals of functional, popular constitutional democracy. Indeed he had opposed secession and had accepted personal and political exile from his native Tennessee in testimony of his convictions. While he pursued a policy of "Restoration", Johnson saw the rising tide of opposition grow against him. Washington's birthday found him angry—with the futile anger of the trapped. Several days before he had raised the cudgel of the veto—a weapon as weak as a rope of sand when not backed by a congressional majority or a pivotal minority. Unable to control the rapidly shifting political currents, Johnson called out to the nation, announcing the new political alliance which even he must have known that he could not long successfully oppose.

While Andrew Johnson, in his moment of anger, had said nothing of the western wing of the radical alliance, James Gordon Bennett had called attention to it on the eve of the 39th Congress.[7] Under the title "The State of the Country—the Crisis of the Republican Party", Bennett editorialized:

> "The Republican Party is in the same danger of a ruling radical sectional clique. What the Virginia and South Carolina managing politicians were to the Democracy, the Massachusetts and Ohio leaders threaten to be to the Republicans, with their contracted ideas and their pretentions to authority."

The western leg of the new axis was, like the northeastern leg, personalized in Washington by an understanding between men of the new persuasion. There was the tie of conviction between the bewigged, club-footed giant of the House of Representatives and the polished Sumner from the Athens of America. But there was the tie of friendship between Sumner and John Sherman.[8] All three were pragmatic, as hard as nails in their politics. Sherman's realism was obscured by his genius for high finance, and Sumner cloaked the mailed fist in the velvet glove of a nebulous, starry-eyed idealism.

Led by the giants of the new era, the radical host had misinterpreted Andrew Johnson's position in the first days after Lincoln's death. Their thinly veiled hints and finally threats left the man from Tennessee unmoved in his policy of "Restoration".

Johnson's only basic fault—his error of statesmanship—was in believing, like all idealists, that, despite the real war aims—whatever the popular shibboleths might have been—he could win the peace. Like most democratic liberals, he underestimated the ruthless ingenuity of the opposition; and hence disarmed himself from the start by placing too much trust in legal processes and popular support. Therefore, Johnson was led, on the one hand, to an arid orthodox constitutionalism in his state papers; and on the other, to what was popularly played up as undignified outburst in his public expression.

But in the spring and summer of 1865, Johnson had the radical host frankly worried. Thad Stevens was an old man. His words of political wisdom had carried weight during the Lincoln regime.[9] It came as something of a shock to be ignored by this up-start Democrat to whom only political necessity and an assassin's bullet had given the chief magistry. Old Thad, taking his pride in his hands, wrote Johnson twice in this fateful period, asking the President to stay his hand; both letters were ignored.[10] Then Stevens turned to Sumner to ask, "Is it possible to devise any plan to arrest the government in its ruinous career?" "When will you be in Washington?" Stevens later anxiously inquired, "Could we collect bold men enough to lay the foundation of a party to take the helm of this government and keep it off the rocks?" Late in August Stevens finally suggested to Sumner, "Get the rebel States into a territorial condition and it can easily be managed".

As the thunder heads of Reconstruction gathered on the horizon, it was inevitable that men in the eastern counting houses would take sides. But the maturing politics of business was unwilling to place its destiny in the hands of politicians alone, whatever their importance. In 1860 they had risked a great deal on the throw of the iron dice of war.[11] Nothing must stand in the way of their reaping the full victory. The promoters of the new business-political hegemony were willing to cast their future upon sustained pressure politics. With political instincts

sharpened during the war, men of the new order sensed the
limitations of the ultras in the radical host. The business answer
was simple. Let the political pyrotechnics of the radicals and
their camp followers provide a smoke-screen behind which the
men of the new order might cut across the field to outdistance
agrarianism in the race for supremacy. For their part, the
business politicians would build a fire behind the lions on
capitol hill in their native habitats, and thus place the success
of the new hegemony beyond the caprice of the political fortunes
and personalities of individuals.

"Well may we, not only from moral considerations, but as
representatives of vast material interest, offer our grateful thanks,
that the slave system of this country, the constant opponent of all
national legislation having in view the interest of American industry, the only cause of actual discord in the past, as of possible
conflict in the future, has wholly perished", thus the Philadelphia
masters of capital, along with their brothers the country over,
greeted the cessation of hostilities.

A feeling of relief was all businessmen had in common; for
the war years had brought evidences of sharp division of opinion,
which became marked as they were identified with the elemental
issues of Reconstruction. The Philadelphia Business community
thought the battle for protection was over;[12] but in 1864-65
Philadelphians discovered that New Yorkers, though they had
accepted previously the principle of protection, openly attacked
the war schedules. Touched at their most sensitive spot, Philadelphians were on guard and in a temper. Moreover, contro-
versies arose around the whole issue of the debts owed to Northern capitalists by Southern debtors. The actions of a Provost
Judge at Alexander and suggestion for wider use of such courts
to guard creditor interests brought a sharp exchange between
Philadelphians and "Yorkers".[13] The movement, initiated by
the New York Chamber primarily for the Southern situation,
for a permanent bankrupt law on English principles raised a new
issue.[14] After showing a disposition to agree to the legislation,

Philadelphians had secured the defeat of the measure on the pretext that Congress was too busy to consider it. Bostonians joined Philadelphians in 1865 in objections to the revived Bankrupt Bill, and the former dispatched a powerful lobby to Washington to secure the defeat of the bill. Philadelphians and Bostonians felt that the bill would penalize Northern creditors if its provisions were operative in the Southern states, even after their return to the Union.[15] New Yorkers, at their wits end, believed that the failure to legislate would allow the vast amounts owed to New York creditors by Southerners to be lost.[16]

The problem of confiscation and relief also divided the merchants of the great cities. Attention of Northeastern capitalists was especially centered on this double problem in Savannah, Georgia.[17] The New York capitalists welcomed the opportunity to renew their old business contacts and lectured the Federal government on the need of recognizing private property rights in the South. Bostonians and Philadelphians remained unmoved before the thinly veiled threats of cotton burning if confiscation was continued. While sympathetic with Southern suffering, New England textile barons felt that since treasury agents were confiscating cotton, they might as well ask the Secretary of the Treasury to see to it that a fair share got to the New England mills.

The basic issue involved in the split of the Northeastern business community was obvious. Bostonians and Philadelphians, on the eve of Reconstruction, had already taken the position that the South must be penalized, and thus excluded from the benefits of any new comprehensive legislation until the interest and claims of creditors had been secured. The powerful New York business community, caught between two aggressive rivals and divided within its own domain, was to fight a losing battle for the principle that all aid, legislative or otherwise, should be given toward achieving the quick recovery of the South, and thus the readjustment of the national economy to normal, progressive conditions. Both factions argued from convictions born of interest. New

York, tied to the Southern economy and England in the past, wished to smooth the way to a renewal of that tie.[18] Bostonians and Philadelphians were frankly ambitious for the power and the glory that a new politico-economic hegemony might secure.

The New York business community soon saw the virtue of Johnson's policy of "Restoration". To it, Johnson's movement to decentralize the war-bloated federal power was in keeping with the New York merchant's desire for a quick return to private enterprise over the traditional channels of Southern trade and thus the restoration of pre-war business conditions. In the summer of 1865 William B. Dana opened the New York business propaganda offensive for Johnsonianism in his newly founded *Commercial and Financial Chronicle*.[19] In Dana's opinion, Johnson's policy was sound both in its states-rights orientation and its qualified adherence to confiscation, emancipation, and the enfranchisement of the Negroes.[20] Only the denial of amnesty to rebels possessing $20,000 in property was thought by Dana to be unsound. Since the South had no middle class, Dana was sure that Johnson's idea would exclude "almost every capitalist in the South" and lead to the insecurity of both native and foreign capital. "Beyond this", Dana reasoned, "Mr. Johnson's policy will obtain the hearty acquiescence and support of the industrial and commercial classes of the entire country", and as soon as the President saw his error he would undoubtedly change his policy in this regard.

As August drew to a close and the political barometer was registering storms, Dana decided that the time had come for plain speaking. Falling back on a rather stale dodge Dana editorialized:

> "The Commercial and Financial Chronicle has, and can
> have nothing to do with political questions in any of their
> partisan or sectional aspects. It is only when the move-
> ments and the policy of parties are directly connected with,

and have a positive and vital bearing upon the great permanent material interest of the country that it becomes our duty to consider them . . ." [21]

The editor did not believe that military occupation and confiscation were necessary to keep the peace; for the Southerners were not contemplating rebellion. Indeed, they accepted the decision of the war. "It is, we think" observed Dana, "plain that if they are suffered to reorganize socially, the Southern States will, for sometime to come, treat purely political questions as secondary merely and will devote themselves to economical and industrial issues". To those who asserted that the Negro would not be treated fairly, Dana replied that after all the constitution went only so far; and besides, no outside agency could secure fair treatment for the Negro.

September found Dana off on another path in the propaganda offensive through which the New York business community hoped to buttress their stand for private enterprise as the means of Southern restoration.[22] Dana pointed with hope to the colonization of Swedes and Poles in Virginia, and to the mineral resources of the state and their proximity to transportation facilities. "A yeomanry", asserted Dana, "is of the last importance" to the South because "the freedmen are not sufficient to meet this want". Dana insisted on the industrial future of the South, and cited the enthusiasm of Union officers in East Tennessee as proof. The editor threw out the old climate argument as of no significance, and advised that the "better way to emigrate to the South is by colonies". Thus the moderate policy of the New York business community was fully elaborated.

*   *   *

War Secretary Stanton may have been the radical spy in Johnson's household,[23] but the plan for the Northern merchant regional aggression was hatched in the department of that Indiana banker, Hugh McCulloch. Of the three methods used traditionally by the business politicians, the New York business community had, and was to continue to use, persuasion—the weakest of them all. Bostonians had no compunction about using the more dangerous and effective methods of attrition and concession. If the radical host could find some way of either staying Johnson's hand or undoing what he had already done, Boston capitalists could certainly build a power alliance with Philadelphia capitalists. David Ames Wells, frail but tireless, translated this alliance of convenience into a positive aggressive legislative program.[24]

In 1864 John Sherman advised the creation of a Revenue Commission, which would make a path through the trackless jungle of the Federal finances. Legislation creating such a commission was passed the following year. Wells openly sought the position, and appealed in vain for the aid of New York senators.[25] Since he hailed originally from Massachusetts, Wells turned to Sumner for aid.[26] On the advice of his predecessor, Fessenden of Maine, and from his own knowledge, Hugh McCulloch appointed Wells chairman of the National Revenue Commission. Stephen Colwell, lawyer, iron manufacturer, and friend of Henry C. Carey, was appointed from Pennsylvania; and Samuel S. Hayes, Comptroller of Chicago and a Democrat, represented the Northwest.[27]

In David A. Wells two intellectual forces temporarily met and fused: the one represented by Henry C. Carey—the other by Edward Atkinson. Carey and Atkinson belonged to the group of non-academic theorists arising out of the ranks of successful "practical" businessmen. Carey, son of an Irish political refugee, retired from business with a fortune in 1835 and began writing on economic subjects. When in the early '40's Friedrick List's *National System of Political Economy* came to his hand, Carey, in the face of the overwhelming damnation of the American academicians, immediately threw over the English economists of the Manchester school and launched a writing campaign for the protection of American industry.[28] In 1849 he began to write for Greeley and by 1857 was considered the economic editor of the *Tribune*. At the feet of this high-priest of American protection, whom Duhring and Ferrara in Europe called "master", Wells received a theoretical training, which he had an opportunity to confirm during his junket to England in 1862.

But when Wells became Chairman of the National Revenue Commission, he came into contact with another "practical" economist, Edward Atkinson. Atkinson, among other things, an oil-stove inventor, was not a college man.[29] At the end of the Civil War, though still a comparatively young man, Atkinson had the reputation of being the successful manager of cotton mills and something of an authority on cotton and tariffs in general. At this period Atkinson was trying to reconcile his free-trade leanings with the general New England desire for protection of the textile industry.[30] Wells and Atkinson became warm friends, the former constantly soliciting and following the advice of the latter on all measures pertaining to tariffs and cotton.

By mid-June of 1865, Wells, at the head of his commission housed in the New York Custom-house, was following the method of English Parliamentary commissions in finding a solution to the revenue chaos created by the war. Advice came to him from all quarters; but for general guidance Wells leaned heavily on Edward Atkinson and his New England friends, and upon the Philadelphia circle of Henry C. Carey. Wells elected to study tea, coffee, cotton, sugar, copper, beer and whiskey. Though Hayes was assigned petroleum, he concentrated almost exclusively on property in government securities. Iron and steel, wool and tariff policy generally constituted, as would be expected, the interest of Colwell. It was in connection with Wells' studies of cotton as a source of national revenue that the Boston lobby moved into the enemy camp in October of 1865.

The Boston lobby consisted of seventeen men.[31] Ten were connected directly with the Boston Board of Trade, including

its president, George C. Richardson, and two members of the
Board of Directors, Edward Atkinson and Erastus B. Bigelow.
William King, a Georgia planter with Boston connections, was
there, as was Edward S. Philbrick, who had supervised plantations on the Sea Islands under the government and later under
a group of Boston capitalists, and Albert H. Kelsey, agent of
another capitalist group under Atkinson's leadership in the
Southwest was also present. The remainder of the lobby was
made up of financial managers of cotton or woolen mills,
commission merchants with investments in textile mills and mill
owners. All, save King, were from New England. "These
gentlemen", wrote Wells to Thomas H. Dudley in November,
"have their agents constantly at the South, and have spent more
time and money in investigating the subject, in my opinion,
than any other set of men; consequently, I give great weight
to their judgment".[32]

Whatever else Wells' report might have meant, the special
Report on Cotton was not designed simply to reveal a new
source of government revenue. The suggestion that cotton, at
the prevailing scarcity price, be taxed was tantamount to an
attempt to secure a war indemnity. The testimony of the New
England lobby revealed that the tax had a double purpose.
Not only was the economy of the South to be mortgaged to pay
a sizeable share of the cost of the war, but also to underwrite
the progress Northern industry had made during the war and
might continue to make in the future. In spite of the impetus
given American industrial development by the war, it was still
unable to compete at home or abroad with the industrial output of Europe, and especially England, without governmental
aid.[33] The apostles of the new order were faced with a fundamental dilemma. They must frame an economic policy that
would give the American merchant and industrialist something
approaching hegemony at home and equality of competition in
foreign markets. It was clear that the policy of "protection"
while accomplishing the first goal, might defeat the second.

Economic statesmanship must find an agricultural staple surplus, the very necessity for which would prevent the open retaliation of foreign countries against our policy of protection in their trade policy, which, if carried out, would destroy a lucrative source of foreign exchange and government revenue. The answer to radical economists was obvious—Cotton! Cotton, and that alone, would enable the aggressive regionalists to have their cake and eat it too.

Men of the Boston lobby were sure that American cotton was the most desirable in the world market, and thus could rule it.[34] An export or excise tax could be levied on a two or three million bale crop and the government would profit thereby. Besides taxes would be lifted from American industry and perhaps the government might find it possible to subsidize that industry to help it in its fight for world markets.[35] After all the tax would ultimately be paid by the European consumer of raw cotton. Wells asked Congress to legislate on this collective opinion, and wrote Thad Stevens in February of 1866:

> "I have endeavored to discharge my whole duty both as regards the revenue interest of the Government and the industrial interest of the country." [36]

The New England leaders of the politics of business were clever enough to identify the demands of the textile industry with the industrial needs of the nation. Therefore, they were forced to agree to the application of the gains they had made—draw-backs, deflected taxes, tariffs—to the interest of other sections of the Alliance. There was only one flaw in Atkinson's "system". New England capitalists knew, as well as those in New York, the condition of the South.[37] If cotton lay at the base of the system, it was obvious that it was impossible to use as a weapon what was not available. The initial problem of both lay economists and practical politicians was to devise a means to make the cotton crop for the next "three" or "five" years what it should be.

Only two of the Boston lobby, E. S. Philbrick and William King, the Georgia planter, had mentioned the problem before Wells' commission. But efforts to bring the staple into market on New England terms had begun soon after the opening of the war. Eli Thayer soon went to Washington with a scheme to colonize Florida.[38] Secretary of the Treasury Chase not only showed an interest in this plan, but in any other of a similar nature. Chase held the notion of territorial status for the confederacy which Stevens was to advocate. The very bone and sinew of old planterism had come out of New York,[39] but there was every indication that the New England expansionists and their allies intended to dominate the new. The officers of the nine special agencies of the Treasury did everything possible to help the production and crop movement program of the new imperialists along. With the establishment of the Bureau of Refugees, Freedmen and Abandoned land, letters poured in from every quarter in America and Europe during the summer and fall of 1865 with every conceivable scheme for colonization and general exploitation of the South.[40] The answer of the Washington office to Brevet Major General A. Baird at New Orleans became the fixed policy on investment schemes:

"As any undertaking of this kind absorbs a large proportion of the surplus free labor of a state, it commends itself to the favorable consideration of the Bureau and should have consistently with the interest of all classes, the support of its representatives in the Southern states."

William King, the Georgia planter, opened correspondence with Oliver O. Howard in May of 1865 on a project to better organize the functions of the Freedman's Bureau so that Negro labor might be rendered more serviceable.[41] King represented a group of planters who had met at Savannah for the purpose

of effecting plans to solve the labor problem, and had written
General Howard about it. J. S. Fullerton, answering for
Howard in June was non-committal; but told King, "If you
should happen to come to Washington, General Howard would
be glad to talk with you about the matters mentioned in your
letter". King took advantage of this invitation and, after con-
sultation with General Howard, went north to sound out the
New England capitalists. When he faced Wells at the New
York Custom-house hearing he was prepared to suggest that,
pending adequate white immigration, the Negroes should be
given the status of minors. What were the possibilities of such
an idea? "Well, Sir", said King,

> "I have been in New England over a month and I have
> been very much gratified to find the feeling existing, as I
> do, that if it be necessary they are willing to accede to
> the plan of recognizing and treating the Negroes as minors.
> If General Howard can be sustained by outside approval,
> he will adopt this course."

The problem of stepping up Southern cotton production
was of some interest to English consumers. They recognized
the key position of the Negro in the entire situation. "How
the Negroes will be 'regimented', as Mr. Carlyle calls it, into
industrial gangs or squadrons again", observed the editor of
the London *Economist,* "does not seem clear. That in some
way or other they will be so regimented—and either induced
to work or persuaded to work, we entertain little doubt".[42]
Sir Samuel Morton Peto, English railroad king and M. P. for
Bristol, observed shortly after his arrival in the states in September of 1865,

> "that the commercial and financial interest of the country
> depends very largely upon the organization and develop-
> ment of Southern industry. They are prepared to throw
> capital and enterprise into the Southern states for the
> purpose of producing results on which the prosperity of

the whole nation is acknowledged largely to depend. The
government, no doubt, so far as lies within its legitimate
province will encourage and support those efforts." [43]

There loomed on the horizon one obstacle to any high-handed
solution of the problem—Andrew Johnson. Some plan must
be concocted that would not offend the democratic sensibilities
of the stubborn man in the White House.

By November, 1865, the New England expansionists had
decided that Lincoln's reluctantly created Freedmen's Bureau
should be, with expanded powers, the cornerstone of the new
regionalism. Sumner wrote quixotic John A. Andrew concerning the plan. "As to the Freedmen's Bureau", replied Andrew,
"that is an old project of mine". After suggesting sweeping
changes in the Bureau's organization and power, Andrew explained that he had "earnestly set forth to the President last
week the utter impossibility of success, without sustaining the
Bureau. I insisted that if that failed all would fail".[44]

The plan, on the eve of the 39th Congress was ready;
there need no longer be secrecy. On the 27th of November,
Edward Silas Tobey arose before a special meeting of the
Boston Board of Trade to make his celebrated speech on "The
Industry of the South".[45] Tobey, unlike Atkinson, was no
youngster hovering around the seats of power with a theory
to sell. Tobey's experience, in Washington's war politics and
profits, made him, though a merchant, a practical politician
in every sense of the word. Opening with a touching review
of Southern conditions and the plight of the Negro, Tobey
assured his audience that it was not from a humanitarian basis,

"but it is at present chiefly on the ground of political
economy and commercial and financial interest that I pro-
pose to effect the organization of labor in the Southern
States so as to increase their production as nearly as
possible to the quantity raised before the war."

Tobey was sure that the same population that produced the great pre-war cotton crops was on hand for the crop of 1866. The Boston merchant was willing for private capital to do what it could. However, he knew Southern capital was inadequate and Northern capitalists were reluctant to take the risk. Therefore, "this deficiency in capital and the protection and organization of labor now there", observed Tobey, "can be . . . provided for by the government, and at the present moment, by it only". Then private capital would follow order and security, attracted by low prices of land, a supply of reliable labor, and high prices of products. "Happily for the country," said Tobey, "Congress at its last session created an agency and a power which in the hands of the President may do much toward accomplishing these most important objects through the operations of the Freedmen's Bureau, as a military branch of the government". After extolling the work of General Howard, Fisk and Gordon, Tobey asserted:

> "With enlarged powers, which may be granted early in the next Congress to authorize or permit the Bureau to lease, and possibly in some instances to purchase lands in the Southern States, where abandoned lands may no longer be adequate to the necessities of the case, the Freedmen's Bureau before the next planting season (can) organize and employ such portions of the laborers there as cannot otherwise be employed for want of capital in private hands, and thereby secure to the laborer the rewards of industry and to the national wealth, the results of that industry."

Tobey made much of the cheapness of the whole project, and the government would still not have to interfere with the efforts of private capital. Tobey wanted the government to buy plantations and set them up as departments of the Bureau. Each plantation was to have all of the necessities of complete community life and be presided over by a superintendent. All indigent and maladjusted Negro families and all other refugees

willing to work, might find shelter there. These superplanta-
tions could be placed under the check of a board of visitors,
who would report to the head of the Bureau on their operation.
Such a plan would benefit the country generally and hasten
the return to specie payments.

Edward Atkinson, present at the meeting, objected to the
plan as only a palliative; and suggested that what the Southern
States should do was to pass laws protecting labor. Indeed,
he would not make the Freedmen's Bureau "a great business
enterprise", but would use it simply to secure justice between
man and man. The assembled New England capitalists brushed
aside Atkinson's objections and voted to both approve Tobey's
idea and ask other businessmen's organizations to help put
it over.

Simultaneous with the emergence of the Boston idea, another plan was released by Alanson Penfield of the Treasury
Department in Washington.[46] Penfield hoped that steps would
be taken at a National Cotton-growing Convention to enable
the South to produce five million bales. At prevailing gold
prices, the crop would be worth one billion dollars, and if
three-fourths of the crop was exported, six or seven hundred
million would be returned, thus creating such a state that
foreign exchange would bring specie payments in the spring
of 1867, "without the usual financial revulsions" and the contraction of the currency. European bankers had informed
Federal government messengers that if Federal securities were
to hold in the foreign markets, the country must return to
specie; and Penfield had it on the authority of an Ohio banker
that the nation could not return to specie without heavy cotton
exports. Not only could the convention provide credit and
physical needs, and stimulate immigration into South, but it
could facilitate the extension of cotton culture into Kansas,
Missouri, Illinois, Indiana and Kentucky, enabling the crop
to mature one month earlier. Boston friends told Penfield
that the New York Chamber was the proper body to issue a

call for such a convention and Penfield urged that body to do so immediately.

These schemes, representing the high hopes of the radical party, went out to the nation as the members of the 39th Congress drifted into Washington. Thad Stevens was prepared to start the legislative machinery moving to realize the objects of the politics of business.[47] By December 13th the radical junto had a weapon in its hand—the joint committee of fifteen. Fessenden of Maine was chosen chairman over Charles Sumner, who was anxious for the post. The choice of the moderate Fessenden was in keeping with John A. Andrew's advice,

> "The right position for New England is one of friendliness, not of antagonism. In taking the latter we are defeated, in the former we shall win. And we shall carry our own doctrines into the South."

However, New England leadership was maintained. Whatever Johnson had accomplished would be under fire.

The rapid successful radical offensive in Congress presented the New York business community with a *fait accompli*. With the Southern states out of Congress, New York's business interest was in grave danger. The only hope for the salvation of that interest had rested in the ability of the New York capitalists, under cover of Johnson's lenient policy, to prove that private enterprise was adequate to the task of the economic reconstruction of the Southern states. Time and conditions worked with the new political alliance; and when the testing came the New York argument was inadequate. But the New York capitalists did not go down before the attack of their aggressive rivals for the want of a show of energy and ingenuity.

The investment trust, the American Land Company and Agency, was chartered in New York State with a branch office in Boston. John A. Andrew, war governor of Massachusetts, was chosen president of the company. Andrew hoped to adapt the firm "to the ultimate hopes and purposes of the 'Radical philosophy' ".[48] Yet Andrew thought to gain the friendship of "the enlightened men of the proprietary class" and appear "the truest friends of the laboring freedmen". By channeling capital into the South, Andrew was sure he would be helping to restore Southern industry and aid in making "emancipation prove an early and visible success". The scheme was to provide investment opportunities for Northern and European capital.

New York capitalists also gathered comfort from the propaganda campaign of the American Free-trade League.[49] With William Cullen Bryant, editor of the New York *Evening Post,* as its President, the League opened the attack as early as September of 1865. "The gentlemen whose names are affixed to the declaration of principles of the New York League", observed Frederick Fraley, "represent interests which depend upon the sale of foreign commodities, or are agents of foreign manufacturers, who wish to bring in the products of other countries". Feeling that peace offered the nation an opportunity to establish a commercial policy for the new age, the League's pamphleteers proposed that "Free Trade" be added to the trilogy—"Free speech, free soil, and free labor". They held that protection to the producer was robbery to the consumer, "with the added hypocrisy of pretending to look after the latter's interest". Pay necessary taxes, said Leaguers, but "not one cent" for protection. This campaign continued unabated.

Organized New York capitalists were heartened when one from the enemy camp seemed to be won over to this idea. Thomas W. Conway, "late" assistant commissioner of the Freedmen's Bureau in Louisiana and one of the most slippery of them all, appealed to the New York Chamber in December of 1865 for approval of his mission to England.[50] Conway's purpose was to secure the introduction of British capital into the Southern states. Pointing out the relation of cotton culture to national prosperity and the limited acreage of the cotton kingdom, Conway was sure that the extensive production of the staple would hasten the return to specie payments by filling the European market demand. Failure in this regard, as far as the South was concerned, would lead to a "war of the races". Conway already had the approval of powerful private interests and Federal officialdom. The New York Chamber gladly endorsed the mission.

By January of 1866, it appeared that the New York theory might be overworked.[51] Intelligence from all parts of the South indicated extensive preparations for the next planting season. Hopes were high in Tennessee, Northern Alabama, Georgia, South Carolina and Florida. Speculation in plantation buying was at fever pitch; and Dana warned that an excessive yield would bring low prices and ruin. "Green" venturers were paying extravagant prices for land and labor. Indeed, even British capital was showing interest. A Mr. Oliver of Georgia had the backing of a wealthy group who had formed a company in Manchester, England. Oliver, accompanied by servants of the firm, had $350,000 to purchase and cultivate 20,000 acres of Georgia land.[52] The notorious Spence of Liverpool and the son of Viscount Pootman of London, both old blockade runners during the war, were among the leading English capitalists interested in buying up cotton lands and making advances for cotton production.[53] With such evidence of the successful efforts of private enterprise in the restoration of wrecked Southern economy, the New York Chamber was prepared to answer Penfield and Edward Silas Tobey.[54]

George Opdyke, lay economist, merchant and politician was the chairman of the Executive Committee to which Penfield's and Tobey's ideas had been referred.[55] While agreeing with many of the views of Penfield and Tobey, Opdyke's committee differed "on the means of securing the desired object". They knew that a good crop of cotton would influence foreign trade, and through that the currency and national finances,

since it would so raise exports as would change the flow of
precious metals in America's favor and thus aid a quick return to specie payments. They knew also that the war had
destroyed much of the capital employed in cotton; that the
abolition of slavery had destroyed the previous condition of
capital and labor in the South; that the restricted cotton
supply had raised the price to four times its normal level, and
hence made cotton a good investment field for years to come.

"But", read Opdyke:

> "your committee are, nevertheless, firmly persuaded that
> any interference on the part of the United States govern-
> ment, save for the preservation of order and the enforce-
> ment of the respective rights of capital and labor, would
> mar, rather than facilitate the increased production of
> cotton. Nor can they believe that a national convention
> would be productive of salutary results. It would be likely
> as all such popular movements are, to discourage indi-
> vidual efforts through the fear of competition, by exciting
> expectations from cooperative action, which, in the end,
> would prove to be, as they generally are, altogether illu-
> sory."

Since the South presented such a rich investment field, let
sagacity and personal interest do the rest. "We are not without evidence", said Opdyke, "that this motive is already attracting to that quarter the capital requisite to produce a
fair crop of cotton for the coming season".

There had been a time when the objection of the New
York Chamber literally delivered the *coup de grâce* to most
schemes. But the aggressive rivals of the commercial internationalists of New York City could depend on radical politicians
and bureaucrats to translate the aggressive regional politics of
business into the law of the land. General O. O. Howard,
head of the Freedmen's Bureau, was already in close conference with Senator Lyman Trumbull drafting the new Bureau
bill.[56] The Bureau was not to be discontinued unless such

was provided for by Congressional action; it was to embrace the entire country and be operative wherever there were Negroes and refugees; Bureau agents were to get from $500 to $1,200 annually; the president was to set aside for the use of Freedmen and loyal refugees unoccupied lands in the Southern states, which Bureau commissioners would cause to be allocated in parcels not exceeding forty acres each; that land titles, authorized by General Sherman be made valid; that schools and asylums for dependent Freedmen and refugees, in accordance with congressional recommendation, be built; and that the Bureau should have extensive judicial powers.[57] By the 6th of February this bill had passed both Houses of Congress and was sent to Johnson for his signature.

Frederick W. A. Bruce, British Minister, sent a note to the Earl of Clarendon to the effect that:

> "It may be said at present with more truth than during the war that the institutions of this country are on trial. The Executive and Congress are in antagonism on the most vital questions . . ." [58]

The crisis had come. Andrew Johnson awaiting his chance, had seemed to agree with the radical schemers, only to throw up his strongest constitutional barrier before the crashing radical juggernaut. Johnson, to borrow Mrs. R. B. Hayes' quaint phrase, was out of "the bosom of his family".[59] But the radicals had neatly turned the blow before it was struck. Let Johnson prate of the constitutional issues involved; quibble over the empty issue in public law as to when the war ceased; take, as a politician, the tenuous ground of a President magnanimously divesting himself of power; argue over cost, courts—anything. The radicals and Johnson both knew that whatever the President said, before the bar of Northern public opinion—still luxuriating in the maudlin, self-righteous sentiments engendered by the shibboleths of a successful political war—

Andrew Johnson would appear to be selling short the moral victory purchased with such a cost of blood and treasure.

With the veto and Johnson's Washington's birthday speech, a storm arose in the warring camps and found voice in their respective press.[60] The editor of the Boston *Advertiser* threw off the guard of altruism and justice for the Negro and flatly stated:

> "We cannot afford to have several millions of men idle. We cannot afford to have the whole industrial interest of the South thrown into confusion."

Greeley spoke plainer still.[61] "What we most regret in this veto", observed the editor, "is its tendency to unsettle the industry of the South". The Negroes would not work without the protection of the Bureau. What of the cotton crop of 1866 and the prosperity and solvency based thereon? "Industrial anarchy in Mississippi draws after it mercantile bankruptcy in New York. And to this results the veto powerfully tends." E. H. Godkin took New York businessmen sharply to task for their "restoration" attitude.[62] He flayed them for the pre-war pampering of the "Toombses, Wigfalls and Yanceys". "We trust", said Godkin, "we shall not witness the repetition of this mistake". What could be lost by delaying the admittance of the rebel states?

Free-Trade Leaguer William Cullen Bryant said in Johnson's defense:

> "It should not be forgotten that the more Freedmen's Bureaus we have, the less we shall have of that private effort which is now doing so wonderfully well, and which is destined to do infinitely more. The more Freedmen's Bureaus we have the less we shall have of free men among the late slaves." [63]

Even the politically acute James Gordon Bennett said that if the Bureau was upheld "we need not think of returning to specie payments during the present generation".[64] But a more fundamental issue was raised when the editor of the *World,* after indicating that all shades of Republican opinion had attended the first passage of the Second Bureau bill, stated—

> "It was also avowedly the first of a series of measures conceived in the same spirit, and intended to complete a policy for the government of the Southern states. The veto is a blow at the whole system." [65]

After the veto was not overridden, Seward, Raymond, and others left the capitol for New York City. George Opdyke and other pro-Johnson capitalists were holding a meeting to support the President's position. Following Seward's "nervous man and man of nerve" speech,[66] Henry J. Raymond demanded:

> "But why this hot haste, this impatient determination of Congress to pass a new law a year before it be required?"

"Dead Duck" Forney had the answer.[67] Said he:

> "The measure itself was not particularly acceptable to the radicals, but was accepted by them as an expedient preparatory to the adoption of a more drastic and permanent system."

Charles Sumner wrote W. W. Story, "I sorrow for Seward . . . He never understood our war and he does not now understand how peace is to be secured".[68] If Seward did not, Andrew Johnson did understand perfectly.[69] Johnson told Governor Cox of Ohio, that while he was not against the Bureau, he was against the "Bureau" bill in the form it had passed Congress and if it became permanent. However, it was out at the St. Louis stopover, in the President's tragic swing around the circle, that Johnson showed he clearly perceived the plans of the Tobeys. Said the bitter Tennesseean:[70]

> "Now, my countrymen let me call your attention to a single fact, the Freedmen's Bureau. Slavery was an accursed institution until emancipation took place. It was an accursed institution while one set of men worked them and got the profits. But after emancipation took place they gave us the Freedmen's Bureau; they gave us these agents to go into every county, every township . . . and especially the Southern States; they gave us commissioners; they gave us $12,000,000 and placed the power in the hands of the executive, who was to work the machinery with the army brought to his aid to sustain it. They let us run it with $12,000,000 as a beginning, and in the end receive fifty or sixty million, and let us work the four millions of slaves. In fine, the Freedmen's Bureau was a simple proposition to transfer four millions of slaves in the United States from their original owners to a new set of taskmasters. I have been laboring for years to emancipate them; and then I was opposed to seeing them transferred to a new set of taskmasters, to be worked with more rigor than they had been worked heretofore. Yes, under this new system, they would work the slaves, and call on the government to bear all the expenses, and if there were any profits left, why they would pocket them."

Johnson's veto of the Second Freedmen's Bureau bill brought a flood of speeches and meetings throughout the city and state of New York,[71] reflecting, among other things, the hope entertained by the more sanguine of the international merchants, especially after the veto was sustained, that perhaps the radical juggernaut might be halted. The planting season was already at hand, and the veto practically insured, the legislative process being what it was, that there would be no high handed organization of Negro labor, under government auspices, for the crop of '66. The Bureau bill, like the issue of suffrage for Negroes in the District of Columbia, contained the ingenious traditional Northern sham of political rights for the Negro combined with an inferior economic position. Johnson was not thoroughly committed to either idea and sought to wreck the legislative tour de force, of which this notion formed a basic element.

But Johnson's hour of victory was not destined to be prolonged. Two days before the veto, William B. Dana noted that Wells' report, recommending a tax of five cents per pound on raw cotton, was before the committee of Ways and Means.[72] The obvious relation of Wells' recommendation with the Second Freedmen's Bureau bill was clear to Johnson.[73] Wells' scheme was clear also to the international business community of New York City. Dana immediately opened an attack upon the cotton tax. The government revenues were important, thought Dana; but radical congressmen were as deluded as the Confederates before them if they presumed that American cotton ever had been, and still was, "King". Competition in producing areas abroad had increased during the war and steps should be taken to recapture American primacy in the international raw cotton market. "But", said Dana, "if we attempt now, to tax this industry as proposed by commissioners, we shall surely delay the accomplishment of this much desired object". Besides, Dana thought—

> "We cannot safely permit a colonial system to grow up among us, tending as it does to concentrate power in the hands of the executive, and to enlarge it even to the dimensions of imperialism."

The political situation continued to grow more tense. The fight between the President and Congress moved from the Civil Rights Bill crisis, through the 14th Amendment and into preliminary plans for the test of strength in the Congressional elections of 1866. However, through the sound and fury of bitter radical personal politics the business politicians did not let themselves become confused. Keeping their eye upon the issues that most concerned them, capitalists watched the economic measures roll from the committees to the floor of Congress for debate.

Johnson's veto of the Bureau bill led to immediate efforts to revive the measure. Major General O. O. Howard wrote Assistant Commissioners that "The President has assured the commissioner that he regards the present law as continuing the existence of the Bureau at least a year from this time". In April Howard was cautioning T. D. Elliot, Chairman of the House Committee on Freedmen affairs, of the inadequacy of abandoned lands and the advisability of using public lands for the further development of their program.[74] Under searching executive scrutiny O. O. Howard found it necessary in late May to issue Circular No. 4 in an effort to rid the agency of the sources of public criticism.[75] All of these efforts were well taken because May 7th brought the finance bill onto the floor of Congress. The following day, the highly controversial recommendation of a tax on cotton was before the House. A mature understanding of the Southern situation had caused Atkinson and Wells to change their minds; but the politicians were in no mood for economics.

Old Thad and the radical junto hurled defiance at moderate temporizers. After Upson had taken a stand for a three instead of a five cents tax, Stevens, asking for an eight cents tax said:[76]

> "I think there is very good reason why this one article should pay a very large portion of the taxation which we are obliged to raise. If we had a right to lay an export duty, which the constitution at present forbids, we could, with an export duty of ten cents per pound, raise $200,-000,000 annually, while at the same time protecting our own manufacturers and selling abroad just as much cotton as we do now. Under the circumstances we must do the best we can. The only thing we can do is to lay an internal duty and then allow a drawback upon the production of

the manufactured article which is exported. That is the only mode by which we can now do what we ought to do."

Sir Samuel Morton Peto, representing English sympathy with New York's international capitalists, had suspected Stevens' revelation all along.[77] After talking with radical capitalists, Peto observed:

"It is much to be feared that the feelings which enter into consideration of this question are far from pure. It is not any mere question of revenue or taxation that is thought of, so much as a means of shifting the burden from one portion of the country to another. But I put it to the people of the United States, if higher and nobler feelings ought not to prevail in the adjustment of this great question? . . . The national taxation should not be adjusted by a conflict of interest, but by a fair equable apportionment of burdens."

The New York Chamber had held its fire for the time when the finance bill would appear. Though William E. Dodge, one of the Chamber's members, had presented the New York argument on May 8th,[78] the Chamber dispatched a powerful memorial on the 10th.

Mathew Maury reported at the special meeting of the Chamber called to consider the subject.[79] Maury assumed that an enlightened community of merchants could see the value in dealing justly with the South. If there was any error at Washington, Maury felt it should not be one of severity. Indeed, if it were necessary to exclude the South politically and legislate on its industry, it should be done with generosity so the sting could be taken from the phrase "taxation without representation is tyranny". With a view to the future, Maury hoped that in after years, when the South was prosperous again, it would not appear that, in the South's hour of trouble, the North and West took undue advantage and imposed no burden on her industry too heavy to be borne.

But Maury's committee had other objections to the five cent tax on cotton. Abnormal prices were bringing Brazil and Egypt into stiff competition with American cotton; and the railroads of India with the adjustment of English textile machinery to the shorter staple were cutting down the demand of the American raw products. In a word, cotton was not still "king". According to New York cotton specialists, anything the planter did at the moment meant long range disaster. A large crop meant falling prices—a small one, the encouragement of foreign marginal producing areas which would rob him of a market. Besides the idea of producing thirty-four millions in revenue was being sponsored by the wealthier portion of the country and thus was unsound. The contemplated reduction of income taxes, the five cent draw-back on cotton goods exports, the abolition of the tax of $1.00 per barrel and $.20 per barrel on crude and refined petroleum respectively would invoke hostility at the South and in all honest minds at the North. This tax would tend only to make the rich richer and the poor of the South poorer. Maury, speaking for the committee, urged a more moderate tax not only for the sake of the South, but for all of the States of the Union. Cyrus Field immediately moved adoption of the report and asked the Chamber to instruct Maury to draw it up in memorial form to be sent Senator E. D. Morgan and Representative William E. Dodge, members of the Chamber, and Secretary of the Treasury, Hugh McCulloch. At the end of a hot debate the memorial was unanimously carried.

The congress passed the tax on cotton. The three cents rate, despite the objections of Wells and the New Yorkers, was to be collected not from the manufacturer, but from the "producer, owner or holder".[80] New Englanders received their kick-back on manufactured goods by the law of July 13, 1866, but other members of the alliance profited from the movement to relieve industry. The excise on pig iron, coal and crude petroleum was repealed. Books, magazines, and their constituent parts were also relieved of internal duties. Exemptions and reduction brought relief to the Railroad, Iron, Steel, Cordage and Slaughtered cattle interests. The rates on boots, shoes and other articles of clothing were reduced two per cent. The tax on unenumerated articles was reduced from six to five per cent. Only the internal duties on sugar, whisky and incomes remained the same.

John Sherman in the last days of May tried to push through the Senate with Charles Sumner's aid, H. R. No. 11 entitled "An Act to Facilitate Commercial, Postal, and Military Communication among the several States".[81] The stated purpose of the bill was to allow railroads to carry freight and passengers from one state to another; and "to connect with roads of other states so as to form continuous lines . . . ". Senator Clark immediately added the amendment:

> "nor shall it be construed to authorize any railroad company to build any new road or connection with any other road without authority from the state in which such railroad or connection may be proposed."

Sherman angrily asserted that he wanted an outlet for Ohio's agricultural products into the New England and Middle states, but "Pennsylvania's one corporation" stood in the way. Clark's amendment requiring the consent of the states was ill considered. On Clark's insistence on his amendment, Sherman threw off the mask:

> "Then the object which I have in view and which the people of Ohio have in view in supporting this bill is confessedly defeated; that is, there is no way to aid any corporation or any individual in opening new channels of intercourse."

But moderates were not completely blind to the economic implications of the new radicalism. Senator Cowan boldly stated that the real purpose of the bill was to enlarge the charter of the Delaware and Raritan Bay Railroad Company through New Jersey. Fully cognizant of the many railroad schemes in the air and the communication ambitions of the new economic imperialists, Cowan sought to sound a warning thus:

> "But I beg leave to say, that if this measure is to pass the Senate, it is, even among the important measures that came before this body, the most important by far which has claimed our attention during this session, and will be fraught in the future with results that no man can calculate now. I hope that we shall all pause before we adventure ourselves upon an errand of this kind."

The bill passed in its amended form despite Charles Sumner's best efforts, but the idea was out. Again economic state rights were under the hammer.

As Congress turned attention to the tariff the merchants girded their loins for the battle of "protection." [82] English sympathy with the international capitalists of New York City, tainted of course by the desire to perpetuate for the United States an inferior, colonial economic status, prompted Peto to remark:

> "That any party, in a country of exports, should desire a system of duties, whether upon imports, exports, or raw materials, is a hallucination beyond every reasonable and sensible comprehension. It can only be accounted for by the idea that one section of the community has grown so rich, under a temporary system, that it wishes to perpetuate that system to the disadvantage of every other section."

Andrew Johnson and the British never seemed to have understood that Philadelphians and their fair weather ally to the North had no intention of allowing protection to be so badly put. Indeed, the ability to persuade powerful Western interests of a similar stake in a successful protection offensive constituted the first success of the economic regionalists of the new order.[83]

Having already received a memorial from the Philadelphia Board of Trade expressing its views on the tariff, George Opdyke brought into the New York Chamber a memorial to Congress on the bill then under discussion before the House of Representatives.[84] Opdyke thought "A bill to provide increased revenue from imports and for other purposes" was ill conceived for several reasons. In the first place, the title of the bill was misleading, since the proposed duties were often prohibitive and would lead to a reduction of the revenue. The proposed higher rates were almost exclusively on products like iron, wool, woolens, worsted, linens and cigars, all of which came directly into competition with domestic products and were leading articles in our import trade. Opdyke thought it impolitic to lessen gold revenue at a time when the nation's gold liabilities were increasing "and especially so coincident" with the abandonment of many sources of internal revenue. He feared that the joint effect of the two measures might weaken public credit by making it impossible to meet current expenses and maturing interest.

"But", said Opdyke, "we object on other and broader grounds" to the tariff. The measure would injure every interest affected by it. Commerce would be injured by the bill by diverting it from established channels since foreign trade would be lessened and large mercantile marine would be left without adequate or profitable employment. The measure also would mar the prosperity of agriculture by increasing the cost of its supplies without raising the price of its products, which were governed by the foreign market value. The measure would also injure "mechanics" by increasing the cost of living without raising wages. Finally, Opdyke was sure that, through its exorbitant protection, the tariff bill would endanger the permanent prosperity of the manufacturing interest itself, "which it (sic) specially intended to protect and foster". Framers of the bill proposed to increase protection by adding from ten to fifty per cent to the already high rates of duty, at the moment when the amended internal revenue laws relieved that interest from a heavy excise tax. The joint effect of the two measures would be to confer on the manufacturing interest a rate of protection, ranging from 50 to 100 per cent. Never before, under federal law, had manufacturers enjoyed such protection, and the resulting internal competition would lead to bankruptcy. Sinclair Tousey wanted Opdyke's memorial referred to a commitee, which would report at a fuller meeting of the Chamber. Even over President A. A. Low's objection, Opdyke's plea for haste prevailed; and the Chamber, after unanimous approval, sent the memorial on to Congress.

For a while it seemed that the New York merchants were in for a signal defeat as the tariff bill moved through the House of Representatives.[85] Old Thad, wracked with pain, and supported by William D. Kelley of Philadelphia and James K. Moorhead of Pittsburgh, shouted down his opponents with the remark:

> "We have long enough been tributary to the pauper labor of Europe. We have long enough been deluded by the idle idea that when we put protection upon articles manufactured in this country we injure the consumers here."

Justin Morrill, more and more reluctant to lead the ever grasping raid of Middle Western wool[86] and metals and Pennsylvania metal and coal, rode out the storm to passage on July 10, 1866. The Senate refused to be rushed into passage with only a few hours left of the session. New Yorkers should have drawn consolation from the New England disavowal of paternity of the bill in the face of the obvious alliance with Pennsylvania capitalists. The economic Revolution was halted for the moment. Only the New England wing, after the passage of Public Land bill on the 21st of June and the Second Freedmen's Bureau bill over Johnson's veto July 6, emerged from the grand alliance with all it wanted.

While the editor of the London *Economist* was "expecting a great and pacific victory of Congress over the violent and superficial policy of President Johnson for the reconstruction of the Union",[87] nature was taking a hand in the South to defeat even New England's temporary victory on the floor of Congress.[88] Treasury regulations, inclement weather, the general unsettled conditions of the Southern economy, and the state of the world cotton market conspired to defeat the schemes of the aggressive alliance. On the morrow of the famine year, radical economics, whatever the state of radical politics, faced disastrous defeat. They had sowed the wind and were to reap the whirlwind. The aspiring regents of "King Cotton" were to find that theirs was indeed a "sorry" heritage.

APPENDIX CHAPTER II

NOTES ON THE KING LETTER

The National Archives, Washington, D. C.

Two copies—one original and another made (copy) for the department—(of plan): also one letter by King to Oliver O. Howard.— all in original envelope with the following heading:

Wm. King, Esq., of Georgia—

Letter with reference to the organization of labor in the Southern States (Pencil note—Bring to my attention when the Gen'l returns). On envelope and on transcript copy of plan Adj. Gen. M. Woodhua writes "In my opinion a worse form of slavery than the old one."

Outside cover—"War Department of B. of R. F. etc.

Washington, June 10/65

Respectfully referred to Brev. Maj. Gen'l Saxton, Asst. Com. for So. Carolina & Georgia.
By order of Maj. Gen. O. O. Howard, Com. J. S. Fullerton, Asst. Adj. Gen'l.

On other fly: Savannah, Ga. May 30, 1865 Wm. King relative to Freedmen's Affairs.
On back of the original draft of the plan—

"Plan for organizing labor of the Freedmen submitted by Wm. King of Georgia after extensive interviews with the public men of New England, and generally approved by them. If this system be adopted in time, the Freedmen's lives will be saved, the Government freed from the expense of providing for them and the Southern states will be restored to order, greatness (or quietness) and rapid advancement in prosperity."—

Washington, D. C.—9 Nov. 1865.

Savannah, Geo., 30 May 1865

Washington, D. C.
Maj. Gen'l O. O. Howard

My dear Sir:

I have been much satisfied to learn that to you has been assigned the head of the F. B.—situated as our afflicted country is, I know of no more responsible situation than that of organizing the new relationship which is to exist between the white and colored races in the Southern states that they may be enabled to perform their duties to each other amicably and advantageously to each other and the country great wisdom, moderation, and justice will be necessary to successfully inaugurate such a practical system and you could probably receive much assistance from the suggestions of intelligent and practical men of the South who are familiar with the habits and disposition of the colored people, and thus be much facilitated in forming your plans to enable this unfortunate class to assume a respected and useful position among the whites—If such a position be not obtained by them their fate will be that of the Redman—killed off and driven away from the whites. This sad cruel and injust alternative can be avoided and humanity dictates that every effort should be made to avert it—if I can contribute by any personal experience of my own, or the experience and mature from the Bible and the principles of good order, tending to incite disturbances—could I have spared the time and means, I would have accompanied our country press to afford me the opportunity to have a long personal interview with you on the subject of the well-being of the Negro.

Very respectfully General
Your Observer,

Wm. King.

KING'S PLANS AFTER NEW ENGLAND CONFERENCES

Regulation of Labor for Freedmen, who are possessed of no visible means of support for themselves and families.

1. No rations to be furnished by the Bureau excepting to such cases as are incapable of self support and who have no members of their family able to support them.

2. The able members of families shall be required to provide for the members of their immediate families who are incapable of self support.

3. All Freedmen who have not permanent supporting employment, in cities, towns, and villages, to be required to remove to the country and make engagements for their labor.

4. All capable labor shall at once make engagements to labor in the country or agriculture, or otherwise for a term not less than 12 months from the date of contract at such wages as both parties may agree upon.

5. Should any Freedman not find permanent employment for a year, before the first of January of each year, then the local superintendent, herein after (no) shall bind such person out to labor until the first of January there after to such party as he may think proper and at such wages as he may determine on, but for the interest and profit of the Freedmen so bound out.

6. The immediate families of the Freedmen who may be from youth, old age, or other infirmities, incapable of self support shall always (unless otherwise provided for) accompany the able bodied members of their families and to be supported by them.

7. In all such engagements made for labor on plantations and farms, the laborers shall be required to perform properly and faithfully and all such labor as has been known as farm and plantation work, but not to exceed in labor over the time from sun rise to setting of the sun, allowing two hours from 1st April to 1st October and one hour from 1st October to 1st April during the day for meals. (Married women and women with children shall not be required to labor more than half the time of able bodied laborers nor to receive over half supply rations unless by special

agreements without extra compensation for such additional labor. No farm or plantation work to be required of the laborers on Sundays; and before such contract shall be binding, both contracting parties must sign a formal contract in duplicate and witnessed by the local authorized superintendent. (no)

8. All Freedmen without visible means of support for himself and family who shall neglect or refuse to make a contract for labor for one year, before the first of January of each year, shall be arrested by order of the local superintendent and confined in solitary confinement (and supplied only with bread and water) and not released from prison until a contract for labor for him not to expire before the 1st day of January thereafter shall have been made and signed.

9. Any Freedmen who shall abandon in place of labor or fail to perform properly and faithfully the duties he has contracted to perform, or for other bad conduct, shall be reported to the nearest local superintendent, who shall immediately institute an examination of the case reported, and decide on its merits, and should such superintendent determine and decide, that the Freedman has been guilty of improper or unfaithful conduct, such Freedman shall be immediately placed in solitary confinement (and supplied only with bread and water) for such length of time as may be determined on, not however to exceed the term of his contract, and during the period of such absence from labor his wages shall cease and he shall yet be chargeable with the expense of supporting the non supporting members of his family.

10. Should it occur during the term of contract that from death or other disability on the part of the laboring Freedman, that his service should be so destroyed or diminished, as to reduce his or her wages below the amount needed to provide for their own and their family expense, then the local superintendent shall have such Freedman, with his or her family at the written request of the employer, removed immediately from the premises, and the employer relieved from any further care for responsibility of such Freedman and family; and all time lost from labor in consequence of

sickness and inability as well as absence to be deducted from the wages of such Freedman, information of such loss of time to be given as soon as practicable (in writing) to the local superintendent by the employer or his or her agent.

11. No Freedmen to be allowed to trespass on the property of others, nor to make visits on the plantations or farms on which they are not employed without first obtaining the consent of the owners thereof for such trespass the trespasser shall be arrested and punished by the local superintendent.

12. All employers of Freedmen make contracts for labor, as required in the foregoing articles, and therein set forth the amount of wages agreed on and the manner of payment. The crops to be cultivated shall be held responsible and liable for the payment of such wages.

13. The employer shall provide for the Freedman and his family, a comfortable house, and not less than half acre of land for each family to cultivate. Each full hand shall be provided and supplied with 3 lbs. of bacon and ten quarts of corn meal, or their equivalent in other possessions, all to be good quality; other laborers not full hands to be furnished each week with one peck of corn meal and such amount of meat as may be agreed on in the contract and shall allow the Freedmen to cut and use all the necessary fire wood to be used by them on the premises; all of which shall be allowed free of charge.

14. The employer shall also provide the adult man laboring members of the Freedmen families, with one peck of corn meal for each one for each week, and to the children too young to labor with a proper supply of cornmeal needed for their subsistence, the expenses of which shall be charged to and deducted from the wages of the laboring Freedmen connected with such families. He shall also provide the Freedmen and their families with medicines and proper attention during their sickness, to be paid for by and deducted from the wages of the laboring Freedmen of such families.

15. The employer shall protect and bestow friendly care over the Freedmen and their farms, so long as they are engaged

in his service, and refrain from inflicting any physical punishment, whenever any cause of complaint occurs he shall make the same known in writing to the nearest local superintendent. He shall allow the local and general superintendents of the Freedmen to visit them on his plantation whenever they shall desire to do so, without interruption, but no other person shall be authorized to go on any plantation or farm without the owner's consent.

16. A superintendent shall be supplied by the Freedmen's Bureau to be located in each county or district of a state whose duty it shall be to examine and witness all contracts made with Freedmen laboring within the bounds of his district, to retain one copy of the same and to enforce the faithful performance of such contracts to hear and examine the complaints of either party, and to decide the justice of such complaints, to protect the rights and interests of the Freedmen in cases of oppression, and whenever necessary, to inflict such punishment on the Freedmen and their families by solitary confinement as justice may demand in conformity with the foregoing regulations and the article of agreement between the two parties. It shall be the duty of the local agents to see that the employer furnishes each Freedman employed by him with a certificate of employment and it shall be their duty to arrest and confine all freedmen within their district who have not made labor contracts for the year unless such Freedman shall give satisfactory evidence of being possessed of visible means to provide for the wants of himself and family.

17. A General Superintendent for each State shall be appointed by the Freedmen's Bureau whose duty it shall be to have oversight and control of the local superintendents of his state; to enforce the proper performance of their duties, to consider, confirm or annul the decisions of the local superintendent in all cases of dissatisfaction which may be referred to him by either party, to superintend, direct and protect the safety and interest of the Freedmen, to direct their intellectual and moral training, to appoint, control, or exclude all teachers of Freedmen who are located among them.

18. A charge of 25 cents shall be made and collected by the local Superintendent at the time of making the contract

from all employers for each Freedman signing such contracts. (10) ten cents of which charge for each Freedman shall be retained by the local Superintendent and five cents for each Freedman shall be paid over to the General Superintendent for their services, and no other charge or payment to be made for the performance of their duties, the balance of the funds so collected to be applied towards the expense of establishing prisons and providing for the support and care of prisoners.

3.   The Famine Year and After

The best laid schemes of mice and men gang aft agley.

—Robert Burns
"To a Mouse"

Triumphant radicalism, enthroned at Washington, was knee-deep in plans to reward the economic faithful. The system of tariffs, drawbacks, tax reductions, bounties, and government organized exploitation of the Southern region, sponsored by the Boston-Philadelphia-Northwestern merchant-dominated political alliance, was being pushed to completion with every pressure tactic known to the habituees of the imperial city. To be sure, despite the heroic efforts of the Freedmen's Bureau, the Southern situation upon which most of the new plans depended continued chaotic. But Southern chaos was obviously a passing phase which only the calamity-howlers were trying to exploit. Devotees of the new radicalism were optimistic. Arms and the law had destroyed the hated political supremacy of King Cotton at Washington and its socio-economic supremacy in the Southern region. What arms and the law had destroyed, thought radicals in their naivete, arms and the law could create. After all, two and a quarter million bales of cotton sold in 1865 for four hundred millions of dollars.[1] Why should planter and politician be anything but optimistic?

Planter and entrepreneur alike, unmindful of chaotic conditions and past failures, to say nothing of the unsettled labor situation in the South, reinvested immediately in the 1866 cotton crop. The worst fears of the Cassandras were fulfilled. Unseasonable drought, rain, and the army worm destroyed the crop of 1866. By late fall it was clear to the most casual observer that the artificial post-war boom in cotton was over.[2] Indeed as early as June, George H. Morgan was receiving calls from the people of Georgia and Alabama for supplies to alleviate the suffering.[3] July found Governor Patton, of Alabama, on

76

his way to St. Louis to raise money by the sale of bonds for the purchase of food for the destitute of that state. Patton met with the Directory of the Exchange and presented his predicament. The appointed committee soon sent along at reduced rates the corn and provisions purchased from the sale of $41,000 of Alabama bonds.

As fall and winter came on the situation in the cotton states became critical. Governor J. L. Orr of South Carolina in November suggested a state bond issue to purchase corn for the poor.[4] Senator Henderson received a sharp letter in January from James E. Yeatman of St. Louis. Yeatman said that the preoccupation of the Radical Congress with purely political matters had caused it to be unaware of the eminent famine and ruin in the South. He blamed Northeastern capitalists and adventurers from the North and Mid-west for bringing famine by concentrating on cotton production. Yeatman saw the '67 season approaching with the planters in debt and unable to get credit, without which it would be impossible to employ and feed labor.[5] The merchants, having lost heavily during the '66 season, even if disposed could not make advances or render any assistance to the planter. There was no prospect but for idle lands and unemployment.

Governor Patton wired the Southern Relief Commission on January 30, 1867, that he must have help to relieve the destitute of Alabama.[6] Patton was faced with an empty state treasury and he wanted as much free service as he could get. The Harper Brothers turned the influence of their popular *Weekly* to the task of Southern relief.[7] The editors wanted to make it clear that their interest in relieving the suffering of the South was not intended to be a reflection upon the philosophy or practices of Radical reconstruction in the South. *Harpers'* correspondents revealed that Alabama's grain was very light and fully half of the necessary supply would have to be shipped in. Every county had its destitute and more than 40,000 would have to be fed by public charity. In 1866, 42,000 had been helped in Georgia, and indications were that more than that would have to be in '67. Yet in that state, according to a relief commissioner, there was no more grain than would last to the end of the month. In one county there were 1,200 persons who needed relief immediately. From another county a physician wrote that within four weeks he feared that the poorer people would "be dying like the Hindus in the late famine".

From many parts of South Carolina the reports were harrowing and the "universal cry is 'Help! Help! for God's sake, Help!' " The situation was not without its anomalies. While Savannah hotels were feeding their guests on spring lamb with mint sauce, green peas, lettuce, radishes, tomatoes and all of the delicacies of the summer season, the people of middle Georgia were starving. Six weeks, it was said, would exhaust the last supply of corn in that section.[8]

Faced with this problem, Georgia's legislature passed a "lien law", by which loans made for live stock, implements of agriculture, seed, labor and farm production should constitute the first lien upon incoming crops.[9] This state, confronted with the vengeful politics at the north, had already adopted the practice of appealing to its friends, the merchants above the Mason-Dixon line.[10] Armed with the lien law, the Board of Trade of Macon appealed to the Chamber of Commerce of the State of New York and other northern commercial organizations to initiate measures by which loans could be effected and capital obtained under the lien law.

Such universal suffering in the land of the defeated touched the nation's heart. The masters of capital did not fail to heed. Captain J. W. Luke, Chairman of St. Louis' Merchant Exchange Committee, worked tirelessly to raise funds and, almost single-handed, purchased, forwarded, and distributed supplies.[11] A relief commission, made up of Louisville's leading merchants, used the Board of Trade rooms in the Kentucky metropolis as headquarters.[12] James M. Brown, treasurer of the Relief Commission in New York City, had received by March of '67,

$55,000 and had purchased nearly 50,000 bushels of corn.[13] March 17, 1867, a Sunday, was the day set aside for a general contribution by the churches of the nation for the South. In May, 1867, the Southern Famine Association at Washington received $47,000 from California.[14] As late as May, 1868, the "Ladies Southern Relief Society of Baltimore" sent to Savannah five hundred barrels of flour, meal and bacon "for poor and deserving whites".[15]

Triumphant Radicalism at Washington paused long enough, in its drive to create a politico-economic formula for the nation based on Northern regional needs and interest, to help alleviate Southern conditions. Congress passed an amendment to the bankruptcy law, exempting $500 in property from execution, in '67.[16] March 30 brought approval of an act of Congress setting aside $500,000 to relieve destitution in the South.[17] Congress transferred to the Department of Agriculture $50,000 more to furnish seed for the Southern states. These measures served to prevent widespread property loss which destitution brought in its wake.

As the famine year drew to a close, Southerners got an opportunity to see in what direction they might look for aid and comfort. Angry since the close of the war about their Southern-owed debts,[18] Northeastern merchants at the 1868 Boston Commercial Convention threw off the mask.[19] When Tait of the Louisville Board of Trade offered an ill-timed resolution to the effect that Congress loan the Cotton States $20,000,000 for a year to be secured by either a crop lien or otherwise, Philadelphia's John Price Wetherill tried to block it.

Tait defended his resolution with the observation that the South was neither represented in Congress nor at the Boston meeting, and that the proposed loan would go a long way toward making the South feel better. He knew that there was some such scheme before Congress at the time, but he wanted "to know the sentiments of the merchants throughout the country". Tait noticed that only the interest of the east and the west had consumed the interest of the convention, and in the proposition adopted on direct importation Louisville had not been included. But the lingering bitterness of the war was still near the surface in the minds of the assembled capitalists and found ready expression. That the east and west were going to split on this point was soon apparent. Though Northeasterners were currently looking askance at all such schemes, Western capitalists with heads full of plans for exploiting the Southern market, favored anything that would give the planter buying power in their city markets.

Mr. Alexander of the aggressive St. Louis delegation took up the cudgels for Tait's idea. Arguing from the experience of St. Louis adventurers in the South "for the past two years" and the reticence of Northern capital to aid the planter, Alexander openly championed the Tait scheme. Nazro and Ward of the Boston delegation attempted a conciliatory compromise, but Edward Atkinson was openly hostile. "I look upon this attempt", said he

> to obtain a loan for the South as the last struggle of the plantation system, which in my judgment was doomed by the war. Twenty millions would continue the barbarism of the South for part of a year perhaps.

Atkinson stood firm on his hope for a South of small farmers. Philadelphia's John Price Wetherill, also hostile to the scheme, thought that northern post-war dislocations and debt should persuade "Northern men" to be "sectional in a case of this kind". The Louisville delegate had to be content with a resolution sympathizing with the South and hoping Congress would do something, "without loss to the government", to help the industry and the permanent prosperity of the South.

The non-committal resolution should have indicated to the Southern capitalists that the new politics of business was unwilling to use its power in the interest of Southern needs.[20] Indeed, as time went on, Southern canal schemes, proposed state-federal bond issues to strengthen the Mississippi levees, endorsement of semi-public schemes to improve the rivers and bays leading to Southern port cities—all received the veiled thumbs-down treatment of merchants who knew that the power and glory now lay in another quarter.

The famine year not only brought this result. In the first hours of the Reconstruction victory, the Radicals schemed, in their naivete, with an infallibility born of inspiration. There were a few, the most outstanding example being Andrew Johnson, who himself had barely survived the politics of vengeance, who understood reconstruction for what it was—a Yankee euphemism for capitalist expansion.[21] "The aristocracy" observed Johnson,

> based on $3,000,000,000 of property in slaves south of the Mason and Dixon line has disappeared; but an aristocracy, based on over $2,500,000,000 of national securities, has arisen in the Northern states, to assume that political control which the consolidation of great financial and political interest formerly gave to the slave oligarchy of the late rebel states. The aristocracy based on Negro property disappears at the southern end of the line, but only to reappear in an oligarchy of bonds and national securities in the states which suppressed the rebellion.

Johnson told Halpine that the war of finance was the next war the nation would have to fight. The famine year should have brought some consolation to the Johnsonians; for while it left the South staggering with a mountain of problems, it also put to confusion the plans of the radical host for a painless economic solution of post-war problems.

John A. Andrew, sitting in the ruin of his much touted "Land Agency", wrote Montgomery Blair in January of 1867:

> I felt that the questions ought to be simply economical ones, to receive economical solution; that war had disposed of the old, political questions and had left no good

> ground for new ones, of a political character. If I was
> wrong, I am glad that it was my heart that erred, and
> not my head.

In his attempt to straddle the New England and New York
positions on the nature of reconstruction, Andrew had mis-
calculated the possibilities of the new sectionalism. New England merchant-capitalists were clever enough to identify their
cotton manufacturing interest with the other manufacturing
interests of the nation. Upon this identity of interest, they had
built an alliance with Pennsylvania and the West on the broad
principle of protection from hostile action both at home and
abroad, and quick amelioration of the economic dislocations
of the war. New Englanders took care that much of this system, especially that dealing with the encouragement of the
growth of "King Cotton", was translated into legislation. The
cornerstones of this "cotton policy" were the Freedmen's Bureau
and the "Cotton tax". The logic of policy demanded that when
one of these became impolitic, the other must go.

The famine year brought in its train a serious reconsideration
of the cotton tax. The international merchants of New York,
despite divided councils, had fought the cotton tax on high
ground from the time of its introduction.[22] Again and again
they had hammered home the points that the tax was unjust,
since no other agricultural staple was so burdened; that it was
oppressive, because the planters, operating in a falling price
period, were not realizing enough to cover cost exclusive of
the tax; that it was oppressive because, operating as a dis-
couragement upon production, the tax tended to divert the
industry of the South to other pursuits than raising cotton—de-
priving the South of what had theretofore been an important
source of profit, and thus diminishing the resources of the
country in curtailing the growth of its great export staple; that
it was oppressive because, finally, the discouraging of cultivation
in the South encouraged production in other parts of the world,

to the end that American shipping, commercial interest and internal trade were injured. Indeed, it was equally clear that the tax was injurious to the Freedmen.[23] Therefore, it should be repealed at once.

There were few who were willing to listen to the international merchants of New York during the bitter years of 1866-67. But the Boston merchant community suddenly awoke to the realization that the world cotton market was not dependent upon the necessities of American merchant politics.[24] Reports from New England textile manufacturers, who had travelled in England, to Boston's Board's committee on the Cotton Tax, made it clear that the cotton policy, as New York merchants insisted all along, had been conceived on inadequate data.[25]

William H. Thomas, one of the reporting New England manufacturers, drew an interesting contrast between conditions in England in 1864 and 1867. When he was there in 1864, English manufacturers were altering their machinery to use Indian "Surat" in vain. The staple was so badly baled and cut up in ginning that it was hardly fit for coarse fabrics. Only the necessity of keeping the mills open for the sake of the operatives, in the face of the scarcity of the American crop, caused "Surat" to be used at all. But by 1866-67 British inventive genius had so altered the textile machines that "Surat" proved quite useful in coarse and medium numbers.

Moreover, "Surat" had improved in quality. The introduction of the Macarthy gin, manufactured in England, was responsible for this.[26] This new twelve-inch wide gin allowed one man to clean eight pounds of cotton per hour; and when forty inches wide and adapted to power, thirty pounds of cotton could be ginned per hour. Macarthy's gin was said to work the staple as gently as human fingers; it saved all of the staple and left the seed in better condition than did the "saw" gin. Adapted to all staples of cotton, this new gin proved useful to small cotton raisers in America. Indeed, D. Keith, Esq., of Columbus, Georgia, already had one in use. However, the Macarthy gin had been going to India for the past four years at the rate of one thousand per month. English manufacturers assured Thompson that Macarthy-ginned "Surat" brought 1½ pence more per pound than American "saw" ginned cotton. Therefore, if Americans could not lay down the Southern staple in Liverpool at 10 or 11 cents per pound, the English were prepared to use the better grades and Sea Island for finer cloths and make up the coarser stuffs from "Surat".

A. D. Lockwood summed up Thompson's argument very well with an observation which the New York merchants had made long ago. Said he:

> It is a great mistake to suppose that the world is dependent upon the United States for cotton, even for fine numbers; for notwithstanding there is a good deal of poor cotton grown in India and other countries, there is also a large amount of better grades produced. Egyptian and South American cotton are of very superior quality—fully equal, if not superior to the best grown in the United States, except Sea Island; and I found in spinning 80's to 120's the Egyptian was preferred to almost any other.

Before going to England in 1866, Lockwood studied the possible uses of "Surat" and other foreign cottons. Up to No. 25, he found that "Surat worked well".[27] After going abroad, Lockwood found English labor and supplies 25% cheaper on a gold basis; but more important, raw cotton was 25% cheaper for all numbers in competition with American mills.[28] Lockwood felt that "Surat" not only could be used in print cloths, sheeting, and drills (No. 12 to 25) coarse yarns and bags; but he would not "hesitate to work the higher grades of "Surat" for filling into such goods as Androscoggin L's, Bates XX, and Hill Semper Idems.[29] Then came the happy thought: if the American manufacturer could procure "Surat" as cheap as the English, they might well use it.

Boston's Board's committee had not rested on its oars.[30] February of 1867 found two of the committee in Washington working hand-in-glove with James G. Blaine to secure passage of a bill abolishing the tax on cotton. The bill, bringing repeal either immediately or by September 1, 1867, emerged from the committee of the whole, but was thrown out by a close vote in the House. Boston's merchants, never daunted, continued the preparation of their report. The bill for repeal passed the House in the interim; and it was the position of the bill in the Senate which secured, on December 16, 1867, the acceptance by the full Board of the Committee's report.

It was clear from the report that the committee, taking advantage of the tide of similar protests rolling up from the South,[31] had a double motive. Boston merchants wanted to obtain cheap India cotton on the same terms with English manufacturers in order to compete successfully with them in the world market for cheap cotton manufactures. This, Senators were given to understand, could not be done if the excise on cotton remained. New England textile barons said they wanted to see cheap coarse cotton milling move West and South. This would never come about if India cotton, which would expand the growing cheap fabric trade in China and South America, could not generally be used to reduce the competition with the skillfully handled low cost, heavy spindled New England mills. Indeed, the New Englanders hoped eventually to go on to finer fabrics. In the meantime, India cotton would permit the manufacture of the seamless grain bags, so universally used, at a much lower cost than they could otherwise be made.

It was also clear that Boston merchants wished to give aid and comfort to the socio-economic revolution in the South which emancipation so violently introduced. Believing that "when slavery was abolished, the plantation system was doomed", Boston merchants professed to have "entire confidence in the ultimate cheapness and economy of free labor as compared with slave labor". They were sure that America, with its superior climate and soil, would eventually supply as large a proportion of the demand for cotton, at as low prices and with

more profit than formerly. Boston's merchants saw the South
as a land of small farms, cultivated by educated black and white
farmers with adequate tools. "Until it secures a more dense
and better-educated population, its (the South's) crops must be
such as can be raised by what may be called the ruder or simpler
methods of cultivation, and such crops are grain and cotton."
The merchants were sure that Southern producers would not
be able to compete with the West in grain production; hence,
"their only alternative for saleable commodity must be cotton,
for years to come". But during this transition from the plantation to the farm system, the cost of cultivation would be high,
and thus "every impediment should be removed". The merchants, aided by the universal protest, carried their point.
February 3, 1868, brought approval of the measure abolishing
the Cotton Tax. [32]

But political and economic radicals were not together on
the aims of reconstruction. Charles Sumner, explaining the
aims of reconstruction to John Bright from his point of view,
said: [33]

> Thus far our great change at the South promises well.
> Without the colored vote the white unionists would have
> been left in the hands of the rebels; loyal governments
> could not be organized; this I saw at the beginning, and
> insisted pertinaciously that it should be secured. It was
> on this ground, rather than principle, that I relied most;
> but the argument was like a reinforcement.

The Freedmen's Bureau and the Union League had been the
radical's long arm to establish political hegemony in the South.
But economic radicals, less doctrinaire than their political fellow
travellers, had been willing to use the Bureau as long as it served
their purpose.[34]

The repeal of the cotton tax was a clear indication that
the cotton policy had failed. Its justification rested on the assumption that a large cotton crop could be produced in the

South, which, under famine price conditions in the world
market, would bring the government a sizeable revenue and
underwrite New England leadership in the international cheap
finished cotton markets. This assumption proved fallacious.
Whatever its political uses might be,[35] there was no longer any
immediate economic justification for the Freedmen's Bureau.
The super-plantation-under-government-supervision idea went
down as if nature and world conditions had conspired against
it. In anticipation of the forthcoming legislation a circular
letter, dated December 11, 1867, went out from headquarters
notifying all Bureau officials that after February 15, 1868,
all officials in Maryland, West Virginia, Kentucky, and Tennessee, save Superintendents of Education, would be dismissed.[36]
July 25, 1868, brought approval of the act abolishing the major
functions of the Bureau save in Virginia, Mississippi, and Texas
pending their restoration to the Union.[37]

New England merchant capitalists and industrialists were
rid of the mistake in judgment which threatened the very existence of their interest. But, in their hot haste, they forgot that
it had taken friends to build the alliance in Washington. New
England capitalists had entered an alliance of expedience with
Philadelphia protectionists to secure the necessary pressure to
put over their plans. Philadelphians watched with dismay
the intellectual gymnastics by which their former ally swung
over to the doctrines of "Free Trade". Indeed, when Philadelphians scanned the membership list of the American Free
Trade League, they found some of the oldest alliance makers.[38]

Andrew Johnson, in his interview with Halpine, spoke out
against the protectionists thus:

> The manufacturers and men of capital in the Eastern
> states and the states along the Atlantic seaboard—a mere
> strip or fringe on the broad mantle of our country, if you
> will examine the map—these are in favor of high protec-
> tive, and, in fact, prohibitory tariffs.

Philadelphians were not ashamed to own their interest in the tariff. The Board of Trade let it be understood that as far as it, the city and the state of Pennsylvania were concerned "Protection" was no longer an open question.[39] This unalterable position found justification in the current state of national finances, and in an interest in continued progress and the national credit. Quaker capitalists were determined that no step would be taken to abandon "Protection" without their opposition. Philadelphians had had need to be on guard since 1865. It was to be expected that New York's international merchants, once committed to the principle of protection, would abandon it.[40] Bostonians, having helped frame the post-war policy, seemed bent on shifting the responsibility to other shoulders. In the opening months of the tariff fight of 1867, Edward Atkinson read his paper "On the Collection of Revenue" before the economic section of the American Social Science Association.[41]

His paper was written "to destroy prejudices erroneously held against New England manufacturers". Having already written David A. Wells, "I have finally planted myself on British free trade", Atkinson could say of protective and bounty laws, on the eve of the liquidation of the cotton policy, "I am satisfied that justice of the whole people never required such laws".

The nation, according to Atkinson, had accepted a high tariff as a war measure. He was sure that no man in Congress understood the basic assumptions of the Protection-Free Trade controversy. Atkinson drew comfort from the fact that David A. Wells, Tariff Revision Commissioner for the 40th Congress,[42] was changing his mind. Wells, said Atkinson, was right in assuming "that free trade and not protection, is the proper basis from which to enact a tariff law for the collection of revenue." Professor Perry, William Cullen Bryant, Charles Nordhoff, and the New York Free Trade League were in ecstasies over this signal stroke for free trade. But David A. Wells was not so sure. Fearing the wrath of Henry C. Carey, High Priest of American protection, Wells let it be understood that he was not "dangerous and hostile to the best interest of American industry" and had no intention of being "read out of the ranks of my old friends and supporters". Wells was for relief for domestic industry through the reduction of taxes on raw materials, machinery, and finished products. With currency contraction, the resumption of specie payments, the admission of essential raw materials on the free list, and the reduction of duties on other imports to the lowest point consistent with revenue requirements, Wells thought the tariff problem would be solved.[43]

There was every reason to fear Henry C. Carey. Wells must have understood the nature of the original alliance between Boston and Philadelphia capitalists. If he did not, Henry C. Carey did, and the cavalier attitude of Boston's merchants and politicians toward the alliance drove the high priest of protection to plain speaking.[44] Carey viewed with contempt "the cheap raw material system" advocated by the Atkinsonians. Examining the record as far back as the eve of the Civil War, Carey found that both Henry Wilson and Charles Sumner had taken the cheap-raw-material position, and the tariff debate in the Senate in July of 1866 found Wilson unchanged in his views. Wilson had voted to commit the tariff bill for several reasons, among which was the following:

> What I objected to the other day, and what I object to now, is, that New England should be singled out and charged with the sin of the paternity of this measure. While the representatives of Massachusetts and of New England have voted on general principles for this bill, they have so voted with a great deal of hesitation, doubt, and reluctance. They saw what was clear to gentlemen of ordinary intelligence, that this measure imposed increased duties upon raw materials, increased largely the cost of production, and subjected the manufacturing and mechanical interest of their section to the censure and hostility of those who spare no occasion to manifest their hostility to that section of the country.

If it was asked whether or not the cotton manufacturers suffered like the rest, Carey's answer was no. "Having secured almost entire monopoly", said Carey,

> all he desires is that nothing shall be done that will stimulate domestic competition and to that end, as I understand, New England men have shown themselves inflexibly opposed to granting any more protection than that which they themselves required, or little more than that allowed them.

New Englanders had much capital at low interest, and a highly efficient industrial plant. They were a little embarrassed at that moment, but were consoled because domestic competition was practically dead—or so it was in Pennsylvania. That great industrial plant—the arsenal of Freedom—which Quaker ingenuity had reared up to turn back Jefferson Davis' grey horde, was at a standstill.

Carey, calling up all of the moral indignation of his Revolutionary Irish ancestors, demanded of New Englanders their reaction if they were placed in the same position of Philadelphia capitalists. "Might they not" said Carey, "be led to think that further political connection with us was a thing to be dreaded and not desired?" Carey thought that sectionalism at the north was as much to be dreaded as sectionalism at the south. Indeed, he felt that the work of Reconstruction could not be regarded as having been achieved so long as the whole nation should be required to aid in the construction of an inverted pyramid, the the little apex of which was to find its place among the mills of Lowell and Manchester.

The high priest of protection had spoken for the industrial interest. But the mercantile interest, realizing that American industry and internal trade walked hand in hand—that both had been subject to the whim of foreign manufacturers and merchants in the fight for the American market—also were for a broader reading of the principles of protection. Stephen

Colwell of the Carey circle already had spoken out against
the stranglehold foreign capitalists had on the American economy
entrenched as they were in New York City.[45] The English
were especially suspect because of their inordinate interest in
American tariff legislation.[46] The fact that the American market
absorbed one-fourth of the British manufactures was enough
reason for Britishers to rejoice over the defeat of the tariff
of July, 1866. Fearing the prospective duties of 1867, British
manufacturers and their agents were rushing frantically to dump
their surplus upon the American market before the ruinous
duties went into effect.

Englishmen were overjoyed when intelligence reached the
island in March of 1867 that the tariff bill had failed.[47] Thomas
H. Dudley wrote Seward that

> Every effort will be made in this country to prevent
> any increase in our tariff. Many of the leading manufac-
> turers here have agencies and houses in the states; they
> will work principally through these. So much depends
> upon their retaining their markets in the States that no
> means will be spared or stone left unturned to defeat any
> and all laws that will in anyway interfere with it.

Indeed the much heralded Cobden Treaty turned out to be, as
far as the British commercial and manufacturing interests were
concerned, no unmixed blessing and they confidently expected
to dump in America to make up their loss in Europe.[48]

If the opinion of American consuls in England could be
trusted, Philadelphians believed that they were on sound ground
in their bid for economic nationalism. Indeed, American consuls became alarmed at attempts by British merchants to avoid
accuracy in invoicing their American exports.[49] A large portion
of the British exports to America was in the hands of foreigners
who would not sell their goods for America in England, but
consigned them to their own agents in America for sale there
on their own account. It was discovered that exporters in Eng-

land were invoicing their goods much below their market value, thus realizing the entire profit on American sales.[50]

Despite the continued cooperation between New York merchants and foreign agents in the perpetuation of the "invoice" trick[51] imports of foreign manufactures fell off.[52] Reports of depression due to the decline in American exports rolled in from London, Manchester, Cardiff, Bradford, Liverpool, and Glasgow. America's consul general at London "remained of the opinion . . . confirmed . . . by statements . . . of Mr. Consul at Manchester and Sheffield, that the improvement in American manufactures has very much to do with the extinction of some branches of the export trade from Great Britain, and its decline in nearly all. I imagine that under improved commercial circumstances some of these branches will never revive."

Philadelphians were justified at last when the British press acknowledged the virtue and success of their "idea". The *Times,* acknowledging the stiffness of German and American competition, was especially struck by the superiority of American tools and machinery in Canada, Australia, and especially at home.[53] Editors of the *Times* admitted that England had had no competition until the Civil War closed, "when the Americans who also (had) iron and coal and Anglo-Saxon energy and who were relieved from the incubus of slavery began to strain every nerve to become a great manufacturing nation. Having surrounded their country with a barrier of protective duties, and being temporarily strengthened by a large immigration of trained workmen from the older centers of industry they applied themselves to the improvement of machinery, and to the production at home of almost all the manufactured goods which they formerly bought from us."[54]

Thus the bid for economic nationalism on the part of merchants and manufacturers of Philadelphia in the first bitter years after the Civil War was eventually realized. Moreover the Philadelphia idea proved to be the soundest basis for a liance making with Western capitalists. Only with diminishing of the influence of foreign capital, commercial and industrial, in the American economic scene could the building of a bourgeois society, so typical of the age, be realized in America. Time and circumstance dictated that the new men in the new society must build that society over the bleaching bones and devastated way of life of the giants of the former agrarian era.

4. Creating the Sellers' Market

The famine year was a catastrophe that left the South with many problems. The cumulative effects of the futile attempts on the part of Southerners to solve the manifold basic problems attendant upon the Northern politics of vengeance and a progressively disorganized socio-economic situation was to leave the South a debtor region. This status as a "debtor", while leading directly to the region becoming an economic vassal to other regions, was not due to an absence of a show of energy on the part of Southerners. The failure of the ill-planned immigration program, the absence of capital, the rise of a diabolical system of credit, the continued production of cotton in preference to a diversified agriculture, the mobility of its black and white population, the panic of 1873 with the resulting restrictive "hard money" policy of the federal government—all of these were basic factors in the failure of the Southerners to secure the Southern market for largely Southern exploitation. To be sure obsolete traditions and an ignorance of "Know-how" figured largely in this defeat. But equally important were factors over which the wisdom of a Solomon among the Southerners would not have prevailed. However, this failure to secure semi-economic autonomy in the Southern region by Southerners made the South open territory for the entrepreneurs and capitalists above the Mason-Dixon line.

Looming large among the factors which led to the creation of the "Sellers' market" in the Southern region was the factor of shifting population. The famine year did not begin this problem, but simply aggravated it.

One of the immediate effects of this disastrous period was a population shift from the older Southern region. White and black alike, during and after 1867, began to drift toward Latin America, the Southwest, and the border states. Southern whites were migrating in larger numbers than Negroes; and the

94

resulting effect upon land values and political life was far reaching.

This population shift was not exactly a new situation. The census of 1860 had already revealed the movement.[1] The planter system was still forcing out the small landholder. South Carolina, the census revealed, had lost 193,000 of the 277,000 born within its bounds; North Carolina 272,000 of its 643,000; and Virginia 400,000 of its 1,000,000. But with the debacle of 1867, Freedmen and farmer alike fled from the older cotton areas. The whites took "Texas fever" and headed for the trans-Mississippi. South Carolina alone lost 40,000 whites during the famine year.[2] Some of the planters, in despair, fled to Córdova, Mexico.

The Freedmen had scattered in all directions before the famine—to Texas, the bottom lands of Mississippi, Arkansas, and Tennessee. In the period immediately after the war, the first reaction of the Southern whites was to be rid of the Negroes. Northerners were not entirely without sympathy with the South in this matter. For a while, emigration schemes blossomed thick and fast. Some thought that the Negro should be sent to Mexico, to the Carribean, back to Africa,[3] to British Guiana[4]—anywhere.[5] But necessity put such visionary schemes to flight. The lands must be worked, and who was to work them save Negroes? Nevertheless, the idea persisted that the Negro, by the force of his improvident habits, would soon become extinct and thus the racial problem would be solved.

The more realistic Southerners turned to economic enslavement. To be sure the Negro was free by government fiat, but that could be gotten around. Many of the Southern states, in 1865, resorted to the vagrancy law as a solution to the problem.[6] During his inspection tour of the South at the Radicals' behest, Carl Schurz found Southerners manipulating labor contracts and juggling supply figures to create virtual peonage for the Negroes.[7] Then too, there were the political pressures. Freedmen found themselves victims of the political necessities of planters, carpetbaggers and scalawags. The Freedman's Bureau made a futile attempt to act as a buffer between Southern social collapse and the Negroes.

But the severities of the famine year brought on a crisis. South Carolina alone lost 60,000 Negroes.[8] Out of the Atlantic seaboard freedmen fled to less distracted areas. The activities of the Freedman's Bureau and the march of debt had delivered Tennessee into the hands of the small farmer class, and there the Negro might find work on railroads and farms.[9] Mississippi, Texas and Arkansas offered fresh lands.[10] Perhaps too, they would escape the bitter politics of the older areas.

In some areas white depopulation was taking place so rapidly as to leave more Negroes than was comfortable either for the political or economic situation. The South's necessity proved to be the Negroes' opportunity. Often Negroes could get jobs when the white could not,[11] and white artisans frequently had to go north for employment. Moreover Negroes found the radical reconstruction measures profitable.[12] The Federal tax gatherer, local sheriff or Freedmen's Bureau agent made it possible for the Negroes to acquire some land.[13] The sharp decline in land values throughout the South doubtless aided this development.[14] Something had to be done to stop white emigration. An appeal to Southern whites to remain and thus stave off Negro domination went out. Southern whites must remember, so ran the plea, that the fight had not ceased with the surrender of Lee. It had just begun and would have to be carried to a finish.

The new Southern governments that emerged under the rule of the Major Generals fell heir to all of the post war problems aggravated by the famine year. Their task was not easy. These governments were asked in many instances to act with promptness and decision where their predecessors had followed a policy of procrastination. Their policy was dictated to them—it was to be a policy of necessity. The Carpet-bag regimes were faced with two problems. First, something had to be done to stave off widespread loss of property. Then steps had to be taken to attract new capital and labor to revive the South economically.

Johnsonian "restoration" governments had resorted to the "stay law" to solve the problem of mounting property loss. A storm of protest from the North greeted the use of this expedient.[15] Texas and Alabama had abolished imprisonment for debt earlier in the century and reaffirmed that action in their constitutions of 1866 and 1865 respectively.[16] It was possible for distracted Southern legislatures to draw upon the statutory provisions, dating back to the panic of 1837, dealing with "Homesteads" and "Exemptions". Texas in 1866 "exempted" land only from execution and sale for debt.[17] North Carolina established a total exemption of $500.[18] Governor Pierpont of Virginia advised the Legislature of his doubt of the validity of "Exemption" provisions. Despite some objections, Alabama's "exemption" law was introduced into the Legislature in the fall of 1866, and became a constitutional provision in 1867.[19] Governor J. L. Orr, of South Carolina, called the attention of the legislature both to the necessity of abolishing imprisonment for debt and "to the propriety of passing a homestead law and of extending the value of articles exempt from levy and sale for the head of each family". Orr claimed that most of the states had been much more liberal about such things than had South Carolina.[20]

The chief difficulty of the provisional governments in this matter was Northern fear that every attempt to solve the problem prior to the carpet bag period was wild repudiation. If the carpet bag governments performed no other service, they brought the opportunity for a positive stability and adjustment into the South which only a confidence at Washington, and in the North, in the economic orthodoxy of the Southern governments could make possible.

The carpet bag governments in the South began the task of tempering the wind to the shorn lamb in the new constitu-

tions of 1867-8. Imprisonment for debt passed away and thus
a great evil was abolished.[21] Then the carpet bag governments,
in hot haste, passed a set of laws that perhaps sealed their
doom. Circumstances were accomplishing the liquidation of
the planter when the carpetbaggers staged a rescue. "Homestead" and "Exemptions" provisions were expanded tremen-
dously by both radical constitutions and statutes.[22] Congress
contributed to relief efforts a $500 exemption in the 1867
bankrupt amendment. Federal district courts in the South
sustained all of these provisions. Offices of Registers in Bankruptcy in the South openly advertised in the press this escape
from financial difficulties, past and present.[23]

These laws proved to be a mixed blessing. In Florida
the courts, standing on a ridiculous legal point, refused to
support the constitutional provisions on "homesteads". Governor Bullock of Georgia pointed out that contract debts were
still crowding the dockets of the courts. He said that the
pressing creditors were old secessionists and suggested that the
mass of farmers and merchants, who were opposed to the
"dogma of secession" before the War, should be protected from
these "Shylocks who demand the full measure of their bond." [24]
Governor Scott, of South Carolina, could not see why the professional man, the mechanic, the farmer, and the laborer should
not enjoy some kind of exemption.[25] Governor Reed of Florida
suspected that planters were themselves openly violating the
law.[26] Reed discovered in many counties, no doubt through
his privately hired detectives, that homestead and exemption
laws were being openly violated, especially where Negroes were
concerned. He demanded stringent legislation against such
violations. Radicals in the southern legislatures, it began to
appear, had overreached themselves. They had entrenched their
implacable foe.

The flight of blacks and whites created the second task of
the carpetbag governments. The population of the South, already too small to fill the vast expanses of available land, was

spread as a result of the flight from the seaboard, all the more thinly. "What we need is capital and population" became a byword in southern circles. There were two schools of thought in the South on the meaning of "capital" and "labor". To one group, thinking in the slavery tradition, "labor" and "capital" were two distinct ideas; yet there was division in this group over the meaning of "capital". Perhaps the majority of this second group thought in terms of moderate capital in the tradition of the country squire. The other wing of this second group was the Southern prototype of the northern merchant, for they welcomed capital regardless of its source. They saw only the end to be attained—the economic reconstruction of the South through extensive exploitation of its resources.

When a member of the Congressional Reconstruction Committee asked General Lee "There is no desire to keep out labor and capital?" Lee's answer was "Not that we know of, on the contrary they are very anxious to get capital in the South".[27] There was some justification for Lee's answer. Though the motive was to be rid of the Freedmen, the South Carolina Legislature on December 20, 1866, passed an act for "the protection and encouragement of European immigration." [28] The act established a commissioner at a salary of $1,500 and an expense account of $110,000 per year. On December 21, 1866, the State chartered the "South Carolina Land and Emigration Company" to bring in new people. Georgia in the same year passed an act "to encourage immigration into the State of Georgia and the investment of capital in lands." [29] The act set up a joint "foreign" and "domestic" Commission, whereby the two received $3,000 and $2,000 per year respectively. Alabama established a commissioner February 11, 1865,[30] while Louisiana likewise established a commissioner two years later and placed $20,000 at his disposal.[31]

These early efforts at self-help found northern capital of the "restoration" persuasion ready to lend aid. John A. Andrew's American Land Company and Agency was simply one example of the New York business community's economic reading of Johnsonian policies. Persuaded that private capital could do the job better than governmental bureaucracy, Andrew's agency was willing to act as the funnel through which capital and labor were poured into the South.[32] Northern efforts, while needed, were at first not exactly welcomed. Indeed the southerners evinced a disposition to ostracize northern men and viewed with complacency the lawlessness that kept out northern capital.[33] The depopulation that came with the famine year brought an end to this attiude.

The carpetbag governments were forced to do something about the capital-population problem. A solution did not come from the sporadic relief efforts of 1867-8. The flight proved to stem from more fundamental causes than a temporary shortage of food. Whites moved across Alabama and Mississippi to the west bank of the Mississippi. Their movement, especially into Arkansas, Louisiana, and Texas was a sustained one.[34] The Emigration Commissioner of Louisiana said that the movement resulted from "a natural reluctance to cultivate worn out cotton fields and clear the forest from the rich river bottoms, when fertile prairies lie beyond, all ready for crops of cotton, sugar, rice, and fruit." Indeed, the migrants had gone beyond Louisiana. Negroes from Virginia and the border states, or those brought out of the Northeast by the Freedman's Bureau, together could not hope to fill up the localities stripped by the population shifts. New people, willing to work, became imperative.

Cotton, the soil miner, had laid waste much cultivated land in the South.[35] But the Cotton Kingdom had occupied only a small part of the available land in the region. The South, then, had much to offer prospective capital and labor in the way of natural wealth. According to General Land Office Commissioner Joseph S. Wilson,[36]

> In all of the states involved in the recent war against the government including Alabama, Arkansas, Florida, Georgia, Louisiana, Mississippi, North Carolina, South Carolina, Tennessee, Texas, and Virginia, large tracts of unimproved and unoccupied land exist which may be purchased from individuals at prices ranging from $.50 to $10 per acre, and wild lands are seldom held at so high a figure as that last named price.

Indeed seven-eighths of the land of the eleven rebel states remained wild and uncultivated, and the mineral deposits of the South were known to be rich. As late as 1869 not one-fourth of South Carolina had been brought under cultivation and approximately two-thirds of Virginia's land was in the same condition.

Efforts to bring immigrants into the South became intense after the famine year. "The Mississippi American Industrial Agency", with sweeping powers over the total economy of the state, was incorporated February 19, 1867.[37] The organization was an outgrowth of a meeting of a number of influential men in Jackson the previous November. These men organized under the name—"Central Industrial Association of Mississippi" and proposed "to encourage, develop, and improve the agriculture, horticulture, and the manufacturing and mechanic arts of the state, as those upon which the comfort, prosperity and happiness of all classes primarily depend".[38] Governor Scott asked the Legislature of South Carolina to follow Georgia's lead by exempting outside capital, used in establishing manufactures in the state, from taxes for five years. Scott further suggested that the appropriation for the Land Commission be increased for the purpose of

> securing homes for the worthy and industrious mechanic and laborer which will establish many small farmers . . . and will consequently secure better cultivation of the soil and the expenditure of a greater portion of their earnings at home.[39]

W. L. Trenholm, addressing the Charleston Board of Trade
during its third anniversary observance, said:

> We need population and capital. The one will come if we
> open our doors; the other will follow if we assure it of
> protection. The great popular mind has fastened upon
> immigration as the foremost measure of the day.[40]

The South broke out in a rash of agricultural societies, immigration societies, Granges, and fairs.[41] The General Land
Office Commissioner reserved a special place in his report for
1869 "to call attention to the inducements presented in the
Southern states . . . to immigrants either from the northern
states or from Europe, to the end that their industrial interest
may be established and the cultivation of the valuable staples
carried to an extent far exceeding former times". Representatives of the railroads met at Atlanta and framed a scheme to
aid southern immigration. They established a ticket rate of
two cents per mile and arranged for a series of hotel stop-
overs, at reduced rates, anywhere on the lines. A Convention
on Chinese immigration was held at Memphis. Moses Greenwood, chairman of the delegation from the New Orleans
Chamber of Commerce, returned jubilant over the prospect
of Chinese laborers to aid cotton, sugar, rice, and tobacco
culture.[42]

The newcomers arrived in due time. Many of the European
immigrants in Georgia settled close to the towns and engaged
in market gardening. A good portion of this produce was
shipped to the North.[43] The Swiss Consul bought in 1869,
at 50 cents per acre, 10,000 acres in Grundy county, Tennessee.[44] He established a colony—"Grueth"—where each colo-
nist was allotted one hundred acres. The thrifty Swiss specialized
in cattle, grapes, and fruits. The community of between four
and five hundred moral "folk" established schools that were
the envy of the surrounding territory. John G. Cullman, an
influential German, bought 300,000 acres thirty-three miles

south of Decatur, from the South and North Alabama railroad, a link in the great chain of railroads connecting Montgomery with Louisville, Kentucky.[45] Cullman selected a high, healthy, and heavily wooded plateau for his colony and began with five German families. It was not long before the community increased to six hundred families, and the forest was transformed into lush farms, surrounding the thriving town named for its founder. The town had streets one hundred feet wide, a handsome railroad station, telegraph and express office, three good hotels, a large steam flour mill, two wagon factories, cigar manufactory, tanneries, eight saw mills, lime kiln and brickyards, shingle-barrel and furniture factories, planing mill, fruit canning and drying establishment. There were Protestant and Catholic churches.

Other immigrants did not fare so well. In some respects the South's attitude toward free labor lacked maturity. This became evident when a group of Germans arrived in Charleston in 1867. They were employed by planters in the interior for $12 per month and provisions. The Germans were unfamiliar with English, and were astounded when rations of "fat back", corn meal, salt and molasses were issued. The planters were equally surprised that the Germans did not like their rations. Negroes had survived on such fare without complaint—and were not these Germans laborers too? In a short time the Germans went back to Charleston to be provided for by the German settlement there. The efforts to bring laborers from Portugal and Spain failed for the same reason. Besides the Chinese coolie, who was more amenable to an invidious social and economic status, soon proved to be a perfect failure and was decidedly in disfavor by the early '70's.[46] Indeed, the "coolie trade" had begun to rival in horror the African Slave Trade, and the "British and Foreign Anti-Slavery Society" had already issued a sharp warning to American authorities. Chinese were decidedly not the type of labor wanted.

The type of labor the South did want was hindered by two conditions—a discriminating social status and the lawlessness of the southern communities. Governor Tod R. Caldwell told the North Carolina Legislature, after commenting on the lawlessness of the state, "What we need most is capital. Our condition will for a long time remain as it is unless we send words of encouragement, cordial in their widest sense to those abroad" inviting them to come and insuring them "that our laws shall protect them and that no invidious distinction shall be made to their social or political prejudice". Governor Kellogg pointed out to Louisiana solons that "riots, massacres and assassination must cease. Capital, naturally so sensitive, "shuns a community where turbulence and violence are tolerated".[47] Governor Davis of Texas, believing that "Every industrious, ablebodied adult added to our population may be considered an addition of fifteen hundred dollars to the wealth of the state," admonished the legislature that government "must establish, first, law and order" throughout the state.[48]

Social proscription and lawlessness were not the only obstacles to immigration. As the '70's wore on, other serious problems arose. Outside opinion had always been divided as to the possibilities of immigration to the South. British consuls, located in southern cities, were not at all united on this question. Consuls Barnes and Donahoe, at Galveston and New Orleans respectively thought that immigration into the South was feasible and profitable.[49] Donahoe had changed his mind by 1869.[50] He felt that the steaming, fever-ridden Mississippi bottom could not compete with "the salubrious climate of the Western states" in attracting European immigrants. Consul Credland, at Mobile, was a little hopeful, as was the "Board of Trade and Order of Grangers" of the same city, over the reports of certain responsible persons as to the possibilities for small farming in the Gulf pine region.[51] Despite Somers' belief in the superiority of the fertile Mississippi bottom,[52] de Fonblanque, the successor to Donahoe at New Orleans, not only echoed his predecessor's objections, but added a few of his own.[53]

De Fonblanque, located at one of the crossroads of America, had seen every wrinkle in the Southern immigration effort. He had seen the funds for immigration relief, raised by a "commutation" tax on ships,[54] squandered on immigration officials' salaries, while the immigrant was either put into a workhouse as a vagrant or fed at a public soup kitchen. He, from his limited funds, had helped many English artisans who had wandered from New York to New Orleans looking for work, and many others incapacitated by fever. Other immigrants had signed what purported to be labor contracts in England; on arriving and going into the interior, they found no job awaiting them. The southern "societies" and planters merely advertised and seemingly did little else about the immigrants; for certainly no pains were taken to provide for the wants and remove the prejudices against the different nationalities immigrating. Then came the old story. "Planters to whom I have spoken on the subject", said de Fonblanque, "seemed perfectly satisfied that a dietary of pork and beans for breakfast, dinner, and supper, seven days in the week was not improved. It is what the Negro had, and a laborer, be he British, French, Italian, or Swede, is a laborer; he does the same work and is to be treated in the same way". De Fonblanque was sure that Negro slavery had "spoiled" the planters. He had also seen women, who came out to America as trained house servants, driven, by the enormous amount of field labor imposed upon them, either to prostitution or to a bed in a charity hospital.

The theory of the entire Southern immigration idea had been predicated, as far as the immigrant was concerned, on two assumptions: first, he could get better wages than were possible in Europe; and second, he would be given land around his "cabin" to raise a bale of cotton worth £20, and where his wife and children could raise vegetables, chickens and pigs for home use or sale. Thus the immigrant eventually would become an independent farmer himself. It had seldom worked out that way in de Fonblanque's experience. Said New Orleans' British Consul:

> At first all may go well, especially if his employer be a reasonable man who will not expect him to work in the extreme heat of the day, but the cotton patch, the vegetables, and the livestock and chicken schemes have to be given up . . . Then comes the inevitable chills and fever. The laborer is no longer able to work and loses his employment; his wife and children sicken also, and there is no one to care for them. They sell all they have and painfully make their way to a charity hospital or throw themselves on the Consul who can do little or nothing for them. This is the beginning of the end. The end itself is too sad to contemplate. I do not know what becomes of scores of such unfortunates.

As the '70's wore on some Southerners were no longer so sure of the benefits of immigration.[55] The tide of people that swept over the Southern region was a penniless horde, bringing added burdens to a region wracked by depression and torn by bitter political factions. But there was to be no respite from the contagion. The demand was for still more people.[56] In the Mississippi area in 1879 the population shortage was dramatized by the great exodus of Negroes into Arkansas. Freedmen feared that the coming of the Democratic regime in the area meant re-enslavement. The whites promised everything to no avail. The movement was sponsored by Conway, former carpetbag school fund commissioner of Louisiana. His agents, acting as sewing machine salesmen, went among the Negro field hands distributing palm-sized flags as passports into the Arkansas region. The whole thing was conducted on revivalist principles, and abrupt wholesale abandonment of farms and plantations ensued.

The attitude toward labor that made the field hand class possible was bearing bitter fruit. One of the British consuls observed:[57]

> It would not be permitted in any Southern state to say that the Negro race has improved since the war in a greater ratio than the white laborer, but so far as my observation goes it would nevertheless be true. The planters say that he is lazy and irresponsible, but don't admit that the good ones now own their own farms or have learned a trade and are in the towns and cities, leaving lazy ones behind as field hands.

It was the field hand, so easily misled, that rose up and fled, thus creating a new labor shortage.

The problem of increasing the capital of the South through the improvement of land and the increasing of the labor supply had proved difficult of solution and heightened the possibilities of the region's economic vassalage. Pointing in the same direction was the more pressing and difficult problem of fluid or operating capital. Before the Civil War many of the Southern States—Georgia, South Carolina, Virginia, and Louisiana—either had owned all or a majority of the stock in an official state bank.[58] The notes of these banks especially after the Jacksonian period, had, in their free circulation, provided the liquid capital for business operations. To be sure, many of the state governments unloaded their holdings in these institutions before the Civil War. Nevertheless most of these powerful banks were, on the opening of the war, still strong. But their strength was tied up with the social configuration of the planter-slavery system. When that pattern was shattered the doom of these banks was sealed.

Many of the great banking institutions in the North date their origin from the banking act of 1863. Had the Lincoln administration, the northern merchants, or the Reconstruction radicals plumbed the depths of ingenuity, they could not have

conceived of any measure that would have had as far reaching
implications for the exploitation of the South, than the ten per
cent tax on state bank notes imposed by amendments to the
new act. Governor J. L. Orr told the South Carolina Legislature that the loss of assets and the heavy tax on state bank
notes made it clear that the state bank could never resume
business. He therefore recommended that "its charter be re-
voked . . . and its books, papers, and assets (be) put in the
hands of commissioners for the early liquidation as may be
practicable." [59] The solution of this problem proposed by
Governor Jonathan Worth, of North Carolina, was an obvious
one—the state must secure a national bank.[60] He realized that,
with the state bank having only $800,000 in specie and pos-
sessing claims by depositors and note holders amounting to
$8,500,000, thus making it possible to liquidate only 10 cents
on the dollar, the ruin resulting would be terrible. Worth
suggested that the charters of banks and railroads, where
the state held bonds, be amended to allow the $800,000 in
specie to be subscribed to a national bank.

As circumstances were to prove, the national banks, while
necessary to provide the circulating medium, were useless in
an agrarian situation. The banks could lend money on personal security, but not on land. The banks tended therefore,
to be located in the large trading cities of the South and
served only their interests.[61] Some planters could raise the
necessary personal security for loans from these banks, but the
majority of planters and small farmers had to look to other
sources. The southern governments turned to the expedient
of extending banking privileges to strong corporations. The
"Central Railroad Bank" of Georgia, which had survived the
debacle of the Civil War by keeping a capital reserve in England, was only one of the many examples of such combinations.[62]

Banking capital, despite the adoption of many expedients,
continued to be scarce in the South. Somers found the typical
southern banking picture of the early '70's in Charleston. The

city had had a banking capital of $13,000,000 before the War, and after it, only $1,892,000. Indeed the State of South Carolina, outside of Charleston, had before the war $3,000,000 in banking capital and only $300,000 thereafter.[63] Going on to Alabama, Somers remarked: "There are no banking funds visible in such places as Selma adequate to the amount of trade". In Georgia he discovered the same condition; and at a stopover in Mississippi he observed, "There are no banking accommodations in this and many other districts of the state of Mississippi". In New Orleans, Somers found not only a banking capital of $7,497,182 and deposits to $15,039,499 but a valuable fund of credit in foreign exchange as well. Mr. Consul Lynn at Galveston reported five national banks in Texas, with $525,000 capitalization and twenty-four other private banking companies of prominence.[64]

It was obvious, then, that something had to be done about credit facilities. The situation was complicated by the extremely high prices that prevailed in the South for many years, resulting from the scarcity of goods and services after the war. The state governments immediately relaxed the strict corporation regulations, and swept the usury laws from the books under the pretext that this was necessary to get capital into the region.[65] The door had been kicked open! Loan sharks flocked to the southern towns to begin the bloodsucking, and clung like leeches to the farmers. From the Carolinas to Mississippi, complaints were bitter about the 25 and 30 per cent being taken by every one that had money to lend, even on transactions where there was little or no risk.[66] In immediate post war years political conditions encouraged this situation, and the "cavalier indifference" of the planters to the necessities of bookkeeping prolonged the practice. However, the fact remains that investments in a practically one-crop economy were risky, and they continued to be recognized as such in the South throughout this whole period.

The merchants, particularly, were conscious of the fact tha
an act of God might push them to the wall. The famine yea.
brought them to the brink of ruin in the best southern tradi
tion. Many of the southern merchants that had survived the
War were ruined in 1867. Those who took their places were
loud in their demand for additional safeguards. The new
usury laws helped, but the Lien law of Georgia, passed ir
1867 as the possible quid pro quo of Northern financial as
sistance, pointed the way. The planters first asked and go
laws regulating the relations of "landlords and tenants" ir
order to have better control over the production of a crop.[67]
The principle of "landlord and tenant" was expanded with pro
visions making a crop lien for advances superior to all othe
attachments save taxes. Georgia was soon followed by Virginia
North Carolina, South Carolina, and Mississippi.[68] Georgia'
provisions are typical:

> Landlords furnishing supplies, money, farming utensils or
> other articles of necessity to make crops and also all per-
> sons furnishing clothing and medicine, supplies or provi-
> sions for the support of families, or medical services,
> tuition or school books, shall have a right to secure them-
> selves from the crops at the year in which such things
> are done or furnished, upon such terms as may be agreed
> upon by the parties . . .

The law had spoken. All the merchants had to do then wa:
to stock their shelves and proceed to do business. The stage
was set for "The New Imperialism".

The furious rush for commercial routes into the South by
the merchants of the Northeast and Middle West, was for the
wholesale trade. They wished to supply the factors and planter
storekeepers with necessary supplies, and in exchange the
"foreign" merchants demanded and got the old staple for the
manufactures of the North and Europe. In the isolated dis
tricts of many of the Southern states, personally poor young
Jewish storekeepers, acting as the closely supervised agents o

merchants in the large cities, operated with great power over the plantation.[69] The business was risky at best and much of it was simply "on the books". Thus in the face of such a system the demand for diversification was futile. Year after year, under the whiplash of Northern and Middlewestern demand, the Southern cotton crop grew.

In 1870 came the roll of thunder. The Franco-Prussian War caught the South with a huge crop of cotton. Prices began to fluctuate dizzily and "hard times" immediately set in. The Commissioner of Agriculture, with the lack of imagination so characteristic of a bureaucrat, but not without a touch of prophecy said, in his annual report:

> I regret to observe, from official correspondence and during a brief tour through the cotton states, the tendency to neglect other crops and concentrate all available labor and capital upon a single product, however profitable. The inevitable results will be more cotton and smaller net returns in money after the purchase of needed supplies and as a result, a slower improvement of neglected lands. This bane of southern agriculture is still operative and may cease to exist only when low prices, disaster and despondency shall again arrest the impolitic and irrational course of production.[70]

He was not alone in this opinion. *The South,* a journal published in New York, ran the comment that "cotton was a curse, and that its exclusive cultivation had led to the enslavement of the South." [71] Despite these warnings, cotton cultivation, as the reports of Her Majesty's Consuls in the southern states show, was on the increase. This condition existed in almost open defiance of frost and floods and the political conditions which depressed trade and property values.[72]

In 1873 the storm broke. Friday, September 18, 1873, the famous banking house of Jay Cooke & Company of New York closed its doors. The next day Fisk and Hatch, one of the soundest banking firms of New York collapsed, and that gloomy afternoon the Stock Exchange ceased trading. In the South the effect was immediate. Staple prices dropped precipitously. From Baltimore to Galveston business went into a slump. Consul Credland reported from Mobile, a paralysis of all money transactions and the cessation interfered greatly with the cotton trade, "the main dependence of the state".[73] Consul de Fonblanque of the Mississippi-New Orleans area, recorded that the crop year 1873-4

> was marked by more suspensions in business, more disastrous failures, and more general disappointment amongst merchants and commission agents, and both wholesale and retail dealers than has ever been known . . . Real estate and securities have shrunk even from the depressed quotations of 1872-3 and political troubles, which appear to have become chronic, discourage capitalists and defeat projects of improvement.[74]

Consul Lynn of Galveston vouched for similar conditions.

The Panic brought a flood of suggestions to Washington. The solution lay, said one group, in the reduction of the "greenback" circulation to the point where the bills could be exchanged at par with gold. Needless to say this idea came from the northeastern money men. The West clamored for more money. Congress, while temporarily expanding the "greenback" circulation in an attempt to stem the tide of the depression, passed acts demonetizing silver and fixing the date 1879 for the resumption of specie payments.

The money policy of the Federal government was felt throughout the South. The contraction of the currency only aggravated further the limited legitimate banking facilities and made a reliance on barter, or the merchant system imperative. State money schemes popped up in the South. When James L. Kemper took office as Governor of Virginia, he pointed out, in his inaugural address, what he considered an inequitable distribution in the national currency.[75] By the December session Kemper was in an angry mood. He had asked R. M. T. Hunter, the state treasurer, to prepare a state money scheme, which was ready for the consideration of the Legislature. To be sure the national banks in the South had survived the panic, but this was no good to Virginia. Said Kemper:

> It is in vain we are told that a supply of national currency can be obtained by first complying with the requirements of the national banking law. Such counsel is as ineffectual as the advice to a starving and destitute man to buy bread for cash. It is impossible for a people, stripped of their means and loaded with debt, to procure national bonds, to be exchanged for national currency. Among the people of the interior, in many portions of the state, the business of society is transacted on the most primitive principles of barter.[76]

Texas solons had the same idea, but their plan was immediately called class legislation and wildcat money.[77]

As the depression deepened, the South turned to the old devices of the late '60's. South Carolina seized upon the stay law, and again the cry of class legislation went up.[78] The State later put a $500 ceiling to its exemption provisions.[79] North Carolina exempted all real and personal property and homesteads, except for liens, taxes, and mortgages, from execution for debt.[80] In the Constitution of 1875, Alabama extended the 1867 constitutional provision on exemptions.[81] In 1873 Virginia found it necessary to exempt the wages of laborers, not exceeding $50 per month, from execution.[82] Mississippi expanded her homestead provision and exemptions beyond any proportion thought of before,[83] and Texas found it necessary to exempt both public and private property from execution.[84]

The southern merchants joined the general clamor for protection against the caprice of fate. The tide had set in another direction. There was to be no repetition of '67 save in North Carolina, where the legislature, seemingly, made it a point to be all things to all men. Southern legislatures made an examination of merchant demands and decided that their influence was a menace. A cry went up in many quarters for a repeal of the "Lien Law" that had fastened the merchant and the credit system, like the old man of the sea, onto the shoulders of the South. Voices also reached a strident pitch over the usury laws, which had allowed merchant and banker alike to bleed the South white.[85]

Governor Moses, of South Carolina, called the attention of his legislature to the Lien law problem in 1873:

> In this view, and in the common interest of the agricultural laborer and the land owner, I earnestly recommend a speedy change in our existing agricultural lien laws. We are now working chiefly on the share system in the raising of crops. This is known as the 'Italian' plan of cropping, and it has kept the agricultural laborers of Italy poor for the past three centuries . . .

Moses found that the system led to friction and litigation between laborer and landowner. Besides, the laborer seldom had a surplus at the end of the season. He recommended the fostering of the English system of tenantry with its yearly rents on a cash basis. Governor Adelbert Ames of Mississippi called attention to the problem in his inaugural address:

> But what is, if possible, a still greater evil, and perhaps a natural consequence of a single product, is the credit system, upon which all planting interests are conducted. Not only is the planter embarrassed by a mortgage on his crop almost a year before it is ready for market, but he is also burdened with high rates of interest on advancements and charged exorbitant prices for supplies by the merchant, who thus protects himself against possible losses. This manner of planting is fraught with much evil, experience teaching that an unpropitious season necessarily causes financial ruin.[86]

In 1878 Mississippi was still agitated about the question. Rumor had it, in many sections, that the prostration of business and the poverty of the laboring class, were mainly caused by the law which enabled the laborer to mortgage the crop months in advance of its planting. The people asked for relief from this condition, which could come by repealing the Lien law.[87] However, by 1884 Governor Robert Lowry was sure that repeal was useless.[88] The same conclusion was reached in South Carolina. The reform party of South Carolina went into power with the desire to repeal the Lien law; in fact, it was a plank in the party platform. But to have done so in the depressed condition of "things" would have brought utter ruin to the poor man and would have injured the man who advanced to him.[89] The State Agriculture Society and the Commission of Agriculture sought the repeal of the law or changes therein in the early '80's to no avail.[90] The doctrine of diversification began to fall on receptive ground, but the fertility had gone. The Southern town and crossroads merchants were in too deep. They did not care particularly which way the crop of cotton moved as long as they did the business. Commercial brains and transportation facilities would determine whether merchants of the Northeast or Middle West would win out in the competition for the trade in the sellers' market of the South, which time and conditions had created.

Parliamentary Papers 1875—Vol. 75 H. of C., p. 453.

Osyka (Mississippi)
December 18th, 1873.

To the British Counsel Residing in the City of New Orleans:

Dear Sir,—I wish to inform you that I am a British subject and was employed by an agent in Liverpool called George Torrey to come out to this country with my family, eight in number. We were engaged by one, Mrs. Rebecca Cox, to work in Amite County in the State of Mississippi. We left home on the third of November, and arrived in New Orleans on the 30th of same month by steamer "Mississippi"; we were forwarded by the agents in New Orleans and well cared for and kindly treated until we arrived at our destination, but when there Mrs. Cox said she was not able to support us and grumbled for the nine or ten days we were there all the time; she has given us our discharge that we are able and willing to work. She sent her team of mules in with us last saturday to Osyka, and we arrived late at night, and threw our luggage out upon the street without one cent in our pockets or a place to go to for to shelter us from the inclemency of the weather on that cold and frosty night. One gentleman, an Englishman, came forward and took the women and children in for to stop until Monday morning. The men of us were taken by her agent, Mr Torrey, and put in his hayloft without meat of any kind, and we stopped until four o'clock in the morning after being nearly frozen to death with cold and walked about on the streets until seven o'clock. We then went to where the gentleman, that where the women and children stopped, and he admitted us and put a fire on and gave us some breakfast. We have searched all around the county for sixteen miles, and cannot find any work. We have no money to buy victuals, or etc., of any kind, only as we beg it from the inhabitants which we were never used to do, and one gentle man has given us the use of an empty house for to shelter us, and all we have to lie on is a bed of leaves. We did not think when we left our comfortable homes that we would have such hardship to endure in this country. Dear Sir, would you be kind enough to give our case your most serious consideration, and if we could have got employment we would have never acquainted you with our case, but it is our last and only remedy. We had to borrow this paper, ink, and pens to write to you and remain your humble servants in need

George Purdy and Family

Dear Sir—if you take any notice of our case would you be kind enough to direct your letter to Osyka Post Office till called for.

APPENDIX B

State	Agricultural Rank			Manufacturing Rank			10th Census
Alabama	17	15	28	16	29	30	32
Connecticut	28	32	22	31	16	6	7
Delaware	37	35	34	35	35	24	28
Florida	34	33	37	34	37	36	37
Georgia	13	13	23	10	20	22	22
Illinois	4	1	3	4	4	5	4
Indiana	6	6	5	6	6	12	6
Kentucky	8	9	10	12	15	17	17
Louisiana	22	25	32	22	30	27	25
Maryland	23	26	18	26	12	14	13
Massachusetts	7	27	19	27	5	3	3
Michigan	9	12	7	8	7	8	9
Mississippi	18	18	27	13	31	34	35
New York	1	3	2	2	1	1	1
North Carolina	15	11	20	18	19	26	29
Ohio	2	2	1	3	3	4	5
Pennsylvania	2	5	4	5	2	2	2
So. Carolina	21	20	31	23	28	28	30
Tennessee	12	10	14	14	18	23	21
Texas	11	8	17	11	23	31	27
Virginia	14	17	13	20	14	20	20
W. Virginia	29	24	21	30	26	25	26
Wisconsin	16	16	9	9	9	10	11

* Columns one through seven in the above chart refer to the rank of the various states as follows:

Column 1. In population
Column 2. In number of farms
Column 3. In aggregate value of farms
Column 4. In aggregate value of products
Column 5. In number of establishments
Column 6. In capital
Column 7. In value of product

5. Westward the Star of Empire
Takes Its Way

*"Let the growth of the great cities of Chicago and Mil-
waukee, and many other of these inland marts of trade
which have sprung up, as it were, in a day, be an incen-
tive to greater exertion on our part; and although the
older cities of St. Louis, Cincinnati and others, are yet
rising in the scale and competing for the palm of victory,
and notwithstanding that 'Westward the Star of Empire
takes its way' . . . yet let us seek to bind closer and firmer
the fraternal bonds of friendly intercourse and more extended commercial relations . . ."*

Charles G. Nazro, President
Boston Board of Trade

The failure of the "Cotton policy" of the Boston-
Philadelphia merchant-dominated alliance and the successful
bid made by the merchants of New York for the trade of the
Southern ports after the war did little to seal the breach existing in the ranks of north-eastern merchants. Indeed the
fruits of the alliance between Boston and Philadelphia had
almost brought an angry quarrel between the two. There was
a growing feeling among Philadelphia protectionists that they
had "sold out" to Boston to no purpose. Philadelphians failed
to understand the "Free trade" leanings of Boston's leading
businessmen and considered them traitors to the alliance.[1]
However Boston's masters of capital felt that, in this first
attempt to create a politico-economic formula for the nation
on northern regional needs and interest, they had made a
mistake, and with typical Yankee candor, they were willing to
liquidate the entire scheme from Washington down.

Bostonians did not like the necessity of having to abandon
their regional aggression in the face of the triumph of their
oldest rival. The New York merchants had been guilty of an
unforgivable sin. New Yorkers had said all along that the
"Cotton Policy" was bad economics and statesmanship. They
had argued their case from a background of superior banking

and credit facilities, both at home and abroad; and from established contacts with the source of the nation's largest and
most profitable staple export, both at its source and in the
world market. In the face of a triumphant politico-economic
radicalism favoring the Boston-Philadelphia alliance enthroned
in Washington, New York capitalists showed a superior business acumen. Though protectionist industrialists around Philadelphia were offended by the cavalier attitude of their New
England ally, the greater number of merchants among Philadelphia's organized capitalists made possible the continuation
of the "Quaker-Yankee" alliance. The alliance now had a
new aim—to destroy the power of the proud international
merchants by reducing New York port from a commercial turn-
pike to a mere gateway.

This was not to be an easy task. Habit and tradition in
business practices and governmental machinery argued against
so bold a stroke. From the first, Philadelphians understood
that such a partisan issue would need friends on both sides
of the Alleghenies. Only then would it take on the dignity
of national interest.[2] Northeastern regionalists were schooled
in the old sectional tradition. The genius of pre-war sectional
statesmanship was to be found in an exchange of favors which
served to harmonize regional interest into national policy.
Radical politicians had thus won the trans-Allegheny for the test
of strength in Mr. Lincoln's war. Northeastern politics of
business decided to go down the same path to win the peace.

Coeval with struggle of the political giants, northeast and
south, to make a deal with the ambitious young Titan beyond the Alleghenies[3] was a growing awareness by the merchants of the seaboard of the decisive importance of the Middle
West in the economic life of the nation.[4] To be sure the
romance of the great staple, "King Cotton", still held the
allegiance and imagination of the best political and commercial
brains of the Northeast.[5] But the growing pull of old emigration
and trade routes,[6] the exchange of courtesies on common com-

mercial problems, and the bold bid for power by the giants
of the west in the national councils all served, as the crisis
over slavery grew and flowered, to make the West more attractive.

In the summer of 1863 at Chicago, the first move in the
direction of undergirding the East-west political alliance with
commercial timbers was made at the politically inspired, abortive "National Ship Canal" convention. The movement began
in 1862 with a bill to construct a ship-canal from the Mississippi river to Lake Michigan.

In June, New Yorkers sent a memorial to Lincoln, proposing adopting the state's canals to the lake's defense. However it was not until March 1863 that ninety-eight members
of Congress published a "Call" for a convention to meet on
the first Tuesday in June at Chicago.[7] The convention, so
ran the "Call", was designed to effect measures for the prosperity, unity, and military protection of the nation, and all
Boards of Trade, Chambers of Commerce, Agricultural Societies, and Business Associations were invited.

Having received, as usual, a rather flattering call, members
of the New York Chamber met, accepted resolutions approving
the project,[8] and appointed twenty-five members to attend.
They were instructed to push the enlargement of the Erie and
Oswego canals to admit vessels twenty-five feet broad and two
hundred feet long, so that the lakes could be defended and
cheap transportation to the seaboard for the increasing volume
of western produce could be provided. The New Yorkers expected the federal government to pay for the locks in this
enlarged canal system. Samuel Ruggles himself was dispatched
to Albany to represent the chamber on this canal scheme. Ere
long an act to incorporate a "Niagara Ship Canal Company"
was in process.[9]

From the outset the faint hint of rivalry was apparent.
Philadelphia merchants met in solemn conclave, and after one
look at the "Call" instructed Secretary Lorin Blodget to ex-

press their regret at not being able to send a delegation.[10] As
much as they were in sympathy with the problem, Philadelphians
were forced to tell the organized capitalists of Cincinnati,
Pittsburgh and Milwaukee that they were afraid that a bad prec-
edent was being set. Arguing in the old pattern of Eastern
antipathy to federal sponsored internal improvements, Philadelphians thought such projects would encourage schemers to
promiscuously seek government backing. Boston capitalists had
the same attitude.

Boston's masters of capital had known moral objections to
this species of Treasury raiding. Therefore they had no invitation to what their secretary, Lorenzo Sabine, was contemptuously
to call later, the "Mass meeting." President Converse, with
several other members, went out to Chicago as unofficial delegates. The Boston delegation had not been in Chicago long
before preceiving "that the sole design was the aggrandizement
of (New York and Chicago sic) at the expense of the United
States under the veil of 'National military necessity' both foreign and domestic." Bostonians were amazed to find New York
and Chicago trying "to turn the entire trade of the West to
and through" their marts. More shocking still was the fact
that both Charles Sumner and Henry Wilson were present at
such a convention. If the plans of this convention materialized
it was futile for Boston capitalists to continue the building of
railroad lines to tap the West and the elevators to accommodate
the grain to be received over these lines. Indeed Boston's
merchants were shocked at the localism of men of Ohio, Indiana,
and Illinois who, were seemingly willing to squander federal
funds on every "backwater" in their states.

But Converse and his men were not without consolation.
Taylor of the Minnesota delegation, delivered the *coup de grace*
to the scheme with the remark:[11]

   "Illinois, with her great wealth and resources, . . . should
   not stand, like a pitiful mendicant, asking Congress to do

what she should do for herself; and New York should not
be here in support of that contemptible effort."

The Chicago Idea went down to defeat; and the convention
broke up with only a resolution for a ship canal around Niagara
and the improvement of the St. Lawrence waterway. The West,
however, had spoken, and the men of the seaboard perceived
that, in economics, as in politics, her voice must be heard. Out
of the experience came one conundrum to Northeastern merchant
capitalists of the seaboard cities outside New York—how was the
power of attraction of America's first port city to be destroyed?

Early in 1865 Boston merchants found an opportunity to
take steps toward the solution of the problem of New York.
Already the cleavage in business circles over government policy
for southern "Restoration" or "Reconstruction" was becoming
apparent, and the Massachusetts-Ohio axis in politics might
well be strengthened on the commercial level.[12] Remembering
the lesson of the abortive "Chicago" idea, Boston's Board, in
February of 1865, went on record as favoring a ship canal
around the American side of Niagara Falls. "It is for the interest of New England," the honest Yankees thought "that
vessels from the lakes should come as near the Atlantic as possible before discharging at Railroad stations", and hoped that
the canal and a bridge over the Hudson at Albany would make
the west, at least in part, a Boston back-country.[13] News came
from the north that Portland, Maine's Chamber of Commerce
was inviting merchants from the west, and Boston's merchants
seized immediately upon this device for creating good will.[14]

In the same month of February, Boston's Board invited
the Union Merchant's Exchange of St. Louis, the Cincinnati
and Milwaukee Chambers of Commerce, and the Boards of
Trade of Chicago and Detroit to visit Boston the following
June. These associations accepted, and on June 6, 1865 their
delegates arrived. On the following day, the delegates were
presented to the mayor and the city government.[15] Boston's

Board president, George C. Richardson, opened the first session
on a broad fraternal note:

> "The producing interest of this country, as well we know
> by the statistics, are getting to be equal to those of any
> other country on the face of the earth. And we as repre-
> sentatives of the commercial interest of the country, are
> so intimately connected in the promotion of the producing
> interest, that we can hardly separate the responsibility of
> doing our whole duty in this work."

Men of commerce in the Athens of America should have
been pleased at the response of their guest to the "Boston
welcomes the West" gesture. George F. Davis, from the Cincinnati Chamber of Commerce, responded properly to the broad
Boston hint when he said:

> "And we feel, that in coming to the East, we do not come
> all of us as strangers. Living here in the days of our youth,
> we feel, that, as we come back once more to press the soil
> of old Massachusetts, we are coming home again."

Better still was the observation of President Miles of the Milwaukee Chamber of Commerce. While Milwaukee was known
primarily as a wheat market, said Miles,

> "The great number of Boston men among us has infused
> there a spirit of ambition to be the manufacturing city
> of the West; and we trust the commencement already
> made in that direction may be enlarged by the capitalists
> of New England."

While northeastern capitalists continued down the old path
of sectional alliance and individual organizational pressure at
Washington, a new idea was taking form in the West. Presaged
by the Chicago "Ship Canal" convention of 1863, the impulse
for national organization of business men to achieve common
goals came out of the river and lake region beyond the Alle-

ghenies. At a meeting of the Detroit Board of Trade, February 28, 1865, H. P. Bridge introduced resolutions proposing a convention of Boards of Trade for the purpose of deliberating upon important subjects "intimately" connected with the great business interest of the country.[16] President Joseph Aspinall was instructed to send a circular letter to the Boards of Trade in the "Loyal" states and the British provinces, asking their attendance the following summer. Centrally and conveniently located, and feeling that the time had come for business men to unite to give the nation the benefit of their experience, the Detroit Board suggested the discussion center around "commerce, finance, communications of transit from the West to the seaboard, reciprocal trade between the United States and the British provinces, and such other business as may come before the convention not of a local or political character."

By late May, most of the business organizations had responded favorably to Detroit's suggestion, and passes were arranged for the delegates over the important trunk and steamship lines leading into the city. At the appointed time four hundred sixty-two delegates, representing forty-five commercial organizations in the United States and Canada assembled for action. The leading newspapers of New York, Chicago, Cincinnati, Cleveland, Boston, Philadelphia, and Detroit had reporters on hand to cover the meeting. In his address at the opening session, Joseph Aspinall sounded the keynote thus:

> "Commerce must bear the burden of taxation and business men are the best judges of their own wants, and what will most conduce to this prosperity; therefore it behooves them to take a deeper interest in governmental affairs."

After a remark on the need of a firm and stable currency, in his further remarks on the objects of the convention,[17] Aspinall went to the heart of the western problem when he said:

"The West has long felt the exorbitant transfer charges and
tax levied by the state of New York upon its products
passing through the Erie canal, which is assessed regardless
to the demand or value of the property or place of destination."

These charges absorbed all of the profit. Indeed, at Buffalo
the charges were so high that elevator owners realized the total
value of their property every two years.

After the election of the Honorable Hiram Walbridge of
the New York Chamber as Permanent President and other
officers judiciously distributed among the various organizations
attending, the Detroit convention settled down to business.[18]
Despite the understanding that nothing of a "local or political"
character was to enter the deliberations, the Philadelphia delegation, sensing the presence of the "Free Trade" heresy, quickly
moved for and got an endorsement of the principle of protection. As was to be expected, Philadelphia merchants stood opposed to the Niagara ship canal because of its "local" importance. But Boston merchants saw an opportunity to press for
recognition and approval a scheme that had lain dormant in
the minds of northeastern merchants since before the Civil
War. James C. Converse, of the Boston delegation, proposed
that a new department be established at Washington, "to promote, by permanent plans of action, the commercial, financial
and industrial interest of the United States."

Lorin Blodget, Philadelphia's Board great secretary suggested, in 1859, that the Federal Government give the Boards of
Trade of the large cities the necessary funds to carry out the functions of a government commercial bureau; and had complimented
the western commercial organizations on the superior accuracy
of their trade reports and general commercial statistics. In the
same year, Lorenzo Sabine, of Boston's Board seeing the neglect
of the commercial interest by the Federal Government, had
advocated that the Treasury Department be relieved of what
trade jurisdiction it had, and another department be established

possessing "as close as the nature of our institutions will allow, the powers of the Board of Trade of England." [19]

Sabine saw then, and the war years bore him out, that the issues handled by the individual organizations, either directly or indirectly, were concerned with national problems or interest. He did not think this implied the liquidation of the local commercial organizations. Local Boards were needed to remove the evils in trade which the national organization could not reach; to devise ways of "safe, speedy, and cheap transportation inland; to produce uniformity in commercial customs and charge of factorage; and to form and concentrate commercial opinion." "Nay more", said Sabine with his flair for history, "just one quarter part of the signers of the Declaration of Independence were bread merchants or shipmasters, and men of these classes, retained in Congress after the adoption of the Constitution, helped materially to shape the policy of the country; but as neither are hardly represented in the public councils now, the abolition of these (local) Chambers and Boards would deprive them of their principal remaining power in legislation."

Lorenzo Sabine may have had truth on his side when he asserted in 1859 that organized capitalists were "out of politics." But that same assertion in the prospectus of the Detroit Commercial Convention was a fiction that did not fit the facts of 1865. Nevertheless, the committee in charge of Converse's reading of Sabine's old argument "enlarged its views" and proposed two agencies; one, a federal government department, as in England, was to be called the United States Board of Trade; and the other, with Chamber of Commerce functions on a national scale, to be called the National Board of Trade. The Detroit convention entrusted to Boston's Board the power to lay the foundation for a national organization of business men. The Board was instructed to invite the commercial associations of the United States to submit plans for the organization, and after comparing them, to select the one, which in their judgment, was best adapted to the purpose. Failing to be satisfied with any of the plans, the Board was at liberty to adopt the local plan of any organization, which, after the approval of two-thirds of the associations, would be the plan of the national organization.

Thus the ideas of East and West met and fused at Detroit. Merchants of the seaboard placed their faith, in this period of triumphant radicalism at Washington, in government institutions deeply entrenched in the basic law of the land, and buttressed by pressure of local politicians at the National Capitol for the realization of their goals. Merchants of the Trans-Allegheny saw that the new power rested primarily upon an understanding among the masters of capital themselves the nation over as to the goals of the new business society. Men of the West vaguely sensed that the old individual democracy had passed away and that they were on the threshold of a new period of group demoncracy, in which every special interest group emerging from the new revolution must close ranks, both in their own regions and with their fellows elsewhere, if the dispossessed of the old and the new order were not to rise up to challenge their dominance.

The Detroit Board was not to be "out-done" by the Boston merchants. The University of Michigan, at Ann Arbor, was duly shown off; and the Bostonians were greatly impressed, not only with the University's facilities, but also with the fact that it had sent 649 graduates and undergraduates to the war, exactly 121 more than Harvard. Detroit also gave the delegates a boat ride. Three boats, decorated with evergreens, flags and Michigan belles, were lashed together, and two thousand boarded at the Detroit and Milwaukee Railroad wharf between five and six o'clock in the evening. For five hours, amid music and dancing, surrounded by good food, and thrilled by patriotic speeches, the delegates cruised about. Honorable Jacob M. Howard, United States Senator from Michigan, took occasion to make hands-across-the-border remarks to the effect of United States wanting to be a good neighbor. However,

generally speaking, the Detroit convention had been a workin
convention. It was a clear indication that the Northwest ha
no intention of letting an opportunity pass to press its clain
upon the attention of the older regions.

Having been given the mandate, Lorenzo Sabine went im
mediately to work.[20] In spite of his best efforts to bring abou
the realization of his dream, Boston's great secretary was force
by failing health, to retire before the heartbreaking delays i
confirming the Detroit mandate could be overcome.[21] Th
Detroit merchants, becoming impatient, had turned to Ne
York; but the New York Chamber showed a peculiar reluctanc
to be connected with the whole movement.[22] Pride in i
own prestige—jealously at not having been asked at first t
arrange the organization—or was it fear, premonition, tha
prompted this reticence? George Opdyke, speaking for th
Chamber's Executive Committee, felt "that it was not probab
that any good would result from a convention of so gener
a character;" yet the chamber agreed to send delegates. O
the other hand, Philadelphia merchants were anxious fc
Bostonians to get on with the arrangements, and had bee
prompt in sending their plan for a national organization alor
to Boston for perusal.[23] Boston merchants were also anxio
for this new organization.

Developments between the Detroit convention and th
Boston meeting in February of 1868 made it especially ir
portant to Boston and Philadelphia merchants that nation
organization of business men be perfected. The "cotton polic
had failed and with it had gone the hope of Boston and Phil
delphia merchants to rival New York in building a new cott
triangle between their ports and Europe. Both associatio
had initiated plans for coastwise and European Steamship lines
But the New York firms had, by superior facilities in provi
ing the manufactured articles and other conveniences of lil
captured anew the trade of the southern ports.[25] This conc
tion made imperative a rethinking of the commercial poli

of the two rivals of New York. Taking a leaf from the book of the politicians, Boston and Philadelphia merchants called in their brothers of the new commercial empire of the West to adjust the balance of the old.

Boston's efforts in 1865 to attract the trade of the West drew an apt retort from a western editor thus:

> "If there is one thing the Boston commercial soul desires more than any other, . . . it is increased trade with the West . . . Board of Trade merry-makings are very well in their way. But there is a sequel sure to come in when trade and sentiment set out to do a good thing together without carefully secured partnership arrangements." [26]

The New York railroads blocked the trade to Boston by the simple device of holding up freight at the Albany terminal. Westerners were "altogether amiably inclined toward Boston," but its facilities for trade constituted a "narrow and too often choked channel through which the bountiful trade of the West must be strained to reach Boston bay." "Let Boston and the Bay State", so ran the admonition, "if they wish to solicit Western trade, commence with the railroads of their own state, and be sure they make them what they are not now, Avenues of Trade."

The warning did not fall on deaf ears. Bostonians knew the value of good-will and knew how to build it.[27] The changes must be rung on the right things in a propaganda offensive. Charles G. Nazro put it typically and well when he said,

> "The natural affinities of the great West are with New England. Their people and ours are, in a great degree, homogeneous; and if we extend to them facilities for intercourse which may be mutually beneficial, they will gladly avail themselves of them."

However, Nazro was able to announce that the Albany bottleneck had been broken with a bridge across the Hudson river.

It was possible to send Boston freight westward, without breaking bulk, over three through transportation lines.[28]

Boston's capitalists were split on the question of commercial expansion and rivalry with New York capitalists, especially since the port city drew, with irresistible force, capital
and business from every quarter. After all, so ran the argument of the industrialist, was it not enough for Boston to be
the seat of ownership and management for New England
manufactures and railroads? Indeed, did not the Hudson river
and the Erie canal "settle absolutely the question of its (New
York's sic) commercial supremacy and of its all-absorbing capacity in the future?" To be sure, Boston owed her greatness
to foreign trade; but that was thirty years ago and it was
"futile" and "undesirable" to try to build up the foreign commerce of Boston port.

But Boston merchants had an answer for the complacent
manufacturers. "Is it not apparent" said the barons of commerce "that the manufacturers of Boston require the cooperation of a strong commercial interest, to enable them to
withstand the tendency toward New York, which in common
with others they also feel?" Were not rivers and canals becoming relatively less and less important year by year? Railroads were changing everything. Baltimore was thriving because
of the B. & O., and Boston and the West, as New York admitted were profiting by her railroads. Besides merchants were
of the conviction that when Boston ceased to be the channel
through which western produce sought its foreign markets, it
would be dangerous, manufacturing competition being what it
was, to rely wholly upon industrial pursuits for the economic
expression of the business community.[29] Railroads westward
became an obsession of the merchants of Boston. As late as
1876 they were still clamoring for direct communications to
the West to buttress the foreign trade of the port;[30] for to
them "there (was) no question but that this lack of efficient
and adequate means of communication has been the great and

only obstacle to the growth of our export trade, more especially in the provisions and cereals of the West and the cotton of the South." As our period draws to a close, Boston merchants still held that "it (was sic) for the interest of Boston and the state today to have an independent through line to the West, and our position will never be secure until we have it."

There was no difference of opinion in the ranks of Philadelphia masters of capital as to the destiny of their city. Devotees of protection almost to a man, Philadelphia's Board had not missed many opportunities to press its "idea" upon the haves and have nots of the new era.[31] Philadelphia was earlier than Boston in sensing the connection between domestic and foreign commerce, and as early as 1865 advocated a railroad from Knoxville, Tennessee, to the Ohio river, no doubt to supplement her east-west trunk line.[32] The passage, on July 28, 1866, of an obscure section in a miscellaneous bill, through Congress with little debate gave Philadelphians their cue. This section of the bill gave the Secretary of the Treasury the power to designate certain ports where goods, destined for Canada and Mexico, might be entered, on arrival, at the custom house, and might be carried, in transit, duty free, under rules to protect the revenue, to the destination on the bill of lading.[33]

In the fall of 1866, Philadelphia's Board's attention was called to this measure and immediately it occurred to them that the same provision might be extended for the interstate trade in imported merchandise. The foreign trade of Philadelphia was handled, for the most part as was Boston's, through New York.[34] Delays, and charges for storage, cartage, general order, the impossibility of obtaining insurance, the difficulty of rectifying errors in valuation and often fraud—all this together urged Philadelphia merchants to positive action. The Board drew up a memorial and a bill and forwarded it to "our efficient representative, Leonard Myers," who saw to it that it was referred to the appropriate committees of both houses of Congress.

Behind this pious solicitude for efficiency in the custom service lay other motives. The registering of Philadelphia imports at New York prevented the Philadelphia merchants from showing their customers that theirs was an original, metropolitan port of foreign commerce. Besides, this abnormal arrangement kept Philadelphians from rushing their imports to inland merchants long before the New Yorkers could "fairly and honestly" get their imports through "that overcrowded and corrupt custom-house." [35] But more important still was the consideration that "by the adoption of this system, direct importers in Cincinnati, Chicago, St. Louis and other places, may come soon to prefer Philadelphia to New York as a port through which to receive their goods, by means of the Pennsylvania Railroad; and thus direct importations, by ocean steamships, be expedited by the very means which might at first seem to be the building up of a rival channel of trade."

Philadelphia's Board got in touch with the St. Louis Merchant's Exchange and the Boston Board of Trade on the proposition. George H. Morgan out at St. Louis answered that, if St. Louis was to be named as an internal port of entry, he thought the proposition was satisfactory; and counseled that New York's merchants' opposition to the scheme could be overcome if all interior cities having government collectors were included. [36] Boston's Board immediately gave its approval and empowered the president to memorialize Congress in favor of the enactment of the bill. [37] Bill No. 788 started through the lower House. Secretary of the Treasury Hugh McCulloch objected to the measure only because he feared it would encourage evasion of custom duties. Philadelphians were sure that bonded carriers into the interior would solve that problem. Thus on the eve of the long awaited national commercial convention Philadelphia and Boston had a real issue.

Having received evidences of businessmen's enthusiasm for the project, Boston's Board framed an agenda and set February 5, 1868, as the date. [38] Hamilton Hill, worthy successor to Lorenzo Sabine as Boston's Board's secretary, felt that "it (was) eminently desirable that expressions of opinions sent to Washington from business men, having reference to measures pending or to changes in contemplation should go from the mercantile community as a whole, and not from any one or more branches or sections of it." Hill was not sure how the convention was coming out, but he had "full confidence in the ability and sagacity of those who control the domestic and the foreign commerce of the country, who employ its capital, who largely sustain its taxation, who stimulate its industry, and whose welfare is dependent on its prosperity, to discuss lucidly and to decide wisely what to them are not speculative abstractions, but practical and vital questions."

Charles G. Nazro, Boston's Board president, at 10:00 A.M. Wednesday, the fifth day of February 1868, greeted the representatives of trade associations from fourteen states.[39] A clear indication of the drift of the convention was the election of E. W. Fox of St. Louis, President; Samuel Vaughn Merrick of Philadelphia and Joseph Bagley of Detroit Vice Presidents-at-large; and Hamilton Hill of Boston, Secretary. Boston's original agenda was supplemented with three items showing clearly the Philadelphia and western influence.[40] The members of the convention silenced, with an innocuous resolution to Congress, an attempt by Mr. Tait of Kentucky to put them on record as favoring a $20,000,000 loan for one year to the southern cotton producers by the Federal government, to be secured by a lien on the crop. Hiram Walbridge's majority report on the notion of Federal regulation of interstate commerce so as to prevent monopolies of through railroads restricting the development of other lines also raised a storm and brought plain speaking.[41] Philadelphia, granting the premises, quickly pushed through to acceptance a classic argument for protection.[42]

In due time, gentlemen of the counting-house took up the business of providing for the organization of the "associated

National Board of Trade," the purpose of which was the "promotion and harmonizing of the Industrial and Commercial interests of the country." Boston's Board was again asked "to take measures to carry out . . . the plan," and set the time and place for the first meeting. Though the original plan was essentially that suggested by the Philadelphia Board, the convention "strongly recommended to the delegates of the National Board of Trade that the basis of constitution shall be the plan prepared by Mr. Gano of Cincinnati." With an eye to the best in the historic traditions of America, the masters of capital again chose Philadelphia as the place to organize their national body.

The convention did not close without New York being settled with. John Price Wetherill of Philadelphia's board introduced the following resolution:

> "Whereas, the cities of Boston, Philadelphia, Cincinnati, and St. Louis have through their Boards of Trade, desired a change in the laws regulating foreign importations; therefore, resolved by this convention, that in our opinion Congress should, by necessary legislation, secure such change in the laws regulating foreign importations as shall authorize invoices of merchandise arriving at one port but designed for another to be directly forwarded from the ships side to ultimate ports and custom-houses for entry, and without warehousing or other detention at the port of arrival."

Hincken of New York, in high scorn, called the whole scheme absurd. It would be laughed at by Washington officialdom. Every importer in the country would agree that such could not be done without a change in the entire revenue system of the United States. President Fox abandoned the chair to pay his respects to the "superior knowledge of the New York broker." "For many years," said Fox, "we have collected our customs under revenue laws calculated and managed for the cities of the seaboard. The West comes here

oday, Mr. Chairman, and desires some change in the laws."
On the New York suggestion that the Federal revenue might
be endangered, Guthrie asked if imports would be any safer
with New York draymen than with the Pennsylvania, New
York Central, Erie, or Baltimore and Ohio railroads under
bond. Charles G. Nazro, in the best spirit of sweet mag-
nanimity, championed Wetherill's resolution and Fox's idea.
To be sure the scheme might injure Boston, Philadelphia and
New York; but theirs was a local interest which could be
waived at that juncture. To New York's Babcock's suggestion
that there would be difficulties with bonding from the ship's
side to the ultimate warehouse, Hersey of Portland claimed
no such were encountered in Maine. "I will ask Mr. Fox,"
queried Hiram Walbridge, "if he wants, for the cities of the
West, any advantages over New York?" "I will say without
hesitation", answered Fox, "we do not." The resolution was
carried. New York was under the hammer.

Boston could not end this convention without the usual
frolicking in the established pattern. But Walbridge and the
rest of the New York delegation, who went to laugh and stayed
to pray, were quite impressed with the unity and harmony
of the representatives from diverse sections. Indeed "even
from quarters where it might be supposed . . . crude and
unsound views of political economy were general . . ." men
were found, if perhaps a bit radical in politics, not so in
economics. "Should nothing else" said Walbridge in his report to the New York Chamber, "result from this large as-
semblage of earnest business men, this alone may be held as
ample reward for the time and expense incident to the convention."

Boston's Board did not hesitate to put into execution the
new mandate. The Quaker City extended its hospitality and
Boston Board set as the date for the meeting to organize
June 3-7, 1868.[48] Capitalists the country over came from
their local organizations believing that the new organization

would "give assurance to each that, however remote it may be from the older and more densely settled portions of the country, and however limited in its local influence, it (did) not stand alone, and it (was) not working by itself." Men of the counting-house were admonished to subordinate "self, class, locality and section to the general good." One month previously H.R. 788 passed the House of Representatives and entered the Senate. After organization and office electing, the first business transacted by the National Board was the item on direct importations. John Welsh of Philadelphia pushed through an indorsement of the bill then pending before the Senate. Fortunately, the measure was referred to the Finance committee, "of which the Honorable John Sherman, favorable to the bill, was chairman, and of which the Honorable A. G. Cattell, a powerful advocate of it, was a member." Edwin D. Morgan, member of the New York Chamber and Senator from New York on the finance committee opposed the bill of the Ohio-New Jersey faction to the last ditch. With some alterations from the House measure, the Senate bill was reported out for adoption in the spring of 1869; however, that being the short session, no favorable action could be taken. Then it was that the international merchants of New York saw the light.

At the first annual meeting of the National Board out at Cincinnati in December of 1868, the St. Louis Board of Trade carried its advantage in this fight a step farther. In the spirit of George H. Morgan's original suggestion, already adopted by the Philadelphia Board, Clinton B. Fisk wished to add to the cities mentioned in the bill then pending in the Senate, all others with a population of 200,000 or over. Kirkland of Baltimore would have all interior towns included; for it was not the population that mattered—it was adequate custom-house facilities. Baltimore, said Kirkland expansively, was not jealous, and wanted as many interior cities as possible to enjoy the privilege and so moved. W. M. Burwell, knowing full well that St. Louis merchants hoped to cut New Orleans' throat by this measure, tried to put the crescent city in as good a light as possible. But Hincken of New York, who had raised the storm at Boston a few months previously by his antagonism, repeated the process. He thought that this question, really of interest only to people of the interior, was taking too much time. The seaboard frankly did not care one way or the other so long as the duties were paid. Allen of Philadelphia thought Congress was doing fine and nothing more need be done by the Board. On Charles G. Nazro's insistence that Kirkland's classification was too vague, James S. T. Stranahan, of the New York Chamber, suggested "the most important towns and cities," which after Halton's amendment "west and south" was accepted, stood as the decision of the Board. Stranahan's had been a statesmanlike gesture, but the New York Chamber had had enough. When Hamilton Hill had the effrontery to send the Chamber a bill for $380 for its share of the National Board's expenses and a letter requesting suggestions for the Richmond meeting, George Opdyke, speaking from the Executive committee suggested the Chamber withdraw from the National Organization. Opdyke's idea did not carry, but it was clear that New Yorkers knew what was afoot.

The 41st Congress was flooded with bills on direct importation and a measure making the scheme possible became law July 14, 1870. The law went into operation October 1, 1870. Between that time and the Buffalo meeting of the National Board in December, there was every indication that George S. Boutwell, Secretary of the Treasury, was attempting to defeat the measure by administrative regulations.[44] L. R. Shryock, the firebrand from St. Louis, rose to the floor of the Buffalo meeting to demand heatedly:

"Does the Honorable Secretary imagine that the interior merchants are all smugglers and thieves? Does he suppose for one moment that the merchants of the West and South are less honest than the resident merchants of the seaboard . . . Redress is what we ask, and fair and honest dealing is what we demand of government officers, whether they sit under the shade of the Capitol or dwell among the Barbarians of the West. We know our rights and dare maintain them."

William M. McPherson of St. Louis, also in a temper, said that Washingtonians "don't think westerners know anything anyway." While Wetherill and Allen of Philadelphia minced their words, Charles Randolph of Chicago, with typical western candor, said that the whole fault lay with Boutwell, not section 32. That official set himself against the act from the first, and, having failed, took this underhand method to defeat the law. Randolph suggested that Congress give the secretary specific instructions to liberalize his regulations. That the Buffalo meeting did.

But the fight with the Secretary of the Treasury was not over.[45] There developed a running fight from year to year with the Secretary of the Treasury sniping at the law from behind first one regulation after the other. At St. Louis in 1871 Wetherill attacked the Treasury ruling (Section 29) on Wines, distilled Spirits and articles in bulk; for the last provision especially hit salt and pig iron. The secretary raised objections also to transferring goods from one type of bonded carrier to another, both going in the same direction to an ultimate known destination. That provision, said W. M. Burwell was killing off New Orleans as a terminal point for foreign trade. Section 7 of the secretary's regulations made registering of imports at the port of arrival so difficult as to consume as much time as the old system. Besides that Wetherill found that the port of Mobile had been slighted in the law and interior merchants were forbidden to import through that port.

The Executive Committee of the National Board went
fore the committees of commerce of both houses of Congress
get the St. Louis meeting's complaints straightened out.
his issue had no more than been cleared up before the
cretary's reading of Section 2927 of the revised statutes
the spirit of the 1799 revenue act, instead of that of 1870,
ised a new storm at the Philadelphia meeting in 1875.
nder Section 2927 no damages could be claimed on imports
ter the imports had been at their destination longer than
n days. There was really no point in the Secretary ruling
at destination meant arrival at the seaboard port, instead
the destination on the bill of lading. Merchants of the
'est were being victimized by this ruling. Indeed, Chicago
ith her annual sale of $12,000,000 in imports, of which
,000,000 were direct, stood to lose a good deal. The Secre-
ry of the Treasury finally agreed to this new construction of
e statute.

The Milwaukee meeting in 1877 found Wetherill still
ying to get the wrinkles out of the law and New Yorkers
ll fighting for the old order. Philadelphians thought the
quirement of posting of bond on the imports at the port
arrival (Section 29 and 30 of 1870 act) was ruinous be-
use it meant the carrier had to pay the bond of the importer
d its own bond as a carrier. Because New York was being
dersold on the same class of goods in the West, Miller of
ew York, openly accused westerners of fraud. The old fight
as on. Gano of Cincinnati, Hayes of Detroit, and Dickinson
Chicago immediately leaped to the breach with the cumula-
ve observation that there certainly was no more fraud outside
New York than in. Indeed the tales were legion in the
ess of the frauds discovered in the New York custom house.
ranahan called for a poll of the delegates, and 24 to 6,
ew York went down.

But neither the Secretary of the Treasury nor the obstruc-
onist forces of New York Lobbyists at Washington, or delegates

to business men's meetings could turn back the tide of trade which, the boon of this law delivered into the ports of western merchants. The Philadelphia "idea" backed by that giant corporation, the Pennsylvania Railroad, meant prosperity to Philadelphia and the West.[46] But it also gave masters of capital beyond the Alleghenies economic hegemony in the Southern sellers market. Yearly their cotton markets grew.[47] New Orleans to the south as well as New York and Boston to the east suffered alike under the aggression this law made possible.[48] Western capitalists were not slow in recognizing the great opportunity that the factional war to the knife among the merchants of the seaboard over the issues of reconstruction had given them. Direct importation into their cities meant, as it did to New York's rivals on the seaboard, that their markets beyond the Alleghenies would take on the character of a world market. Merchants in the west would then be placed on an equal footing with those in New York City, because the prices, facilities, and the revenue from custom duties, formerly enjoyed exclusively by the merchants of the empire city, could now obtain in the western urban commercial centers.

In the post-war struggle to become the Regents of the Cotton Kingdom Direct Importation was of decisive importance. Conceived by the Boston-Philadelphia merchant communities in a spirit of vengeance against their old rival, New York, Direct Importation assured the western commercial centers equality in the competition for the trade of the South. Enjoying an old advantage of greater geographical access to the Southern market, western merchants boldly opened the "Iron Sluice Gates", and threw their "Knights of the Bag" into the Southern sellers' market. Thus the commercial barons beyond the mountains fell heir to the power of "King Cotton", co-regents indeed to an ever dominating degree in the domain laid open by a victorious political war.

Iron Sluice Gates

In railroads, as in politics, true policy demands that locali-
ties and sections shall be forgotten and that the whole
country shall be considered. The day of Chinese walls
has passed. No man can divert or dam up the great
currents that roll restlessly to and fro through this great
continent.

H. Victor Newcomb

The merchants of the middle-western cities had been agitating for years to build railroads into the South. The railroads offered the possibility of bringing the Southern market closer for more thoroughgoing exploitation. Secure in the willingness of New York's rivals to favor the western merchants, and flushed with the victory of the fight for "direct importations", which made their cities internal ports of entry, middle-western merchants prepared to step-up their efforts to sink steel syphons into the Southern promised land.

Already merchants of the eastern Atlantic cities had re-established lines of communication to the Southern trading centers, and their success impressed *western* merchants with the need for prompt action. By establishing fast coast-wise shipping lines to the Southern port cities, New York merchants had outstripped their rivals on the eastern coast after the war, and they held their lead to 1870.[1] However, the capitalists of Philadelphia were not wanting in vision or the agencies for stiff competition in the Southern trade. The Pennsylvania Railroad had been the long arm of the Philadelphia merchant community in the establishing of spheres of commercial influence,[2] and the road did not fail them now in the competition for the Southern trade.

In 1860, there were in actual operation 8,855 miles of railroad in the South,[3] which under the management of many different companies, opened communication through five great channels of trade along and upon which the commercial develop-

ment of the South was to grow.[4] The war left most of th
roads along these routes either bankrupt or in the hands
the receiver. To be sure, some of the Southern roads wei
strong enough to survive the war, and were able to consolida
weaker roads in their territory.[5] But for the most part, Souther
railroads fell like overripe apples into the laps of intereste
investors. After the war, the Pennsylvania Railroad was a heav
investor in lines south of Washington and in important lin
in the Mississippi valley.[6] But the border city merchants ha
no greater example of the full power of eastern capital i
creating channels for the exploitation of the Southern mark
than the Southern Railway Security Company. The obje
and purpose of this organization was "to secure the contr
of such Southern railroads as may be essential to the forma
tion of through lines between New York, Philadelphia, Wash
ington city, and the principal cities of the South by ownershi
of the capital stock of said companies, by leases, and by con
tract relations".[7] The company was not a blind for the Penn
sylvania Railroad.[8] However, it was incorporated in Pennsyl
vania, and George W. Coss, of the Pennsylvania Railroad, wa
its president.[9]

If full advantage was to be realized from the holdin
company's investment, the first duty of the Pennsylvania Rail
road was to reach Richmond. The Northern Central railroa
acquisition pushed the route into Baltimore, but the lack o
cooperation of the Baltimore and Ohio on through tickets
trains and baggage to Washington, D. C., forced the crea
tion of the Baltimore and Potomac Railroad Company in
1868. The State of Maryland granted the right to build a
mainline from Baltimore to Popes Creek, Bowie, and Wash
ington; and Congress admitted the road to the District o
Columbia and allowed it to extend over the Land bridge to
connect with lines into Virginia. When the Baltimore and
Potomac Railroad had reached Washington, it was necessary
to continue the route south to Richmond, via the Alexandria

and Washington Railway and the Alexandria and Fredericksburg (later consolidated into the Washington Southern Railroad) and the Richmond, Fredericksburg, and Potomac Railroad. This would connect with the whole system of the
Southern Railroads controlled by the Southern Railway Security Company in which the Pennsylvania Railroad Company
had become a shareholder to secure the traffic.[10]

The interest of the Pennsylvania Railroad Company in the
Southern Railway Security Company consisted of a one-sixth
ownership of its capital stock, which had cost $783,000 and
an advance of $1,825,000 to be used to assist in the construc-
tion of the Atlanta and Richmond Airline Railroad from
Charlotte, North Carolina, to Atlanta, Georgia, completed
in 1873. The Security Company was an important factor at
the time in promoting railroad construction in the South, and
with the exception of a few intervening links, with which it
had alliances, it controlled three independent routes converging from Richmond, Virginia. The first of these lines was the
Atlantic Coast route, via Weldon and Wilmington to Charleston,
South Carolina, and Augusta, Georgia, connecting there with
the Georgia system of railroads. The second was the middle
route, via Danville, Greensboro, Charlotte, Atlanta, Montgomery, and Mobile, Alabama. The third was the interior
route, via Bristol, Knoxville, Chattanooga to Memphis, Tennessee, on the Mississippi.

As investment by the Pennsylvania Railroad Company,
beginning in 1871, in the Southern Railway Security Company
proved itself of doubtful value, the whole sum was charged to
profit and loss in 1873, although it was believed that the
outlay would in time bring a favorable return and traffic
of considerable value to the roads controlled by the Pennsylvania Railroad, for the benefit of which the investment was
originally made. The Panic of 1873 placed the Security Company in financial difficulties and it had to dispose of all of its
holdings except the Atlantic Coast route. The securities of

the roads in the middle route, consisting principally of stock, bonds, and notes of the Richmond and Danville Railroad Company, and the Atlanta and Richmond Airline Railroad Company, were conveyed to the Pennsylvania Railroad Company in settlement of its claims for $1,825,000. Financial troubles overtaking the Security Company several years later, its remaining roads passed to the Southern Trunk lines.[11] The Pennsylvania disposed of its holdings in the Richmond and Danville for $1,200,000 in 1880, and the latter road also became a part of the Southern Railroad system at a later date.

The effort by Northeastern merchants to draw the trade of the South out into their own markets was not confined to such schemes as the Southern Railway Security Company. The East-West rail lines into the southern port cities could be used as adjuncts to the coastwise steamer lines to accomplish the same results. The South, after the Civil War, had more railroads than it actually needed. As one railway specialist put it:

> There was not as much business as all could do. Indeed any one of these lines, with a comparatively small output for rolling stock can do all the business to any, indeed to all competitive points.[12]

Therefore, each road tried to monopolize the business by rebates and open rate cutting which brought them all to a ruinously low level.

This situation brought many suggestions for agreements to restore and maintain rates, but many managers entered into these agreements with fingers crossed. Starting at an agreed upon high rate and cutting until low rates were again current, these rate wars brought to the southern roads returns 42% below what regular rates would have yielded and represented all too often the whole net earnings of the Southern roads. The roads in the South were, therefore, practically worthless to their owners. In 1876 a committee of stockholders of the Central Railroad and Banking Company of Georgia reported to the company:

It is conceded that the property of your stockholders is on the brink of being sunk forever; and the bankruptcy of a number of your roads is imminent, if not even now a fact.

The prevailing conditions led to the formation of the Southern Railway and Steamship Association.[13]

After several attempts at a modus vivendi, the Railway Steamship Association in October of 1875, elected Albert Fink, general superintendent of the Louisville and Nashville and being familiar with the railroad business of the South, general commissioner.[14] Albert Fink, as agent of all of the Rail and Steamship lines in the system, had the responsibility of "regulating all competitive business, hearing all complaints, taking cognizance of all grievances and adjusting all difficulties". The Southern Railway and Steamship Association owed much of its success to Albert Fink; and save for the Omaha Pool of 1870, Fink's experiment was the first practical pool arrangement in the United States. The Association was to include all transportation companies south of the Ohio and Potomac and east of the Mississippi River, which wished to become members, and any steamship company connecting these roads with Boston, Providence, New York, Philadelphia, or Baltimore was eligible for membership. The Association's purpose was to cut excessive competition by maintaining rates and fairly distributing business. It is highly significant that the pool covered only the business with the eastern cities.[15]

The Association, down to 1880, had a rather checkered career. The fault, to a degree, was to be found in the fact that its key policy committees, executive, rate, etc., could act only by the unanimous consent of all their members, to the end that little could be accomplished. There were also difficulties in securing for inter-association disputes, arbiters acceptable to all parties concerned. The difficulty in adjusting and compromising general merchandise and cotton balances proved a thorny problem. The doubtful operation of the Steamship-Railway scheme, as well as others out of the Eastern cities, served to spur the merchant of the border cities to heroic efforts.

Because of their peculiar location, Cincinnati, Louisville, and St. Louis were in a position to take advantage of the seller's market in the South after the Civil War. Being both distributing and manufacturing centers, these cities held the edge over their neighbors in the Southern commercial competition.[16] Their eventual ascendency, however, was due primarily to the vision and industry of their merchants. It was their merchants' recognition of the commercial destiny of their cities which opened the competition leading to their unsung greatness.

Of the border cities, the merchants of Louisville, Kentucky were the first to enter the Southern field after the war. This leadership had come after years of planning. Louisville was a Southern city, and its business men had looked South almost exclusively for custom and support.[17] The location of Louisville by the falls of the Ohio was of decisive importance. In the days of river traffic, "cargo had to break bulk there, and the merchants of Louisville levied toll on shippers." Around about lay a rich agricultural country. This gateway city, sitting on a hill in a valley, was indeed in the middle; it "lay between the old east and the western wilderness, between the North and the South", a city of middlemen—a broker's paradise, a countinghouse town—acutely conscious of what transportation meant, taking the tithe of every traveler.

The decade from 1850 to 1860, and until the Civil War began, was the period of Louisville's greatest development in the river trade and travel which made the city the "mistress of the commerce of the South".[18] But the combination river-road artery of commerce to the South from Louisville had long since proved inadequate to the demands of time. It became apparent to many that Louisville was slipping. Though the city was situated ideally geographically, "the rapid growth and settlement of the country made it imperative that a quicker way be evolved for exchanging the raw materials of the Southland, such as cotton, pine, tobacco, rice, iron, coal, etc., for the finished products of the factories of the North. There was a grave danger that the streams of trade and commerce might change their course and pass Louisville by".[19] As results of an ever-growing ground swell of agitation, which began in 1832 at Bardstown and spread throughout the State, a charter was secured from Kentucky by James Guthrie and his associates on the 4th of September, 1851, and the subscription books of the Louisville and Nashville Railroad were opened in Guthrie's office.[20] Eight years of effort in the face of terrific difficulties, scarcity of money, shortage of provisions, drought and epidemic saw the completion of the road through the rugged, sparsely settled country to Nashville, then a town of 10,000 population.[21] When the special train, bedecked with American flags fore and aft, left Louisville, October 27, 1859 on the maiden trip, the faith of city fathers and merchants of Louisville in their ability to open the iron gate to a new era of commercial supremacy in the Southern territory was fulfilled.[22]

Just as the city was about to reap the reward of her industry and vision, the thunderheads of the sectional conflict over slavery appeared on the horizon. While statesmen in the imperial city searched among stale political formulae for a solution, merchants in the border cities were rushing orders to the nearest communication artery for transport South amid the bellicose threats of midwestern politicians.[23] The Louisville and Nashville, under the Presidency of the Southern sympathizer, James Guthrie, did a clandestine thriving business for the merchants of the gateway city while the sectional issue was in the valley of decision in the border states. Throwing in his lot finally with the North, Guthrie and his associates participated in the boomtown conditions enjoyed by the merchants and laborers of Louisville as results of profitable army contracts.[24] It was well that the management so chose, for with government aid in construction, profitable contracts, and unusual conditions of debt funding, the Road emerged from the war stronger than before.[25]

As on the eastern seaboard, the war brought to the merchants of the middle western cities a new consciousness of their worth and the necessity for organization to achieve the new goals of a new era. This was certainly true of the merchants of Louisville. In March of 1862 the Louisville Board of Trade was chartered and organized, and though this first effort was so crude that no organizational records exist for it, by the close of the Civil War, the gateway city was alive with the spirit of a commercial imperialism of the first rank.[26] Anxious to regain the ground lost during the war by "trade restrictions, embargoes, permits, licenses, and other hindrances", Andrew Johnson's proclamation of June 13, 1865, opening Southern territory to trade east and west of the Mississippi River, spurred Louisville business men to their most important task—"the restoration of trade with the South, and the reestablishment of old as well as new lines of communication to facilitate the same."

Spreading over thirteen square miles, Louisville, with its good lighting, paved streets, and its reputation of being one of the best policed towns in America, had much to recommend it as a business community. Travelers found the city architecture substantial if not fine. Government buildings, university and high schools, eleemosynary institutions, churches, public libraries and homes, though stained with brown from smoke and mist, gave every aspect of a "coming" city. What with the commercial and manufacturing establishments, banking capital, railroad connections and great staple markets, it is little wonder that men of enterprise were attracted to the gateway city after the war.[27]

The Louisville masters of capital were truly an interesting collection of men of the new era. James Guthrie, railroad builder, entrepreneur, banker, and cabinet member, was a native son who had risen in the best tradition of the West to the seats of the mighty.[28] Horatio Dalton Newcomb, grocer, Guthrie associate in the L. & N., and his successor in the presidency, and his spectacular son, H. Victor Newcomb, statesman, were also men of the new era.[29] John McDougal Atherton, a native son sprung from the Scotch-Irish, represented the distilling interest, twin Bank of Kentucky and L. & N. directorship in finance and state politics, and the public utility interest of Louisville.[30] J. H. Lindenberg, prewar prominent drug merchant, represented the aggressive interstate Merchants National Bank of Louisville, and the tie between regional finance, insurance, and the L and N directorship.[31] George W. Wicks, former steamboat captain, and later identified with Nock and Rawson, one of the largest prewar wholesale grocers, and cotton and tobacco factors in the South, was in 1864 owner of the firm and held its original reputation long after the War.[32] R. A. Robinson and his son, William Alexander, combined with the father's directorship of the L and N, a prewar interest in retail and wholesale drugs, and a postwar family interest in woolen and cotton mills, lime and cement, and wholesale hardware. The Belknaps grew up with hardware and iron manufacturing and their career carried them from Pittsburgh, to the Southwest, and back to Louisville, where they remained one of the most prominent manufacturing families in the border area.[33]

The peace brought to the gateway city Union and Confederate veterans as well as a sprinkling of foreign elements to throw in their lot with its future. Fresh from Appomattox came Lieutenant-Colonel Andrew Cowan of New York to engage in the wholesale hardware, leather, and mill supplies business, with a side interest in printing.[34] James Breckenridge Speed, caught in a Chicago bank-clerkship in 1861, fought in the 27th Kentucky Infantry, and returned in 1865 at 21 to amass a fortune in telephones, street railways, coal, cement, and banks.[35] Pardoned in 1865 by Andrew Johnson, John Breckenridge Castleman returned from European exile for serving in the grey host during the War, took a law degree in the University of Louisville, and accepted the management of the Royal Insurance Company of London for the Southern states, a position which he held ably long after the War.[36] After four years of service with the 8th Infantry in the Virginia theatre of operations, George Chester Norton came to Louisville in 1865 and became a commercial traveller for the gigantic drygoods house, J. M. Robinson & Company. Eventually a partner, then president of the firm, Norton long remained a distinguished merchant of the gateway city.[37] The grain trade in the gateway city was represented by a son of the German element, Herman Verhoeff, Jr., who rose to power by way of the country store;[38] and the remarkable Brandies clan, whose firm became one of the largest in the Ohio valley or the South.[39]

This aggressive group of merchant-capitalists pushed the importance of the Louisville mart throughout the country.[40] Deploring the unsatisfactory conditions of the South in the annee terrible, 1867, and hoping the radicals would institute "a more liberal policy towards the South" to encourage "foreign" capital investment, the gateway city merchants had much to encourage them. "The Louisville and Nashville Railroad (was) . . . the greatest power in the Southwest, and with its progress and extensions the growth and prosperity of (the) city (would) be equally great and progressive." Indeed, these merchants might look forward to their city becoming the storehouse and granary of the Southwest as well as the leading "emporium" for the other leading agricultural products, "chief of which are cotton and tobacco".[41] Taking a cue from

the new wave of national responsibility of business men everywhere, the Louisville masters of capital bombarded Congress
and the President with petitions and suggestions on taxation
and other national policies; and participated in the organization and program of the new national pressure group to voice
the business policy and attitude, the National Board of Trade.[42]

The gods of commerce smiled upon the efforts of the
Louisville merchants and their great ally, the Louisville and
Nashville Railroad. The commerce of the city southward in
1872 amounted to five times its value as of 1866-67. But this
trade tempted the L & N into a dangerous expansion policy.
To be sure, through services, on both passengers and freight,
was available between Louisville and the Gulf ports, but the
route was circuitous and only a small portion of the trackage
involved belonged to the L & N.[43]

The objective was Montgomery, Alabama, 303 miles away;
and officers of the road achieved it by leasing and securing
control, respectively, of the Nashville and Decatur Railroad
Company (122 miles) and the South and North Alabama
Railroad Company (103 miles) in April and May of 1871.
This deal was not closed until good Kentucky bourbon and
the good sense of Albert Fink terminated the stormy negotia-
tions which extended from the Exchange Hotel in Montgomery
to the Blue Parlor of the Galt House in Louisville, where L & N's
aging President H. D. Newcomb almost came to blows with
Sam Tate of the S & N A.

Then the blow fell. The business depression of the seventies,
due almost entirely to over expansion of railway mileage, hit
the ally of the Louisville merchants broadside. At the bottom
of 1873, there was not enough business available on the S & N A
between Decatur and Colera to justify the "operation of more
than one passenger coach a week", and "One freight car a
day was more than adequate". Horatio Dalton Newcomb,[44]
finding the company in desperate straits, pledged his entire
private fortune to maintain the road, but his health was

broken, and means and credit exhausted; Newcomb was, after the most desperate efforts, stalemated, and his own and the L & N bankruptcy seemed inevitable to the managers of the road. His son, Horatio Victor Newcomb, then less than thirty-years old, stepped in and took over.[45]

Hurrying to London, H. Victor placed several million dollars of the road's bonds, with the proceeds of which, he returned in time to save the road. H. D. dying soon after his return, H. Victor inherited his fortune and became managing director of the road. He soon reestablished the L & N's credit, funded its heavy floating debt, and began to improve the property. For a year or two the road just earned its fixed obligations, but under vigorous management, soon began to pay dividends. Its stock moved from thirty cents to par and was generally considered the safest of investments. But Horatio Victor Newcomb began to dream—a dream which so fired the admiration of Henry W. Grady of the Atlanta *Constitution* until the latter dubbed him "The Napoleon of the Railroad World", "the most notable young man in America" not excluding H. Gordon Bennett.[46] For H. Victor Newcomb's dream led him to the same success in the Mississippi Valley and the Southeast long before Jay Gould had realized his dream in the West and Southland.

Newcomb's ambitions exceeded that of the merchants of Louisville. He saw the L & N as the natural artery of trade and travel from the Lakes to the Gulf and from the East to the Southwest; that the best route from Havana and Mexico was across the Gulf; and that the vast carrying trade from the West to New York and to Europe would be partially directed through the South.[47]

In order to protect his road from ruinous competition and enable it to fully achieve its real mission, Newcomb saw that it was necessary to buy up or control several competing lines. The system of roads, to be really efficient and prosperous had to be under one control, protected alike from local jealousies, diverse interests, and prejudicial competition. Newcomb planned to control lines of travel and trade from Chicago to New Orleans, from St. Louis to Savannah, from Memphis to Port Royal, and from Louisville to Pensacola, thus entering every major port between Wilmington and Galveston. There would be steamers plying from Savannah to New York, Jacksonville, Havana, and Liverpool; from Pensacola to Vera Cruz and Havana. There would be special trains for steamers going to Havana and Vera Cruz that would leave New York, St. Louis, and Chicago, and run through without change.

The small, muscular, poker-faced Newcomb, with charming frankness and cultured address, moved with his accustomed speed to make this dream a reality.[48] Seeking to lay the ghost of monopoly power centered in Louisville, Newcomb, at the time of the St. Louis and Southeastern deal, said:

> We have sought to control this important line in the interest of our stockholders, and to maintain the geographical position of Louisville against unjust discriminations. We desire peace and harmony with all our neighbors. The clamor raised by Evansville, St. Louis, and other cities is causeless and without reason; especially is the perturbation displayed by some of our good railroad friends. It shall be our earnest endeavor to harmonize all conflicting interest and render equal and exact justice to all. We shall seek the maintenance of a just and equitable tariff and demand nothing for Louisville other than that which her geographical position entitles her to claim.

Newcomb got not only his Southern roads, but also a line from St. Louis to New York shorter than the Pennsylvania Central line. New steamers and thousands of freight cars were ordered for the great through lines; and an English Company offered to put on a line of steamers to Liverpool whenever they were needed. Under Newcomb's aggressive administration a program of exploitation of mineral deposits and the establishment of settlements was fostered all along the line.[49]

With such a powerful ally, the merchants of Louisville threw
their agents into the crossroads markets with every promise of
success.[50] Their control of the distributive trade covered east
Tennessee, northern Georgia, northern Alabama and Mississippi,
parts of Arkansas and northern Texas.[51] To be sure this trade
area did not coincide with the full extent and ambition of the
L & N, nor did it represent the city's former commercial sphere
of influence. The Cincinnati Southern, building to the East, cut
the trade considerably there; and the difficulties with through
traffic over the St. Louis, Iron Mountain Railroad, built by and
favoring St. Louis merchants, hampered the trade of Louisville
merchants in Arkansas and north Texas.[52] Indeed Louisville
merchants discovered that, though steel rails and yellow fever
might eventually make the gateway city a key cotton mart,
tobacco was her leading staple.[53] However, Louisville manufactures, distributed in the southern market area, compensated
somewhat for general disappointment of not becoming a leading
cotton mart.[54]

But Louisville merchants also were forced to rediscover the
value of united action if the commercial spheres of influence,
theretofore secured and held by the dominance of the L & N
in Southern transportation, were to be maintained. Having
allowed their old Board of Trade to languish, the merchants of
Louisville awoke to discover that "in every direction our business men, fighting their singlehanded battles, come into collision
with the commercial power of rival cities, thus solidly combined,
concentrated and marshalled by united wisdom, capital, and
experience. It is obvious that in such contest the odds are
against us." Indeed, it came as a distinct shock, one year after
the new Board reorganized, to discover that their old ally, the
L & N, was favoring the shipment of merchandise from points
other than from the gateway city.[55] The truth was that
Louisville had come to the end of an era. H. Victor Newcomb,
with his dream of the L & N as a regional institution had fore-

shadowed this end; and the competition of the rivals of Louisville, through rail facilities of their own, made that end a reality.

The city of St. Louis, sitting like a giant spider in a web
of rivers and steel rails, was also a contender for control of the
South's great staple. Ever since a depot was established at the
confluence of the Missouri and Mississippi Rivers on February
15, 1764, by Pierre Loclede Siguest and named in honor of
Louis XV of France, St. Louis has been a name to conjure with.
Long one of the keys to the French Empire in North America,
the city has had a tradition as a crossroad of the world, both
in commerce and high politics. St. Louis was and remains a
vital part of what is generally considered truly American, and
much of the romance and folklore of the young colossus, the
working out of the spirit of western democracy, was a part of
the past of this queen of the rivers. For the river brought to her
doorstep adventurers from all lands and made the city the
natural market for the Mississippi Valley—one of the termini
of the internal triangle of trade so dear to the hearts of economic
historians of the middle period.

In 1861, the South was, and had been, St. Louis' best market
for produce and provisions. "Besides having the lead of all other
western points in these lines and in that direction", the city
also had "the carrying trade".[56] The booming of the guns at
Sumter was the signal for the cessation of all trade activities on
the River. As a contemporary observer remarked:

> For a time the steamboat interest was apparently
> destroyed. Communication with the lower Mississippi was
> entirely cut off, and packet lines were greatly hampered
> by military restrictions. The immense produce and provi-
> sion trade ceased, and the future of St. Louis looked
> gloomy in the extreme. But steamboat owners, merchants,
> and manufacturers in a little while began to experience a
> more hopeful state of affairs. The wants of the govern-
> ment gave employment at remunerative rates to such of
> the steamboats as were not engaged in the carrying trade
> of the city. The grocery merchants, whose supply market

at New Orleans had been cut off, found a more enlarged
depot of supplies in New York, to which place the operations of war turned all wholesale merchandisers.

As the Federal Legions carried the fight further south, both
old and new packet lines on the river out of St. Louis boomed.
The city, as a logical point of supply for the valleys of the "Cumberland and Tennessee Rivers", received that and "a very
considerable trade on the Mississippi below Cairo". From 1862
to the close of the War the trade of the city boomed.

The merchant community in St. Louis emerged from the
War in a very fortunate position. Many factors contributed to
this condition. St. Louis and Missouri escaped most of the worst
effects of "Reconstruction".[57] There was a strange elixir in the
potion imbibed by her sons. Prophets, like L. U. Reavis, were
so smitten with her destiny that they believed St. Louis to be
the logical and eventual seat of the government of the nation.[58]
The merchants of the city were proud of the fact that their
sprawling metropolis was the largest west of the Alleghenies
and the fourth city of America. Bearing themselves with the
self-congratulatory, sanctified air of good conscience as the result
of having supported without stint Mr. Lincoln's war, the merchants of the city, in an expansive mood, extended the "hand
of friendship" to their southern customers and invited them
back to the St. Louis market.

The great promise of the Queen city of the Mississippi
Valley was insured also in the able, aggressive men attracted into
her midst from all over the nation and Europe. George Hagar
Morgan of New York, school teacher, clerk, Building and Loan
Association President in St. Louis, was for 30 years the great secretary of the Union Merchants' Exchange in the best tradition of
Lorenzo Sabine. Edward C. Simmons of Maryland, hardware
merchant extraordinary and the first in the business to use commercial travellers, banker, was one of St. Louis' and America's
leading capitalists.[59] Edwin Obed Stanard, distinguished manu-

facturer, commission merchant and miller, Republican Lieutenant Governor and congressman from Missouri, president of the Merchants Exchange and vice-president of the National Board of Trade, and banker, lent prestige to the city's masters of capital.[60] Thomas Allen of Massachusetts, lawyer, political newspaper publisher and Van Buren confidant in Washington, post-war congressman from Missouri, and connected with every significant pre- and post-war railroad scheme in the valley, was the H. Victor Newcomb of the Trans-Mississippi.[61]

To the ranks of St. Louis' bustling capitalists came Major-General Clinton Bowen Fisk, pre-war Michigan merchant, miller, and banker, and fresh from his stint with the Freedmen's Bureau in Tennessee and Kentucky.[62] From the Confederate army in Virginia and a pre-war newspaper publishing career, came Seth Wallace Cobb, penniless, to the magic city, where he eventually became President of the Merchants Exchange and sat in the 52nd, 53rd, and 54th Congresses, refusing then to be re-elected.[63] Sprung from a pioneer Illinois merchant family, veteran of the Mexican War, consul, and old freighter on the Santa Fe Trail, Edward James Glasgow was for thirty years wholesale grocer merchant with international connections.[64] The market possibilities of St. Louis for paints, oils, chemicals, heavy drugs, and naval stores were demonstrated by Charles W. Barstow, Union veteran from Boston, who owned one of the largest firms in the West and thus stood high among the capitalists of the city.[65]

The cult of the river was older than that of steel rails and devotees of the former flourished in the magic city long after the War. Among them was George Henry Rea, rising from a Massachusetts tanning career to be merchant, banker, president of the Mississippi Valley Transportation Company and Director of the Missouri Pacific Railroad.[66] Kentucky-born John A. Scudder, leading representative of the River Transportation interest of the city, was organizer of the St. Louis and Memphis, and eventually Vicksburg "Anchor Line" as well as President of the Merchants Exchange.[67] With the blood of the Lawrence and Wentworths in his veins, George L. Copen, though risen from the leather and hide trade in Massachusetts, was not content in Marine Insurance and the Mississippi Valley Transportation Company, but expanded into the public utilities of the city, and, with typical Yankee exclusiveness, organized a capitalist club, "The St. Louis Club." [68]

The grain interest of St. Louis, old as a trade interest, was not wanting in aggressive men. Marrying the sister of E. O. Stanard, John W. Kauffman, Union veteran from Iowa, rose to be one of the largest of the Western grain merchants and member of the grain exchanges of both St. Louis and Chicago.[69] Kentucky-born David Rowland Francis, President of the Merchants Exchange, mayor of St. Louis, governor of Missouri, and talked of for the Senate, headed a grain commission business of international reputation.[70] Not the least of the grain barons was George Bain, Scottish-born flour manufacturer and first to make direct shipments to Europe. Director of banks, railroads, and insurance companies, Bain became President of the Merchants Exchange, Vice President of the National Board of Trade, alderman of St. Louis, and leader of the Republican party in Missouri.[71]

Such a galaxy of talent was not sufficient to restore pre-war prosperity to St. Louis in the immediate post-war years. George H. Morgan stated the situation well when he observed:

> Hitherto our great market was in the Southern states, which had given their whole attention to the raising of cotton and sugar, necessitating the importation of breadstuffs. The change in the entire labor system, and the destitution almost universal in the South, has so interfered with the production of their great staples that they have of necessity been small buyers in our market, and have been compelled to raise food to sustain life. It is not unlikely that this change in the agricultural life of the South will continue, even when her old prosperity is regained.[72]

Conditions looked so bad that Morgan seriously suggested the opening of new avenues of trade elsewhere.

But such entrepreneural skill as was concentrated at St. Louis was not willing to surrender the Valley without an effort. For two or three years after the War the city merchants fought the good fight to turn the trade of the Valley back into their market. Possessing already the old spirit of cooperative mercantile action, they, in the face of the gradual return of Southern prosperity, began looking to the building of grain elevators; to explore the possibilities of building cotton factories to snag cotton from New York and New Orleans; and to push the wholesale drygoods, provisions, manufacturing, and, key to the erection of a cotton market, the wholesale grocery trade.[73] But dominating the Valley and its treacherous mistress, the River was being sponsored under the impact of the new national responsibility evidenced by masters of capital everywhere.[74] Believing that "the National Board will doubtless have much influence in directing the legislation of the country . . . and should be sustained", the St. Louis merchants sent delegates to Boston and pledged their allegiance. In the best tradition of the "third chamber", St. Louis merchants also sponsored River conventions for the improvement of the Mississippi waterway at New Orleans and Keokuk, and sent General Vandever of Iowa to Washington to push appropriations for this scheme before Congress.

The commercial god was in his heaven and all was right with the world. Indeed the merchants of the queen of the valley had much to be satisfied about. See him in his daily round.[75] The ladies have done their shopping at an early hour and gone their ways; paterfamilias seeks his avernus of an office, at the height of the trading season, clad only in thinnest of linen, and with a palm leaf fan in his hand. A misty aroma of the Ires of Hillery or Gregory floats before him as he seats himself at his desk and turns over the voluminous correspondence from far Texas, from the vexed Indian territory, from the great North-

west, from Arkansas, or from the host of river towns with
which the metropolis does business.

At eleven the sun has become withering to the unaccustomed
Easterners and Europeans thronging the mart; but the St. Louis
paterfamilias dons his broad straw hat, and, proceeding to the
"Merchants Exchange", a large circular room into which 1300
members vainly try each day to cram themselves, he makes his
way to the corner allotted to his branch of trade. There he
patiently swelters until nearly one o'clock. In this single room
every species of business is transacted; one corner devoted to
flour, a second to grain, a third to provisions, and a fourth
to cotton, etc. Though the noise is not so great as in other exchanges, business of national and international proportion is
carried on amid shouting, mopping of brows and the quiet hum
of waving palm-leaf fans, with large cans of cool sulphur water
to reduce the ardour of the trading process. Then our hero
saunters off to lunch, satisfied with the day's work and contemplating that happy day when the projected new "Exchange",
touted to be the finest on the continent, will be completed.

Within this atmosphere of happy cares that irrepressible
press agent of St. Louis, L. U. Reavis, dropped the electrifying
thought which had hovered like Banquo's ghost in the background all along. Said he: "The people of St. Louis and the
West must learn that next in importance to the Mississippi
River is a railroad through the Southwest to Galveston".[76] The
gradual shift of cotton cultivation to the new, more productive
lands west of the Mississippi and the heavy movement of colonies
of Negroes to these new areas gave St. Louis merchant capitalists their cue.[77] Besides this, the city merchants found the
river much too whimsical for modern business practice. Frozen
in winter, too low, as the result of drought, in summer, destruc-
tively flamboyant between seasons, and clogged at the mouth
year round—a quixotic mistress indeed![78] Then, too, it dawned
on the merchants that perhaps the long held notion of the
identity of interest between New Orleans and St. Louis was a

mistake—perhaps the successful fight to make the queen of the rivers an internal port of entry guaranteed the merchants a larger, separate destiny as rivals of the crescent city's masters of capital.

The merchants of St. Louis realized that if they were to keep pace in the furious competition among the merchants of the border cities for the Southern trade they must open the iron gates. The chief railroad project directly south to the new cotton country dates from the incorporation of St. Louis and Bellevue Mineral Railroad Company, constituting a railroad from St. Louis to Pilot Knob, with possibilities of extending to Cape Girardeau, Missouri, on the Mississippi on to the Southwestern part of the state, in 1837.[79] However, the St. Louis and Iron Mountain Line was chartered March 3, 1851, and amended by special act of 1857, authorizing the company to extend their line to connect with the Cairo and Fulton Railroad, or construct its line or unite and consolidate with it. The project languished to the extent that the close of the war found only eighty-six miles complete, and, because the state held a statutory first mortgage as a result of $3,501,000 purchases of the company's bonds, the legislature of Missouri passed, in February of 1866, an act authorizing the Governor to foreclose the state's lien and offer the road for sale. The Governor advertised and sold the project at public auction on September 27, 1866, at which time it was bid in for the State for the amount of principal and interest due Missouri. The deed was turned over to the State, and three commissioners appointed under the act of February 19, 1866, took possession and managed the road until January, 1867, when it was sold to Thomas Allen and associates.[80]

Thomas Allen, with the backing of the St. Louis merchants, threw himself into the work and by 1869 had extended the line to Belmont opposite Columbus, Kentucky. He already owned a transfer boat and had rail connections with the Baltimore and Ohio at this point; thus, St. Louis freight could be transferred across the River, without breaking bulk, to access to the Southern rail system below the winter ice barrier.[81] But Allen and Superintendent Morley looked toward the Gulf as their goal. They wished to sink the iron siphon deeper to Pilot Knob, into Arkansas, through Little Rock, Fulton, and, by the way of Tyler, Texas, to Houston. Galveston could then be reached over the Texas Central road. Though the Joy road, building out of Chicago and another line to Lawrence, Kansas, might offer competition, Allen was sure that his direct 800 mile scheme would "make St. Louis the natural supply depot of this territory." [82]

While St. Louis merchants were looking hopefully upon the scheme to use Chinese coolie labor in the cotton fields and organizing a "Cotton Association", Allen pushed his line past Pilot Knob into Arkansas.[83] Buying, with the assistance of Marquand, the stocks, bonds, property and franchises of the twenty-mile Cairo and Fulton line in 1872, Allen, by the end of the following year, had pushed 375 miles of rail into Texarkana, Texas.[84] Swiftly on his heels, the merchants swarmed down the line to make contacts and receive a hearty welcome from planters and country merchants. Allen finished his task by consolidating the four companies' 686 miles of road into the St. Louis, Iron Mountain, and Southern Railway in 1874 and became the new company's president.[85]

The end of the first decade after Appomattox found the queen of the valley in possession of a great commercial empire and the second packing and inland cotton market of the nation. The town was bustling with activity. James B. Eads, an engineer native to the city, had been appointed by Congress to open the mouth of the Mississippi at New Orleans. Exchange Hall, reputed to be the grandest in America, was ready for use and fifteen railroads served the city merchants. During the next five years the Southern lines and the River made cotton receipts skyrocket in the St. Louis market. Huge compresses were built, storage space expanded and buyers, exporters, and speculators from the Eastern mills and Europe thronged the market. Ere long direct exports of cotton from far San Antonio and Waco, were consigned to Liverpool, Havre, Bremen, and Vienna.[86] Never once did the St. Louis, Iron Mountain, and Southern betray its trust.[87] From the time of its completion, the road fought the Louisville and Nashville to the East, New Orleans to the South, and extended its connections farther and farther into the new cotton territory, adding $100,000,000 annually to the city's trade.

The Gould deal, establishing the Missouri Pacific line, properly marks the end of the great merchant capitalist era of St. Louis. But George H. Morgan could be justly proud of his city's Southern commercial empire. He put it well in his letter to Joseph Nimmo thus:[88]

> The Southern trade of St. Louis embraces all that part of the State of Missouri lying south of the latitude of this city, the State of Arkansas, western and northwestern Louisiana and a large part of Texas. East of the Mississippi it embraces a considerable portion of Kentucky and Tennessee, Northwest Georgia, Alabama and Mississippi. St. Louis also virtually controls the trade of the Mississippi River on both banks between Cairo and New Orleans. Our merchants have not the same hold on the trade east of the Mississippi that they have on the trade of the states west of that river, from the fact that east of the river they meet sharp competition from the merchants of Louisville and Cincinnati. The city of Chicago is also quite an active competitor for the trade east of the Mississippi; and the Northern cities on the Atlantic seaboard also compete for this trade by means of the facilities afforded for direct shipments.

George H. Morgan had mentioned the city named for that veteran's organization of the Revolutionary War, the Society of Cincinnatus. Colonel Israel Ludlow, looking over the fertile land on the banks of the Ohio awaiting his plan, chose well the tradition implicit in name of the great farmer-Emperor of the

Roman Empire. For there was strength rooted in the land and the river for peace and war. This child of the river was the leader in the swift growth of the Trans-Allegheny border cities down to the year when the giants of the passing agrarian age made the compromise that postponed for a decade the booming of the guns of Sumter.[89] The slow measured tread of that agrarian era had been kind to Cincinnati. Had not the dictate of geography thrust greatness and leadership upon the city— had not the logic of expansion assured her prominence in the Ohio Valley?

But the war came and Cincinnati became a boomtown. Under the impact of Government spending and building, wages jumped to new highs and evercoming immigrants found "Porkopolis" a great town in which to settle.[90] Indeed, the ten year rising tide of city prosperity had been considerably implemented by the sale of one-half of the government confiscated cotton of the Confederacy at fabulous prices in her market.[91] Cincinnati merchants viewed with favor Chase's new money and faced the phenomena of a mounting national debt firm in the conviction that thus England had grown great. To be sure, steamboat building and other industries were somewhat curbed by reconversion; but the merchants of Cincinnati faced the new era with confidence, for had not the "rights of man" and "Popular Government" been vindicated?

Beneath the current optimism the realist understood that the boom was over.[92] However, that spirit of high responsibility for merchant capitalist unity in public policy was to be found no stronger anywhere than in Cincinnati.[93] Today they were helping sponsor a river convention in St. Louis to clear all obstructions from the Ohio-Mississippi River system;[94] tomorrow they were directing their representatives in Congress to get repeal of the cotton tax;[95] another time they were seeking a universal standard of grain classification and measurement.[96] But, most important, the merchants felt that the propriety of organizing a "National Chamber of Commerce" made it extremely desirable that the Boards of Trades and Chambers of Commerce should meet at an easily accessible place as soon as possible before Congress met, so that "legislation deemed necessary might be secured". They too, went to Boston and pledged their allegiance, as a devotee to a shrine to renew his faith.[97]

Back in the minds of the merchants engaged in this flurry of activity was the "Cincinnati Problem", becoming more acute every year. Prior to the War, Cincinnati enjoyed a large and important trade with the South. "Its business ramified throughout all parts of the Southern states more generally than that of any other interior city. This was largely conducted through the instrumentality of the Mississippi and Ohio Rivers and their tributaries." [98] These trade relations were somewhat disturbed by the War. When hostilities ceased, the industries of the South were prostrate, and the old business relations were not readily restored. Besides, the necessities of the time had created channels from which trade could not at once be diverted. Previously, Cincinnati had relied mainly on the rivers for transportation to the South, and these, by the changes which railroads had wrought, had lost precedence.[99] They no longer "dictated methods nor rates", but yielded to the quicker facilities which rail transportation furnished to the interior of the South. Railroads Cincinnati did not have. "So far from being independent, it found itself at the mercy of the Louisville and Nashville railroad, which was largely managed in the interest of Louisville and which was playing an important part in building up the trade of that city. The facilities too, of that road at times, were not equal to the performance of the work demanded, so that shipments from Cincinnati and other points north of the Ohio River were delayed, to the embarrassment and ultimate injury of trade." [100]

The condition brought home to Cincinnati's masters of capital the truth that Cincinnati was without a back-country, and had ceased to grow.[101] Facing her at the South was a "vast empire", rich in natural resources, containing a population of four million, and penetrated by four thousand miles of railroad converging at Chattanooga where Cincinnati merchants could have no successful rival. Weary of the talk of the preceding thirty years on the Railroad Projects, the organized merchants took it up, becoming the clearing house for all Southern communications on the scheme and receiving all accredited representatives from Southern Atlantic and Gulf cities in interest thereof. Taking the position that private capital was inadequate to the necessities of such a project, the Chamber of Commerce and Merchants Exchange suggested the repeal of the clause in the Ohio Constitution of 1850 which forbade governmental corporations aiding any private project of this character with its credit.

After many proposals and much agitation in the press,[102] a young attorney, Edward Alexander Ferguson, took the initiative in calling a meeting of citizens to secure the passing of a law giving Cincinnnati the power to build the road. The new law would circumvent the state constitutional barrier in question.[103] On November 26, 1868, Ferguson handed the press the bill which was supposed to be presented to the legislature that winter. Amid the resulting speculation and discussion a committee from the city council, the Chamber of Commerce, and Board of Trade, presented at the capital of Ohio a memorial asking that the bill be passed. The idea was, so ran the memorial,

> To enlarge the market for manufactures, to extend the area of commerce, to aid in developing a district of country which is naturally tributary to this city, and by accomplishing this, to give greater employment to labor and increased value to property. In one word, it is to secure greater growth and prosperity to this city.

The bill was passed by the Senate on April 28, 1869, and by the House a week later.[104]

The act stipulated that whenever the city council of Cincinnati (a city of the first class having over 150,000 population) should declare it essential to the city's interest to provide a railway, one terminal of which should be at Cincinnati, and a majority of the city's qualified electors, at a special election held for that purpose, should approve such a declaration, it should be the duty of the Superior Court of that city to appoint five trustees to carry out the will of the electors. The trustees were to hold office during good behavior, were empowered to contract loans, issue bonds, supervise construction, and report their receipts and disbursements annually to the city council. It provided for the issuance of bonds to the amount of $10,000,000 for this purpose. These bonds were secured by mortgage on the road when built, by the good faith of the city, or by an annual tax levy to cover interest charges and provide a sinking fund for their redemption.

The city fathers immediately passed the necessary resolution and on June 26 the special election carried the question. The Superior Court, on the petition of the city solicitor, handed down the names of the first board of trustees.[105] As was to be expected, Edward Alexander Ferguson was one of the trustees and perhaps the only one associated in any way with railroad building and financing.[106] Kentucky-born Richard M. Bishop, wholesale grocery merchant, mayor of Cincinnati, and eventually Governor of the State of Ohio, was also a trustee.[107] Miles Greenwood, iron monger, leading sponsor of the Ohio mechanics' institute, capitalist, was one of the five trustees appointed by the Superior Court of Cincinnati. Philip Heidelbach, a Bavarian by birth, renowned clothier, and banker, was also one of the original trustees. William Hooper, the last of the original trustees, had a long successful business and banking career at the time of his appointment. His connection with the Board was confined to the attempt to negotiate the loan with Baring Brothers and he resigned just as active work of construction commenced.

These original trustees worked with the enthusiastic backing of not only the city merchants, but of the most prominent men in the State. No less a man than John Sherman worked for the success of the scheme at Washington.[108] Coming to Cincinnati from his native Pennsylvania via Kentucky, Henry Lewis, school teacher, banker, interested in public utilities, quarries, tool works, hotels, car works, and the C & O bridge at Cincinnati was prominent in the Chamber of Commerce and was a member of the Common Carrier Company that inaugurated the operation of the Cincinnati Southern Railway.[109] Pennsylvania-born John Skillito, merchant, was founder of one of the greatest drygoods houses in America and for fifty years one of the more aggressive and resourceful city builders.[110] A. T. Goshorn, Civil War veteran, patron of the Arts and Education, public impresario, and foreign traveller, was among the leading city and state builders, as was Joseph Curran Butler, philanthropist, banker, Democrat politician, and so strongly identified with the Chamber of Commerce movement in Cincinnati, becoming president of the Chamber during the first two years of the War.[111]

Cincinnati produced no greater man of the new era than John A. Gano.[112] Educated in the city and for a while its assistant postmaster, he was, on the eve of the secession crisis, financial editor of the Cincinnati *Commercial* and Secretary of the Chamber of Commerce. During the War he was sent to Europe with the Federal bonds for sale in the money markets there. His was a great dream for the commerce of the city and the new ambitions of merchant-capitalists. Gano was one of the first executive committeemen of the National Board of Trade and a part of the Cincinnati delegation to that body until his death. In this same category was Samuel Fulton Covington, Indiana-born Southern flatboat trader, editor, lawyer, county politician, and insurance authority before coming to Cincinnati in 1851.[113] His mastery of insurance law secured him the presidency of the Globe Insurance Company (1865-1888) and of the Board of Underwriters. A writer on political and economic subjects, Covington held local offices in Cincinnati government and the presidency of Chamber of Commerce, as well as being a delegate to the meeting organizing the National Board of Trade and its vice-president from 1873 to 1880. C. Lester Taylor, Canadian-born, cotton commission merchant, and large shipper of cotton to Canadian ports, was also a great city builder and commercial statesman of the new era.[114] With such backing the scheme had every promise of success.

When the special committee of the city council chose, in the resolution calling for the election of June 26, Chattanooga, instead of Nashville or Knoxville, they chose well.[115] Planted at the very mouth of the narrow passes, Chattanooga had sprung, since the War closed, from a village into a prosperous city of 12,000 souls.[116] It had an ever growing aspect of a Northwestern settlement, Northern and Western men having flocked there in large numbers. Union veterans remembered its wonderful advantages as a railway center in one of the "richest mineral regions in the world", and, on being mustered out, settled there. If Cincinnati merchant-capitalists planned to open the "Iron Gate" at Chattanooga, they would connect with five trunk lines of railroad. The Western and Atlantic connected Chattanooga with Atlanta and the South; Nashville and Chattanooga pierced the Cumberland and gave a route to Louisville and the Ohio river; East Tennessee, Virginia and Georgia road reached to Bristol giving direct connection with Lynchburg, Washington, and New York; the Alabama and Chattanooga ran through fabulous coal and iron fields to Meridian, in Mississippi, where there was a direct line to the river proper; and the Memphis and Charleston opened up a rather devastated, once prosperous, plantation area. Chattanooga was also a river center of no little importance and yearly her storehouses were crowded with corn, wheat, and bacon from Kentucky, Virginia, and North Carolina for the Southern trade. But these same lines could also bring the magic staple, back into the market area of Cincinnati.

It was one thing to select a Southern goal and quite another
to achieve it. Kentucky and Tennessee must be persuaded to
grant a charter to the road to run through their respective
territories. Ferguson framed the Tennessee franchise on both
American, Tennessee, and English legal principles to attract
English capital, and on November 9, 1869, went to Nashville
with Heidelback and Bishop to put it over. Bishop returned
to Nashville after the first visit and pushed the bill through to
legislation on January 20, 1870.[117] The assault on Kentucky
in January of 1870 proved to be a more formidable task. On
the presentation of the legislation, it was sent to the committee
on railroads of both the House and Senate. John C. Breckenridge, retained by the trustees, presented, at an open hearing
before a joint meeting of the Senate and House committees on
McKee Bill, the argument for the bill on two alternate days.[118]
Isaac Caldwell, in turn, addressed the general assembly's joint
committee in the interest of Louisville, and carried the day.
Ferguson, in Frankfort all the while, returned to Cincinnati,
defeated.

There was every reason why the scheme should be pushed.[119]
Cincinnati's river traffic was falling off seriously and the discrimination of East-West rail lines in rates relative to Cincinnati
had not been alleviated. The city merchants had ambitions of
making Cincinnati "preeminently the cotton market of the interior"; but it was plain that merchants in the neighboring
border cities with direct Southern rail connections were reaping
the harvest. As if to remedy matters somewhat, the Cotton
Exchange merged with the Chamber of Commerce, and daily
quotations from cotton markets throughout the nation and
Europe improved conditions. Moreover, the merchants went on
a goodwill tour to Savannah and other Southern cities in an
attempt to build their economic fences. The going into operation of the law making the city an internal port of entry, while
not totally satisfactory, was at least encouraging.

A necessary part of the Cincinnati idea involved the building of a bridge across the Ohio river to Kentucky. General Andrew Hickenlooper had already taken the bill for this purpose to Washington, and John Sherman and Job E. Stevenson had already introduced it into the Senate and House, respectively. But the failure of the McKee bill in Kentucky called for heroic measures. In the best spirit of the new radicalism, John Sherman prepared to force Kentucky into compliance by a federal grant of land to an incorporated "Cincinnati and Chattanooga Railroad Company"; and Sherman was persuaded to withdraw his bill only on the condition that another try at Frankfort resulted in success.

In February of 1871, Ferguson drew a bill embracing both the Ohio River bridge and the Kentucky situation entitled "A Bill to Promote the Construction of the Cincinnati Southern Railroad" and, accompanied by Bishop and Heidelback, went to Washington, where Sherman and Stevenson introduced it. Ferguson and Sherman appeared before the Senate Committee and urged passage. Ferguson also appeared before the House Committee on Roads, etc., to explain the Stevenson Bill. The Bill passed the House, after a favorable committee report, by two-thirds vote; and failed in the Senate only for the want of time. The appearance of the McKee bill in Frankfort in December of 1871 caused friends of the scheme to advise that it might be best to let Kentucky settle it. February 13, 1872, saw the bill through in Kentucky and the trustees accepted the same day.[120] Immediately, the merchants of the city pinned all their hopes for the future upon the successful completion of 335 miles of steel rail to Chattanooga.

Work soon began in earnest to complete the line.[121] William Hooper went to Europe to dispose of most of the $10,000,000 bond issue, but in vain. It was just after the trustees were in New York negotiating with Winslow, Lanier and Co., and while Hooper was in London negotiating with the Barings that Jay Cooke & Co. closed their doors. Needless to say that this, like all railroad schemes, came to a halt.[122] Cincinnati merchants took the shock well and failures were few. Indeed after the first scare, most branches of trade in the city steadied except the nationally crippled iron trade. The cotton trade boomed to the extent that S. Lester Taylor saw clearly Cincinnati as the great inland mart for the staple.

Spinners from Ohio, Indiana, Kentucky, and Michigan, as well as Canada, were buying most of their supplies in Cincinnati. Direct shipments were going to Pennsylvania, New York, and New England mills; and Europe, with the then prevailing low rates, was just twenty days away. Steamship lines at the ports of New York, Boston, Philadelphia, Norfolk, Baltimore, Portland, and Montreal had resident agents in the city to bill through the increasing good quality of cotton to their ships and Europe.

Conditions looked more hopeful still when Ferguson and his associates successfully negotiated the $10,000,000 bond issue with the American Exchange Bank of New York in March of 1874.[123] The funds were soon exhausted; and, in spite of general optimism[124] elsewhere, a new fight opened in the state for legislative authorization of $6,000,000 more.[125] A hard fight by the trustees, no doubt aided by the ruinous cut-throat competition and strikes on the East-West rail lines, finally brought, on March 14, 1876, favorable legislative action.[126] Released for action and with the line pushed 163 miles to the green hills of sleepy Somerset, Kentucky, the Trustees leased the road, as the law required, to a group of Cincinnati citizens under the title "The Cincinnati Southern Railroad Company".[127]

The new fund was exhausted in building, and in 1878 a fight both in the legislature and the courts over leasing and completing the road was weathered successfully.[128] The road by 1879 was ready for through business and Cincinnati stood upon the long-awaited threshold. Sidney D. Maxwell, already appointed treasury specialist in the Ohio valley, could proudly write Joseph Nimmo that:[129]

The Southern Trade of Cincinnati embraces Kentucky, Tennessee, West Virginia, Louisiana, Arkansas, Northern Georgia, Alabama, Mississippi, and a part of Texas. The nature and extent of the trade of Cincinnati with the Southern States cannot be specifically defined. In some departments the city penetrates the whole South. Her machinery, implements of husbandry, safes, wood making machinery, furniture, provisions, liquors, clothing, boots and shoes, hardware, candles, soap, and starch, carriages and other classes of goods go to all parts of the Southern States. Her heavy drygoods are largely distributed throughout Kentucky and Tennessee, to some extent in Arkansas, and, in a limited way, in the northern parts of the Gulf states. The same may be said of heavy groceries and drugs, though her light groceries go farther southward, finding liberal outlets in Arkansas, Louisiana, as well as in other parts of the more remote South.

As a fitting finish to this great effort of the merchant-capitalists of Ohio to tap the arteries of Southern trade and thus become the regents of King Cotton, the Cincinnati merchants held a grand banquet on March 18, 1880.[130] Up from the South to be wined and dined in Cincinnati's Music Hall came Governor Blackburn of Kentucky, Governor Colquit of Georgia, Ex-Governor Brown of Georgia, General Wilder of the Roane Iron Works in Chattanooga, Colonel J. W. Grant, President of the Knoxville Board of Trade, Governor Rufus N. Cobb of Alabama, Ben E. Crane, president of the Atlanta Board of Trade, Hon. Leslie E. Brooks, president of the Board of Trade of Mobile, and all of the Knights of the Law and the Press, unabashed camp-followers of these apostles of the New South. The city's hospitality moved W. A. Hemphill, editor of the Atlanta *Constitution,* to say:

> I have felt the pulse of the public sentiment, and the sentiment is that Cincinnati has given the South just what its people wanted, a fine railroad to the largest, wealthiest, and most liberal city in the West, St. Louis not excepted.

But all of this enthusiasm could not obscure the basic truth. To be sure, Cincinnati could then throw, with greater ease, her commercial travellers into the crossroads' market for more effective competition with St. Louis and Louisville. But the merchants realized, in their hour of triumph, that Chattanooga could not be the end. The strength of the city could not be realized until the Gulf was reached; and it would take more capital and less heroic efforts to accomplish this. The merchant-capitalist era in Southern exploitation was over. It took, for the new day, the vast sums of the Erlanger interest of London to build the "Queen and Crescent" or Cincinnati, New Orleans, and Texas Pacific Railway line.

The Newcombs, the Allens, and the Fergusons were radicals, in the truest, if not the more spectacular political sense of this pregnant "reconstruction" word. Urban imperialist to a man, they dared open the iron sluice gates of commerce into the sellers' market of the South. They were not rugged individualists. Their wisdom and courage were that of the naive. Held together by a sense of their new importance, they did not quibble to use government in the new game of amassing wealth and building a new society. But their fierce competition never made them forget that they must work together if the new orientation in the American socio-economic scene was to be secured and maintained. Here is the new politics of modern America. Here indeed is political regionalism triumphant in the Trans-Allegheny river valleys. The Western wing of the American Bourgeoisie had come of age.

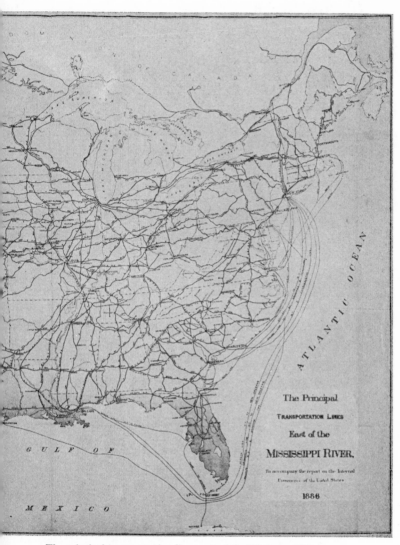

The principal transportation lines east of the Mississippi River.

7. Knights of the Bag

It was not enough for the merchants of the Middle West to sink steel syphons into the South for the purpose of establishing markets. Competition of the seaboard cities, both North and South, was still keen enough to cause concern in the counting-houses of the middle western cities. If the spheres of commercial influence were to be held, it was plain that heroic methods had to be resorted to. A tool made to order lay within the easy reach of the border city merchants, the commercial traveler. Through the iron sluice-gates and out over the hinterland moved these "Knights of the Bag" to secure the economic hegemony of the Middle West in the South.

Around the commercial traveler, as around the railroads over which he traveled, hung an aura of romance. The probable date of his appearance in the United States may be set in the 1850's.[1] Before and long after the '50's the custom prevailed that merchants from the back country, west and south, came to the eastern cities once a year to purchase their supplies and to enjoy a taste of city life. The dealers would attend the annual or semi-annual auctions of the publishers, boot and shoe manufacturers, hardware manufacturers and hatters. They formed the acquaintance of the manufacturers and so could order directly from them. To be sure the principal or some of the junior partners of many firms solicited orders; but most of the manufacturers, importer, jobbers and publishers operated on a small scale, and their representatives reached, at best, only the hundred or two customers they had made for their goods.[2] These representatives were often collecting agents who gave or withheld the firm's credit as the local situation seemed to justify.[3]

In this same period however, the commercial traveler made his appearance. He was an agent or representative of an importer, manufacturer, or other wholesale dealer, who procured and transmitted orders for the goods of the principal, in quantity, by personal solicitation and the exhibition of his samples. There-

176

fore, he was no peddler, carried no goods, or made no direct
sales, and in this period dealt only with the wholesalers. There
were not many more than one thousand of these agents on the
road by the close of the 50's[4] in the entire United States, and
nearly all of this total was from the eastern cities, where were
then located the wholesalers, importers, and a few manufacturers.[5]

The commercial traveler entered the picture at a time when
the continued growth of the country made the annual trip to
the Eastern centers by local merchants, West and South, too
expensive. The larger cities of the West and South were indeed
becoming centers of supply for the towns within a radius of two
hundred or three hundred miles around them; and this very
soon involved, to a considerable extent, their transacting their
own importing and manufacturing. Finding their business was
likely to drift away from them without special efforts on their
part to retain it, "some of the manufacturers and most of the
jobbing houses of New York, Boston and Philadelphia, in the
dry goods, grocery, liquor, drugs, paints, jewelry, books, and
some other trades began to send out their canvassers to solicit
orders from country dealers." [6] At first these were junior partners or some favorite clerk or salesman, who made this an occasional jaunt to escape the confinement of the warehouse. But
so excellent were the results of these partial canvasses that, ere
long, these houses came to employ men skilled in the business
and who had undergone a more or less thorough training for it,
as commercial travelers, through the greater part or the whole
of the year. As it was obviously for the interest of the great
houses of the eastern cities to retain a large proportion of the
custom of the jobbing houses of the western and southern cities,
an understanding was had with the latter that the eastern jobbers would not canvass for customers in the West and South
below a certain grade, leaving these to be supplied by the wholesale dealers in those cities.[7]

The Civil War brought some changes in the whole picture of selling in this fashion. Those eastern firms which had used salesmen in the South before the War were, of course, forced to suspend operations, not only because of the War, but also because the southern cities raised barriers against their agents. But the general prosperity, which followed swiftly on the heels of war, increased the activity of these Knights of the Bag, both East and West.[8] Competition became very keen and the older conservative trusted representative of an established house, who "held a trade" in pre-war years, found himself jostled on trains and in the hotels by new inexperienced young men, often representing no one but themselves.

Around what was patently a prosaic problem of distribution in a period of rapid expansion and wealth accumulation arose a certain glamour because of the personnel of the process of distribution. The men and women who were commercial travellers brought a touch of color and adventure into the rather narrow, humdrum lives of the small town and rural communities in which they operated. Their jargon, their clothes, their very cosmopolitan air, to say nothing of the goods they carried in sample cases, bespoke the fabulous mystery of the distant cites.[9] Who can measure how much the vicarious sharing of that adventure figured in the sales success of these "Knights of the Bag"?

The idealization of the travelling salesman found its best living example in George Peabody, the great Baltimore and Georgetown merchant prince and philanthropist. It naturally followed, then, that a salesman should have had integrity and correct morals; pleasing and winning address and gentlemanly manners; thorough knowledge of his goods—its history—how made—and place of manufacture and all elements affecting their production and cost; and, finally, a wide general culture, not only in business matters, but on topics of state, national, foreign, literary and scientific nature. This paragon of virtue would be, so ran the exhortation, an agreeable and intelligent companion, welcome in all society.[10] Seldom before the Civil War, and even less so after the War, did the mass of salesmen even approach this high standard.

The personal habits of the traveller before the War had already taken on the character which the term as used today readily brings to the popular mind. These folk were then careless in speech and rough in manners. They drank much, gambled often, were not entirely honest in reports to their houses, and often imposed upon their customers a very shortsighted policy. But it could be said to their credit that they were an open-hearted lot of fellows, "breezy and frank with their acquaintances and friends, full of experience and of a kind that quickened them in many ways, excellent story-tellers—though rather of the style of Chaucer than of the later writers", and in their relations to each other generous to a fault.[11]

This pattern, while not entirely universal either before or after the War, continued valid for the mass of salesmen swarming the field. There were a great many post-war travelling salesmen who were well posted in their lines, gentlemanly in their deportment, and who possessed the respect and confidence of their customers and employers; but the majority of men then engaged in salesmanship were densely ignorant of the goods they were handling. They were not selected for any real qualifications as salesmen, but for their ability to talk glibly upon almost any subject and their pertinacity in soliciting orders.[12] The calling seemed to attract such men to represent the commercial houses. These men looked upon such jobs "as a soft place and easy position to fill, and then to be allowed five dollars to eight dollars a day for expenses, just makes them feverish to try it."

The novice on the grip-sack trail soon found that the life was no bed of roses. Few of the first class drummers liked the occupation, and the constant necessity of being away from home, to say nothing of the daily risk of life and health, made the travellers look forward to the time when they could abandon this foot-loose way of life.[13] The novice would find post-war competition ruinous in the towns and villages—price cutting, lying—indeed no device was too cheap to stoop to, to sell. There was no telling in what condition the traveller might find lodging for the night; and a trip into the southern back country in a hired buggy with a Negro driver during reconstruction was a feat which should have been approached with a good deal of misgivings.[14]

There were compensations in the life of the traveller, not the least of which was diversity in the calling.[15] There was the drummer, "the everyday, common sense, hard-working, travel day-or-night fellow, sells lots of 'stuff' on close margins; his career is devoid of all ambition other than that of his profession, and to whom the term *holiday* is a misfit phrase. He wears store-bought clothes, and is—generally broke." Then there was the "commercial traveler, self styled." He was the "most attractive young fellow on earth, takes the world easy, sells the better grade of goods, and does it 'nicely', wears tailor-made clothing." He knew "a few drummers, smokes three-for-a-quarter cigars", was "usually of a cynical turn of mind, but on good terms with the world." His trade looked him up at the hotel after business hours for he was "straight goods" and took "well". Like the drummer, however, he was—generally "broke."

Among this group there was the "travelling representative". He held a small working interest in some big firm for whom he had made "big money"; a firm which needed his services but had adopted this method to keep from paying him the salary he was worth. It reduced "the T. R.'s income; but who would sacrifice income for the glory of being admitted to the firm?" He was generally "a fine handsome young fellow of good address, polished manners, genial, jovial, liberal, (had) a 'mash' on the trade, unexceptional in attire, the idol of the hotel." Yet he too was—generally "broke."

There was also a stilted group who went under the name of "commercial tourists". These men were mostly "middle-aged, very passe",—usually unsuccessful merchants who entered business with the idea of "doing it all". "They still (knew) everything and (told) it; usually recommended from smaller towns by their friends (?) who want to get rid of him." He was the man of "gall", which constituted his stock in trade, and he worked it for all it was worth. "They affect elderly society and don't mix with the drummers; have a look of having seen better days, and their dress shows it." They were generally —"broke."

Finally, the trade looked with scorn on the "commercial angels" who were the whitehaired lads with real alligator grips. They generally travelled for either their fathers or uncles who doted on them and hoped to reform them by experience on the road. They were obviously wellkept and their clothes were called "dainty". These scions really did not work at the business of selling and the money they spent on the fine art of enjoyment irritated the average salesman because these "commercial angels" did not have to earn it.

Among other compensations, the novice would have also the privilege of joining a national or regional organization which looked after his interest. This was especially true as the '70's wore on.[16] These salesmen's organizations had special newspapers, published in New York, Syracuse, and Chicago. The organizations had many purposes, among which were insurance, concessions from railroads and hotels, interchange of information, social benefits, and all the strength and assistance for which every interest in the history of this country has traditionally resorted to organization as soon as it became of any economic or numerical consequence.[17] From the beginning these national and regional organizations had the characteristic of a lodge, paying sick benefits, and making some provisions for the unemployed and the widows and orphans of men killed on the road. The lodge idea proper materialized later in the 1880's in the

Middle West with all of the ritual, paraphernalia, and hierarchy.[18]

*   *   *

As picturesque as the travelling salesman was, as a new factor in the American scene, the fact cannot be obscured that he made up the shock troops in the furious city competition for the trade of the South. It was admitted that the use of travellers as trade seekers was expensive, and often entailed waste, delay and questionable business practices.[19] Yet the merchants felt that competition in the post war South demanded the use of travelling salesmen if old and new spheres of commercial infuence were to be reestablished and held. As we have seen, the merchants of New York, because of previous contacts and better modes of access, reestablished hegemony in the South immediately after the War, and held it down to 1870.[20] As the representative of a New York house revealed:[21]

> "After the war was over I was sent down the Mississippi River to Vicksburg, Natchez, and to New Orleans. I also travelled over the territory along the Atlantic coast, selling in Richmond, Petersburg, Wilmington, Charleston and Savannah and other important towns in the southern Atlantic states. Previous to the war most of the trade of our firm had been with the South and we naturally desired to get all the trade in this territory with which we could profitably deal."

However, the New York merchants faced competition from merchants of Boston and Philadelphia who were likewise interested in the southern trade. Agents of the jobbing houses of the eastern cities found that "there was no careless taking of risk and no wild-eyed slap-dashness about any of the southern storekeepers in the days after the war." Yet it was necessary that the old credit structure be established in the southern states.[22]

The devastation of war, the disorganization in government, and the general condition of labor delayed investment and re-establishment of commercial activity somewhat. But since these conditions were ameliorated, it soon became clear that the new planterism would be in no sense less merchant ridden than the old.

The failure of the "cotton policy" of the Boston-Philadelphia merchant dominated political alliance and the eventual success of the "New York idea" led, as we have seen, to a disposition on the part of the former to break the power of the port city by successful pressure at Washington to recognize the interior cities as ports of entry.[23] This, along with a shift of cotton cultivation westward to the trans-Mississippi, gave the Middle Western merchants, especially after 1870, greater competitive power in the southern market.[24] The swiftly developing railroad projects out of the interior border cities all during the '70's enhanced the advantage that the natural crop shift and federal legislation made possible. The growth of manufacturing centers during the same period in the Middle Western cities seemed to add the final impetus to the new trade offensive.

The Simmons Hardware Company of St. Louis was a good example of the activity of Middle Western merchants in the South during the '70's.[25] This house had goods manufactured "at several of the principal penitentiaries of the country", and shipped in directly, on through bills of lading, goods from England, Germany, France, and Switzerland. Their trade extended as far south as the Gulf of Mexico, and included the states of Alabama, Georgia, Tennessee, Kentucky, North Carolina, Virginia, Mississippi, Arkansas, Louisiana, Kansas and Texas. This widely extended business was "chiefly done through commercial travellers or agents employed by the Simmons house." The southern territory was divided up into districts, each district being in special charge of one of the Simmons agents, who was held responsible for the maintenance and extension of the trade within his district. He was expected also to keep the house informed in regard to the competition which he met from every point from other business houses in St. Louis, and from other cities. The agent also reported concerning the crops and facts of interest touching the influence of competing rail rates;[26] for the limits of Simmons' trade depended very largely upon the rates for transportation which they had to meet from competing business houses in other cities.[27]

Not all of the merchants could operate on the same scale as the Simmons' house; but most of them in the Middle West enjoyed the same facilities for communication and distribution. Many of the principals of the smaller firms could be found on the road with sample case following the trade routes through the southern towns and back country.[28] Southern jobbers and local wholesalers, who thought they had solved the problem of outside competition in their city and back country markets by persuading both city and state governments to pass practically prohibitive legislation during the war, viewed with amazement the horde of salesmen from the North who did not even bother to observe the pre-war gentlemen's agreement not to sell to the local dealer.[29] To be sure, talk of nationalizing business and commerce had drifted southward to them from Washington, but they had it on the authority of the Supreme Court that the heresy of the radical nationalist had been scotched.[30]

Representatives of fire insurance firms had followed northern merchants into the South to guarantee the crop after it was placed in the gin house or in transshipment to the world markets;[31] and life insurance agents were not long in seeing the new field. However, on the third of February, 1866, Virginia passed an insurance act, providing that no insurance company, not incorporated under the laws of the state, could carry on its business within the state without previously obtaining a license. To obtain one, bonds of a specified character ranging in amount from $30,000 to $50,000, according to the

tent of the capital employed, must be deposited with the
ate Treasurer. In the same month, an act was passed
pulating that no person could act as an agent of a "foreign"
surance company without a license from the state.[32] Anyone
acting was to be fined from $50 to $500 for each offense.

In May, 1866, Samuel Paul, a resident of Virginia was
pointed the agent of several insurance companies incorporated
New York State to carry on a general business in insurance
ainst fire.[33] He filed his authority accorded to law, but re-
sed to comply wth the bond stipulations of the act. Thereon the Treasurer refused him license, but he, Paul, defied
e law and issued a policy.[34] He was immediately indicted and
ied in trial $50 by the circuit court of the city of Petersburg.
he Supreme Court finally took the case on a writ of Error
om the Virginia Supreme Court which sustained the convic-
on, and affirmed, by a unanimous court, Virginia's action in
stice Stephen J. Field's ringing decision thus:

"The corporation, being the mere creation of local law,
can have no legal existence beyond the limits of the
sovereignity where created. . . . Having no absolute right
of recognition in other states, but depending for such recognition and the enforcement of its contracts upon their
consent, it follows, as a matter of course, that such assent
may be granted and conditions as those states may think
proper to impose. They may exclude the foreign corporation entirely; they may restrict its business to particular
localities or they may exact such security for the performance of its contracts with their citizens as will in their
judgment best promote the public interest. The whole
matter rests in their discretion."

Since the South had been wrong on so many basic consti-
itional points there-of-late, it was easy for southern capitalists
) chalk up Justice Field's dictum as a victory for economic
ates rights. If, thought Southerners in their constitutional
aivete, it was possible to license or penalize one category of

foreign business and/or its agents it was certainly possib
to do the same to another; but there is no more serio
blunder in any struggle for power in the United States tha
constitutional naivete. However, though many of the northe
and western cities or states had some kind of law relating
non-resident traders, in the South these laws "were enforc
with particular pertinacity" especially in the trading cities
Memphis, Washington, D. C., St. Louis, Charleston, Savanna
Baltimore—indeed, in practically all of the southern cities tl
salesmen might run into a sizeable license fee.[36]

The merchants of the Middle West were in no mood
tolerate such restrictions which stood as a last barrier to tl
promised land, especially since a successful offensive was b
ing carried on in Washington to make their cities ports
entry and thus give them equality in the southern sellers mark
competition. Why not appeal to their northern friends, tl
merchants of Philadelphia and Boston, on the floor of the N
tional Board of Trade, and invoke the necessary pressure
Washington to destroy their obstruction? To that end tl
merchants of the St. Louis Board of Trade hired a lawy
to run the statutes, and after thorough investigation submitte
the idea to the Philadelphia merchants to be presented at tl
Richmond meeting in December of 1869.

John Price Wetherill of the Philadelphia delegation, whe
the issue appeared on the agenda at Richmond, offered
lengthy resolution which appealed to the state legislatures
abolish all restrictive legislation on "foreign" agents doing bus
ness within their borders; and called upon the local board
within the states to press for such action.[37] Though Holto
of Milwaukee agreed that these restrictions were obstruction
to trade, there obviously had been some mistake. Mr. Cullen
the attorney who built the St. Louis Board's case and th
only delegate from the city left at Richmond, opposed th
resolution. The current case in Maryland on the very questio
at issue, thought Cullen, was a clear indication of what coul

e expected from the states, and especially those not engaged
n manufacturing.[38]   Cullen was sure that the government at
Vashington must step in; "and if it be said (and I know it
s said) by the Supreme Court of the United States, that this
uthority only exists in the states, then let us instruct the
epresentative of the states in Congress to enact a law that
he Supreme Court shall not interfere in the matter".[39]   The
nly way to have uniformity, thought Cullen, was to "push"
he Supreme Court aside until a constitutional amendment
ould affirm "that the states stand in the same relation to the
ederal government that the counties do to the states. That is
he bottom doctrine, and I endorse it with all my soul." Cullen
sked that the resolution be addressed to Congress instead of
he state legislatures.

   This outburst in the best spirit of the new radicalism
aught even Wetherill off balance. He, while agreeing in
rinciple with Cullen, hastened to assert that he thought the
tate legislatures ought to be kept intact, and assured a Chi-
ago representative that permanent resident "foreign" traders
vere not under attack. The Detroit delegation had no in-
tructions on this matter and thus expressed divergent opinions.
foseph S. Ropes of Boston, and Simeon B. Chittenden and
george Opdyke of New York could agree with John A. Gano
of Cincinnati on the pernicious effect of these license laws.
But it was left to Mr. Taylor of St. Paul to adequately answer
he outburst of the St. Louis attorney. Taylor cautioned
against efforts to block a recurrence of Paul v. Virginia. It
vas his prophetic opinion that the interstate citizenship pro-
isions in Article 4, section 2, of the Constitution either had
been or would be invoked by the court to destroy the ob-
tructions that states had raised against the free trade the
merchants wanted. The Richmond convention adjourned committed to a resolution appealing to state legislatures for a
repeal of their license laws.[40]

The St. Louis issue at Richmond was obviously new t
the merchants, but the year which elapsed between the Rich
mond and the following meeting at Buffalo gave both th
Middle Western and Southern merchants time to prepare
case.[41] The executive council of the National Board, at it
Washington meeting, had adopted the principle of federal in
tervention, and the Connor Bill, covering the whole problem
was already before the House of Representatives.[42] Mr. Lathers
by request of the Board of Trade of Charleston, of which h
was a member, arose to the floor of the Buffalo meeting t
oppose the resolution brought in by the Philadelphia delega
tion to do what Cullen wanted the previous year—appeal t
Congress to destroy the license laws. Lathers contended that
these license laws were a necessity in the South for the region
was poor and the taxes heavy, especially in Charleston. In
deed, the proposed bill, said Lathers, was class legislation
taking the burden from one class and placing it on another
If the local trader was taxed and the outsider went free
Lathers was sure it would destroy the trade of the local man
in the small southern cities. Falling back on cleverness, Lather
asserted that most of the traders were northerners who had
come south with their families to engage in business and these
merchants in convention surely did not want to penalize them

L. R. Shryock of St. Louis brushed aside Lathers' argu
ment as beside the point. These southern license laws were a
nuisance to northern and western merchants and in most case
prohibitive. While traveling in the South to sell his flour, he
was almost jailed in Atlanta for not paying the tax. Shryock
haughtily explained to the Mayor of Atlanta that it would
be a pretty spectacle to see the president of the St. Louis Board
of Trade in jail in his city. Nevertheless he had to pay the
license fee in Atlanta and in every other city as he progressed
it soon became clear to him that he would have no profit
at that rate and he returned home. That, said Shryock, is
why the St. Louis merchants took this step. Georgia merchants

sserted the St. Louis merchant, wanted their flour and whiskey; et it would cost a merchant $1,000 and three months in jail o sell it there. Such restrictions were clearly unconstitutional.

Lathers replied that he personally welcomed all merchants ith flour and whiskey as long as they were willing to bear qually the burdens of the local trader. Putting his hand on he heart of the argument, Lathers asserted that "these laws vere made because so many (salesmen sic) were coming in nd taking the trade away from the local merchants, who hould have supplied the people with flour and other articles." hough Williams of Baltimore stated that his board had asked Maryland to repeal and was confident that all states would epeal without congressional intervention, John Price Wetherill aid he had changed his mind. Wetherill no longer believed hat the states would act—that had been the mistake at Rich- nond. Since 75 per cent of the jobbing business was done by lrummers, Wetherill thought young men should be encouraged .nd the fence building around cities should be destroyed.

E. O. Stanard of St. Louis took issue with Lathers on the question of to whom the drummer sold. After all, said Stanard, he drummer sold only to the merchant, never to the ultimate :onsumer. That was just it, according to Lathers, the jobber n the cities was killed off and it was the jobber who was epresented in the National Board of Trade. After much dis- :ussion on both sides the vote taken resulted in a loss for the .ppeal to Congress and the Executive Committee was em- >owered to continue activities for state repeal. But all was lot lost. On Friday, December 8, during a discussion of the 3oston Board of Trade's resolution on currency and finance, :omeone placed in the hand of the secretary a telegram from :lement Hugh Hill, assistant Attorney General of the United States which read:

"The Supreme Court has today unanimously decided the case of Ward versus the State of Maryland that state license taxes on non-resident agents or commercial travellers are unconstitutional as conflicting with the fourth article of the federal Constitution which provided that the citizens of each state shall be entitled to all privileges and immunities of citizens of the several states." [43]

The merchants were overjoyed and Wetherill was of the opinion that all merchants owed the National Board congratulation on having spearheaded this entire movement.

The Supreme Court ruling in Ward v. Maryland opened the door to northern merchant activity in the southern promised land. What had gone on formerly in a covert fashion was now sanctioned by law.[44] However, there had never been any unity or understanding between southern jobbers and local merchants on the problem of keeping the "foreign" merchant out. Indeed, Mr. Field, an Arkansas legislator saw a positive benefit in the established system.[45] He observed:

"Five-sixths of the goods now sold are sold by travelers; our country merchant can now, within thirty days, select not only from all competing agents in any line, but from all competing markets, and he can buy this from 3 to 5 per cent cheaper than he could from the jobbers in market."

Commenting on the license tax, Field stated that it tended "to give the large capitalist a monopoly; the traveller system has cheapened goods." Besides the value of the traveller to the hotels and livery stables of the state, Field found in the system a long range value thus:

"Prior to the system, thousands of the best young men of the South went North and found employment and permanent residence as salesmen, but now we not only keep our valuable young men at home but also draw from the North the same class of young men every year, many of whom learn to make their homes with us; under the old system we not only lost thousands of our young men, but our merchants went North for their goods."

Though it could be demonstrated that the license tax was
ten included in the price of commodities from the eastern
d border cities, the notion that the tax should be abolished
ed hard south of the Potomac.[46] As combinations of border
y merchants encouraged the buying up of southern railroads,
they planned greater facilities to handle southern staples
their great city markets,[47] as these same merchants threw
eir agents into the southern crossroads markets, the southern
ober saw his cities, themselves once flourishing markets, slip
wly into decay, and the staples he would control, rushed in
er increasing quantities pass his countinghouse windows on
t freights to the border cities.

However much "The preponderance of evidence" might
ove that the local merchant was "only a part of an inefficient
nishing system rather than being the system", the fact
mains that he was by far the most important link in the
rnicious chain of credit in the planting areas. The necessity
the part of the local merchants to have a marketable staple
settle the accounts made through the commercial traveler
th merchants in distant cities, fastened the one crop system
on the South and set the pattern of exploitation in the
uth to the present day.

The Period 1865-1880 closed with the South an Economic
butary to the North-east and the Middle-west. Men of
mmerce in these regions had truly become the Regents of
former power and wealth of the "Cotton Kingdom". But
steps to this new orientation had arisen from conditions
ated to the broader issues and dynamics of American develop-
nt, and were often directed by the unpredictable logic of
nts implicit in the revolutionary dictate of a politically in-
red war.

The eve of the Civil war found the nation in the grip
the great agrarian politicians. While giving lip service to
tenets of individualistic democracy, the giants of the agrarian
sought vainly to find some formula that would harmonize

the ever-growing inter- and intra-regional conflicts. Their ta
was made difficult by the rise to a new social consciousness
the merchant and industrial groups in the nation. There we
indications that these new men desired power and prestige
the American scene before the out-break of the Civil W
These new men in the older market towns of the Atlan
seaboard already had their group-conscious organizatio
discipline, and leadership. It only took the revolutionary for
of the Civil War to give these new men a consciousness of t
value of their wealth and knowledge, a disrespect for the po
ticians of the agrarian era, and the apprenticeship in gove
ment which they needed to begin the moulding of the Americ
economic and social pattern to their own taste.

The Republican party was their instrument. Alliance w
the forces in that cave of Abdullah gave the prophets of conce
trated-governmental-power-for-nationalistic-economic-ends   t
ideological front behind which the revolution within might
accomplished. Though many men in their ranks believed
the masters of capital had no real quarrel with the way
life of the "Cotton Kingdom." What they resented most v
the power of the Cotton barons in the councils of the natio
To be sure the American staple had given our merchants
strong bargaining point in the markets of the world. But
had been impossible to persuade the Southern agrarians tha
national economy based on staple agriculture, extractive
dustries, and the carrying trade could not hope to surv
in the fierce economic competition of the nineteenth centu
These new men sensed that if we did not begin the restrict
of the American market from European competition and
building of our own industries we could be subject to the wh
of the masters of the economy of England and Europe, a
thus might prolong indefinitely our colonial status. Ne
slavery became identified in a very real sense with the slav
dependence of our economy on the capital of Europe. Tra
lated in terms of the stifling of personal initiative, and ratio

lized into a seeming blot upon the dictate of middle-class liberal democracy, the organized masters of capital in the bustling cities of the North-east and the Middle-west reluctantly decided to help throw the iron dice of war.

The gamble was safe—the war was won. But if the peace was to be won and the economic and political gains were to be consolidated the power of cotton must be used to close the American trade door and prevent retaliation by the commercial powers in the markets of the world. The disorganized economy of the South must be mobilized for high production quotas so that the famine prices in the world market might provide some of the revenue to pay the cost of the war, and also prevent commercial retaliation if the war tariffs hardened into national policy. Masters of Capital, east and west, needed national legislation, and the Republicans were agreeable. The Freedmen's Bureau organized black and white in the South for the needed production, and cooperating with the Union League, helped to keep a fictitious favorable political atmosphere in which the new radicalism, on both the State and National level, might accomplish its designs. While not completely satisfactory to the doctrinaire "Protectionists", the peacetime tariffs began the closing of the American trade door.

The radicals, economic and political, had a good plan in 1865. The aim was legitimate, but the means were subject to conditions over which they had no control. The bitter recriminations of the politics of vengeance, which led to the mobbing of the President of the United States, could be taken in stride. But our economic nationalists had not counted on the rise of Cotton production in the marginal producing areas of the world, or the technological changes which would make that marginal crop usable. They had not seen the economic and social conditions in the South which would bring such heart-breaking delays. This alliance between capital and opportunistic politics had not gauged the possible opposition and quarrels within their own ranks. The Cotton policy was a failure.

The defeat of the Cotton policy in 1866-67 led to the changing of some aspects of the original grand scheme and retention of others by the various members of the alliance. Having "fathered" the Cotton Policy, with its super-plantation scheme under the Freedmen's Bureau, New England capitalists professed a hankering for "Free Trade" and a desire to see the South a region of small peasant proprietors. Philadelphia capitalists clung to "Protection" and did not stop until their goal was reached. New York capitalists opposed the "Cotton Policy" from the start. This position was dictated by the traditional dependence of the international merchants of the "Empire" City upon the plantation economy of the South and the European money market for succor and support. Their opposition had figured largely in the defeat of the "Cotton Policy", and thus provided the basis of a new rapprochement between New England, Pennsylvania, and Middle-western capitalists. The aim of the new alliance was to break the hold of the European merchants and industrialists on the American economy by destroying their connections in the nation's first port city.

An instrument lay ready at hand for the new task of destroying the power of New York port in the economy of the nation. Out of Detroit, Michigan came the idea of a national organization of business men. With such an organization these new men could act as an effective local and national pressure group. They saw themselves as a third "Urban" chamber of national government, bringing to a bankrupt political scene the new politics of a new age. Philadelphians also saw an opportunity to break, with the aid of New England and Middle-western capitalists, the power of New York port with quiet favors and congressional pressure. Bostonians were given the power to plan, and the organization came to light in historic Philadelphia. Immediately the plan was set on foot. Philadelphians and Bostonians hoped that by leading the fight to make middle-western cities internal ports of entry to be the seaboard throat through which the new internal-external trade would be channeled, and thus destroy the monopoly of New York port.

The Philadelphia plan was successful. Opposition of the New York capitalists in the newly organized National Board of Trade and Congress was finally overcome. But the favor extended to the middle-western trading centers fired their merchants' aggressive spirit. The north-eastern centers were forced to share the Southern market with the rising trading and manufacturing centers beyond the Alleghenies. It was from the start an uneven fight. Besides geographical access, middle-western entrepreneurs, often with more zeal than knowledge, established railroads, used commercial travelers, and employed the other arts of trade to secure hegemony in the Southern market. But the "sellers market" of the South was the middle-western capitalist's for the asking not only because of his enterprise. To be sure the Southern business-man proved amenable to the gestures of regional improvement which middle-western railroads and other facilities to bring a favorable market closer implied. But the Southerners had failed, due mostly to factors beyond their control, to secure the Southern market for largely Southern exploitation. Adverse Supreme Court decisions, the failure of an ill-planned immigration program, the absence of capital, the rise of a diabolical system of credit, the continued production of cotton in preference to diversified agriculture, the mobility of its black and white population, the panic of 1873 and the restrictive "hard money" policy of the federal government—all of these delivered the South into the hands of whatever group of exploiters might become the "Regents" of the power of "King Cotton."

Notes

Chapter I: WHO IS THIS NEW MAN?

1 Elie Halevy, *The World Crisis,* 1914-1918 (New York, 1930) passim; Charles A. and Mary Beard, *The Rise of American Civilization,* Vol. II (New York, 1927), pp. 52-121.

2 Arthur C. Cole, "Lincoln's Election an Immediate Menace to Slavery in the States", *American Historical Review* XXXVI, No. 4 (July, 1931) pp. 757-8.

3 Lorenzo Sabine, Sec., *Seventh Annual Report* of the Government, Presented to the Board at the Annual Meeting on January 16, 1861 (Boston, 1861) p. 2. Hereinafter cited *7th Boston Board of Trade* (Date).

4 *Fourth Annual Report* of the Chamber of Commerce of the State of New York for the Year 1861-62 (New York, 1862) p. 8 et passim. Hereinafter cited *4th New York Chamber of Commerce* (date).

5 *Nation,* March 15, 1866.

6 The literature on the *Alabama* in the reports for 1863 and 1864 is the most exhaustive and extensive this writer has seen.

7 The Twenty-ninth *Annual Report* of the Philadelphia Board of Trade prepared for the Executive Council by Lorin Blodget, Secretary and presented to the Association February 3, 1862. (Philadelphia, 1862) p. 8. Hereinafter cited *29th Philadelphia Board of Trade* (Date) Frank Hamilton Taylor, *Philadelphia in the Civil War 1861-1865* (Philadelphia, 1913) pp. 220-1.

8 Arthur M. Schlesinger, "The City in American History", *Mississippi Valley Historical Review* XXVII, No. 1 (June, 1940) pp. 43-66.

9 Schlesinger, *loc. cit.,* p. 57 ff.

10 F. W. Taussig and H. D. White, *Some Aspects of the Tariff Question* (Harvard Economic Studies, vol. XII) (Cambridge, 1931) p. 118 et passim.

11 Richard Hofstadter, "The Tariff Issue and the Civil War", *American Historical Review* 44, No. 1 (Oct., 1938) pp. 50-55; Thomas M. Pitkin, "Western Republicans and the Tariff in 1860", *Mississippi Valley Historical Review* XXVII (1940-41) pp. 401-420.

12 Kenneth Sturges, *American Chambers of Commerce.* (David A. Wells Prize Essay No. 4—printed for the Department of Political

Science of Williams College) (New York, 1915) pp. 33 et passim for the history of businessmen's organizations in Philadelphia before the Civil War and the emergence of the Philadelphia Board of Trade after 1845 as the dominant organization. See also on all business organizations Wilfred H. Schoff, *American Commercial Institutions* (Monograph no. 4 on American Social Economics, Department of Social Economy of the United States Commission for Paris Exhibition of 1900) (Philadelphia, 1900), Passim.

13 *14th Boston Board of Trade* 1868, p. 27. For the efforts in this direction see especially *9th* and *10th Boston Board of Trade,* passim. Further treatment of this point is to be found in Chapter V post.

14 *7th Boston Board of Trade,* 1861, pp. 12-13. Lorenzo Sabine estimated the trade of Boston with New Orleans in 1859 to be $25,000,000, and with other parts of the South, $15,000,000 more; see also Arthur C. Cole, "Lincoln's Election An Immediate Menace to Slavery in the States", *American Historical Review* XXXVI, No. 4 (July, 1931) p. 757. Cole's figure is $60,000,000 plus the stimulation of New England shipbuilding.

15 Robert G. Albion and J. B. Pope, *The Rise of New York Port* (New York, 1939) pp. 95-121; Robert G. Albion, *Square Riggers on Schedule* (Princeton, 1938) pp. 74-76.

16 George French, ed., *New England* (Boston, 1911) pp. 344-360. This book, issued by the Boston Chamber of Commerce, sketches the founding and early history of commercial organizations in New England. See also, Kenneth Sturges, *op. cit.,* pp. 22-31. For the eventual rise of the Boston Board of Trade to first importance among the succeeding commercial organizations, see Chapter V post.

17 Taussig and White, *op. cit.,* pp. 261-278.

18 *Statistical Abstract of the United States* No. 1, 1878. Prepared by Chief of the Bureau of Statistics, Treasury Department (Washington, 1879) pp. 117-18, No. 112-113, "Quantities of Raw Cotton of Domestic Production Exported from the United States to the Principal and Other Foreign Countries during the 20 Years from 1859 to 1878"; No. 114, "Values of Exports of Cottons of Domestic Manufacture from 1859 to 1878".

19 Kenneth Sturges, *op. cit.,* pp. 17-21; Joseph B. Bishop, *A Chronicle of One Hundred and Fifty Years; The Chamber of Commerce of the State of New York, 1768-1918* (New York c 1918) passim.

20   Albion and Pope, *op cit.*, pp. 95-97, 118; Philip Foner, *Business and Slavery* (Chapel Hill, 1941), p. 6.

21   Margaret G. Myers, *The New York Money Market,* vol. I, "Origin and Development" (New York, 1931) pp. 6-9. "The Stock Exchange moved from Philadelphia to New York after the successful floating of the Erie Canal bonds; and the control of commercial credit on a national scale passed also to New York from Philadelphia after the lapse of the charter of the Second National Bank in 1836."

22   Thomas Ellison, *A Handbook of the Cotton Trade* (London, 1858), p. 34; and Chapter II and III post.

23   George McHenry, *The Cotton Trade, Its Bearing Upon the Prosperity of Great Britain and the Commerce of the American Republics* (London, 1863) p. III et passim.

24   Frederick Jackson Turner, *The United States, 1830-1850* (New York, 1935) pp. 225, 323; and Chapter VI, post.

25   Frederick J. Turner, *op. cit.*, pp. 306-7; Thomas M. Pitkin, *loc. cit.*, pp. 401-20.

26   See Chapters V and VI post.

27   Frederick J. Turner, *op. cit.*, p. 266; Chester W. Wright, *Wool Growing and the Tariff* (Boston, 1910) pp. 139-152; Taussig and White, *op. cit.*, pp. 302, 313.

28   The application of this generalization to the new capitalist of the middle west will be found in Chapter VI—"Iron Sluice Gates".

29   Ellis Paxson Oberholtzer, *Philadelphia, A History of the City and its People,* vol. IV (Philadelphia, n. d.) p. 487; *The Biographical Encyclopedia of Pennsylvania of the 19th Century* (Philadelphia, 1874) pp. 35, 49, 426, 433.

30   *National Cyclopaedia of American Biography,* p. 513; hereinafter cited *Nat. Cycl.*

31   One of Morris' ancestors helped William Penn lay out the city of Philadelphia and was its second mayor for a number of years. His great grandfather was bodyguard to George Washington.

The business organization movement that undergirded the revolution of 1860-65 owed a good deal to the vision of the great secretaries of such organizations. Lorin Blodget, statistician and physicist, though a New Yorker by birth, served Philadelphia capitalists well in the crisis. Research Climatologist for the Smithsonian Institution, War Department Surveyor of the Pacific Railroad, Blodget worked as special assistant to the Treasury Department from 1863 to 1877. Blodget was author of *Climatology of the United States,*

Commercial and Financial Resources of the United States, and about 150 volumes of financial and industrial reports and statistics.

Thomas Morris Perot, eventually president of the Board of Trade, served as general secretary of the association. A pharmacist by education, Perot in 1869 became head of the oldest business house in America, being the seventh generation in direct descent from the founder of Francis Perot's Son's Malting Company established in 1687. Yet he found time to be president of the Mercantile Library Company, the Women's Medical College of Philadelphia, and the Pennsylvania Society for the Prevention of Cruelty to Children. The material was taken from *Who Was Who in America,* vol. I, 1897-1942 (Chicago, 1942) p. 961. Hereinafter cited *Who Was Who,* (page).

32 William Binder Wilson, *History of the Pennsylvania Railroad Company,* 2 vols. (Philadelphia, 1895), II, pp. 233-36; *Nat. Cycl.* vol. 13, p. 333. Benjamin Bullock and his six brothers fell heir to the great wool business established by the senior Benjamin in the best tradition of the American industrial development. Of poor parents and limited education, Bullock Senior came to Philadelphia as a grocer's apprentice; and learning wool manufacturing from the ground up, soon was carrying on a vast business from South Front Street and Pittsburgh. On the death of the senior Bullock in 1859, Benjamin and his brothers established Benjamin Bullock's Sons. The firm's great output provided uniforms for Lincoln's blue host and underwrote the post-war philanthropy of the family. Stephen N. Winslow, *Biographies of Successful Philadelphia Merchants* (Philadelphia, 1864) pp. 213-17. One of the brothers was in business in Cincinnati on his own. Richard Wood, merchant and manufacturer, found time to serve as Director of Philadelphia's Provident Life and Trust Company, manage the Haverford *Call,* and serve as trustee of the University of Pennsylvania. From *Who Was Who,* p. 1375.

John Welsh, active in the new regionalism out of Philadelphia capitalist circles, was the scion of a swift growing merchant-banking fortune. Beginning as an apprentice and supercargo to the West Indies for a flour merchant, John's grandfather built the fortune and business in south Warves. With a merchant fortune, the elder Welsh did not find it difficult to help project the hard fought Philadelphia Bank and direct the "Delaware Insurance Company of Philadelphia". In 1834 the sons, Samuel and William, were in charge of the business; and John, William's son, joined the firm in 1857. Acting as commission merchants in the bustling West Indies allowed Samuel, William, and John Welsh to indulge their particular interest. John's father and uncle contributed largely to church extension and fine arts, respectively. John was active in the new politics of business, serving the Board of Trade, the city Council, and the Sinking Fund. All three were bank directors and the family was one of the most influential and respected in the Quaker City. Stephen N. Winslow, *op. cit.*, pp. 161-171.

33 *Ibid.*, pp. 137-40. Philadelphia capitalists in coastwise shipping had no abler man in their ranks than Edmund S. Souder. Son of a merchant prince, Souder's education was cut short by his father's ill considered generosity to his merchant friends; and at fifteen Edmund's education began in the hard merchant school of the Western Trade. Souder completed his education as clerk and bookkeeper for two commission merchants, and in 1829 opened his own commission house on Water Street. Souder pioneered in opening the business contacts and trade relations with New England upon which the politics of business was to build a regional alliance later. Member of the Common Council of the "old city", promoter of the Municipal subscription of the Pennyslvania Railroad, Souder confined his interest to his business and directorships. *Ibid.*, pp. 171-175.

34 George Wilson, comp., *Portrait Gallery of the Chamber of Commerce of the State of New York* (New York, 1890) pp. 30, 170; The Archivist of the New York Chamber has granted use of any of the pictures appearing in *Catalogue of Portraits in the Chamber of Commerce of the State of New York* (New York, 1924), hereinafter cited *N. Y. Catalogue of Portraits*. Up through the apprenticeship of clerkships came Jonathan Sturges to be New York's Coffee and Tea Authority, and founder-director of both the Illinois Central and the New York and New Haven Railroad. Francis Beattie Thurber, Protectionist Republican and Union Leaguer, rose from a clerkship to build the largest wholesale grocery business in the world, create the "American Grocer" and head the nationalistic United States Export Association. From George Wilson, *op. cit.*, p. 59; *Nat. Cyclo.* vol. 22, p. 176.

35 *D. A. B.*, vol. XIII, pp. 168-9; *Biographical Directory of Congress*, p. 1332; George Wilson, *op. cit.*, p. 95. Robert H. McCurdy, scion of a pre-Revolution Connecticut merchant family, won his spurs by opening a Petersburg Virginia branch for his New York drygoods employer. Forming a life-long partnership with

H. D. Aldrich, first as foreign jobber in drygoods, then as wholesaler exclusively in American products, McCurdy retired on the eve of the Rebellion. After attending the ill-fated "Peace Conference", he organized, in his home, the leading citizens of the city for the union Square Mass Meeting following Sumter, and was in the forefront of the merchants' war effort. His postwar years were absorbed by Directorships in the Mutual Life Insurance Company and other financial institutions. *Ibid.,* p. 227.

36   *D. A. B.* Vol. XIV, pp. 45-46; George Wilson, *op. cit.,* p. 60.

37   George Wilson, *op. cit.,* p. 242. Banking and insurance came naturally to those holding large profits made from mercantile pursuits. Frederick A. Conkling made his fortune in the importing and jobbing business as a prelude to his sitting in the New York State Legislature and in the War Senate in Washington. He went on to the presidency of the Aetna Fire Insurance Company, the year the War closed. George William Lane also combined a merchant-banking interest, connected at one time or another with Fulton National Bank, Merchant's National Bank, Seaman's Bank, Continental Fire Insurance, Atlantic Mutual Marine Insurance, and Central Trust Company. Lane was thus enabled to indulge his bent for pious philanthropy. Municipal reformer and leader in the new politics of business, Lane found time to sit on the board of Home Missions of the Presbyterian Church, the American Bible Society, Union Theological Seminary, and preside over the American Port Society. From *N. Y. Catalogue of Portraits,* p. 17.

New York City's unique position owed much to the attention its capitalists gave to communication facilities. George William Blunt's family was the self-appointed guardians of the waters of New York Harbor from 1796 when "Blunt's coast pilot" first appeared. Doing the work of the United States Coast Survey long before its existence, Blunt and his brother served the maritime world, the New York merchants, and in the crisis, Lincoln's Navy. George Wilson, *op. cit.,* p. 127. While the Blunts watched the harbor, Samuel B. Ruggles watched the path west. This precocious Yale graduate and lawyer, helped found the Bank of Commerce and draw New York State's general banking law; Ruggles helped decide on the route of the Erie Railroad, and made his chief contribution as guardian of the interest and development of the Erie Canal. New York legislator and hard money enthusiast, Ruggles spent much time in representing the United States in international commercial and scientific conferences in the postwar years. *Ibid.,* p. 174.

The long arm of mercantile imperialism was the telegraph. The New York Chamber's William Orton came to the leadership in this field by a devious path. Normal graduate school teacher, Orton rose from bookseller in Buffalo and bookmaker in New York City to reform member of the City's Common Council. The Civil War was Orton's opportunity. *Nat. Cyclo.*, vol. 7, p. 502. Appointed in turn Collector of Internal Revenue in New York City by Lincoln, and to the National Internal Revenue Commission by Chase, Orton left Washington because of ill health to assume the presidency of the United States Telegraph Company. On the reorganization of Western Union in 1866 Orton was quickly elected in turn vice-president and president. The money order, the night letter, reduced rates, and the *Journal of Telegraphy* fell quickly from his fertile brain. At Orton's death he headed the International Ocean Telegraph Company, the Gold and Stock Telegraph Company, and the Pacific and Southern Atlantic Telegraph Company, a veritable communication empire. James S. T. Stranahan ended a floating period as school teacher, engineer, and fur trader by helping Gerrit Smith found Florence, New York, in 1832. From *Nat. Cyclo.*, vol. 3, pp. 433-4; *Biographical Directory of Congress*, p. 1579. Sharing for a while an interest in lumber and New York State politics, he moved eventually to railroad building in New Jersey in 1840, and five years later to Brooklyn to head the Union Ferry Company and the Atlantic Dock Company, the finest in the country. Alderman, director of the first Brooklyn Bridge, and creator of Prospect Park, Stranahan was prominent among the fusers of Brooklyn and New York City. Whig member of the 34th Congress, Stranahan went out to Chicago to stand for Lincoln and remain a leader in the new politics of business.

38 George Wilson, *op. cit.*, p. 53. The same pattern is revealed in the careers of Chittenden, Claflin, Stokes, Albridge, Stevens, Maury, Green, and Perit. *Ibid.*, p. 212, Simeon B. Chittenden— Drygoods—Banks and Railroads; p. 217, Horace B. Claflin, $72,-000,000 mercantile house; p. 187, James Stokes, like Dodge, connected with Anson Phelps by marriage and business ties; p. 46, Eton trained Matthew Maury, cotton and tobacco merchant and suggester of Bonded Warehouse; p. 45, John C. Green, of the New York, London, and China House of Russel and Company, banks, railroad, and an interest in Princeton; p. 48, Pelatiah Perit of Presbyterian Missions, seamen, the American Bible Society, and the History of Commerce; *Biographical Directory of Congress*, p. 1656, Hiram Walbridge, merchant, Democrat member of the 33rd

Congress; *Nat. Cyclo.* vol. 13, p. 139; John Austin Stevens, Senior and Junior—see also *D. A. B.,* vol. 17, pp. 616-17. From this group came John Austin Stevens Senior and Junior, great secretaries of the New York Chamber before and during the crisis. Stevens Senior was not only organizer, founder, and first president of the Merchants Exchange and the Bank of Commerce, but was also chairman of the Committee of Bankers of New York, Boston, and Philadelphia which took the union loan of $150,000,000 and arranged the terms of the transaction. His son combined interest in and service to the politics of business with a flair for early American history, writing "Albert Gallatin" in the *American Statesman Series.*

39 Edward E. Hale, "Memoir of the Hon. Lorenzo Sabine A.M.", *Proceedings* of the Massachusetts Historical Society, vol. XVII, 1879-1880 (March, 1880) pp. 371-82; M. L. Simons ed. *Cyclopedia of American Literature,* vol. II (Philadelphia, 1875 p. 450; *Memorial Biographies of the New England Historic Genealogical Society,* vol. VII, 1871-1880 (Boston, 1907) pp. 246-7; Samuel E. Herrick, "Memoir of Hamilton Andrews Hill, LL. D., *Proceedings* of the Massachusetts Historical Society 2nd Series vol. XI (November, 1896), pp. 88-96.

40 Richard Herdon, *Boston of Today: A Glance at Its History and Characteristics, with Biographical Sketches and Portraits of Many of Its Professional and Business Men* (Boston, 1892), pp. 423-5; *Nat. Cyclo.* XIII, 416-17; *D. A. B.,* vol. XVIII, pp. 567-9. Boston capitalist circles were graced by the venerable figure of the inventor-manufacturer Samuel Batchelder. Beginning a long career of mill proprietor—and managership in New Hampshire, he rose to the collective management in his adopted Cambridge, Massachusetts, of mills valued at $5,000,000. Inventor of dynamometer, leading abolitionist, essayist, and legislator in his adopted state, Batchelder handed on a worthy tradition to the younger generation of the politics of business as represented by Edward Atkinson. From *Nat. Cyclo.,* II, p. 16; *Nat. Cyclo.,* IX, p. 416; Harold Francis Williamson, *Edward Atkinson: The Biography of an American Liberal 1827-1905* (Boston, 1934), generally. Economist, publicist, inventor, Atkinson built a reputation as a successful industrial manager and a pioneer specialist in factory mutual insurance. Eventually a free trader and an early proponent of Boston cotton regionalism, Atkinson remained a leading figure among the intellectual capitalists of Boston.

Prominent in transporation circles was Elias Hasket Derby. From *Nat. Cyclo.,* vol. IV, p. 545. Graduated from Harvard with high honors, Derby studied law with Daniel Webster. Derby soon became one of Boston's leading railroad lawyers and succeeded in securing the extension of many lines. Prime mover in the completion of the Hoosac Tunnel, Derby urged during the Civil War the construction of Iron-clad vessels. As United States commissioner in 1867, Derby prepared for State Secretary Seward a report on United States-Canadian Relations and the Fisheries question. Chiefly responsible for the introduction for the use of jute in America, Derby was identified in many ways with the commercial progress of Boston and the nation.

Boston capitalists had no man in their ranks with more Yankee ingenuity than Erastus Brigham Bigelow. From *D. A. B.,* vol. II, pp. 254-5; *Nat. Cyclo.,* vol. VI, p. 20. Bigelow's inventions included a power loom for weaving two-ply ingrain carpets, brussels, wilton, tapestry, and velvet carpetings. During a checkered educational career on the parental farm and cotton factory, and schools, the money for which being earned through "fiddle" playing at dances, Erastus invented a hand loom for weaving suspender webbing and another for piping cord. Further apprenticeship was served as drygoods clerk in Boston, student and teacher-publicist of stenographic methods, and student of medicine before Bigelow made his great inventions. One of the founders of the Massachusetts Institute of Technology and first President of the National Association of Wool Manufacturers, Bigelow had the Republican bias for protection. He stated that there was really no basic principle involved on either side of the protection argument; but rather that Americans should erect a barrier until labor cost, taxation, and capital should become nearly equal in America and Europe.

The traditional combination between banking and transportation found a worthy representative in Samuel Hurd Walley. This native Bostonian was a Harvard graduate and read law. Admitted to the Suffolk bar, Walley combined a Boston-Roxbury practice with treasuryships of the Vermont Central and Wisconsin Central Railroads. Walley was both Speaker and member of the Massachusetts lower house before he went to the 33rd Congress as a Whig. Massachusetts Whiggery was not strong enough to return Walley to Congress or secure him the Governorship. Walley was interested in foreign missions and eventually became president of Boston's Revere National Bank. From *Nat. Cyclo.,* vol. XI, p. 441; *Biographical Directory of the American Congress,* p. 1662.

The rank and file of Boston's merchant capitalists proved equally as interested in creating the new business society. There was the commisison merchant, banker, and business statesman Charles G. Nazro. From *Boston Directory, 1865,* No. LXI, p. 301. James Cogswell Converse of "Converse, Blanchard, and Company", the "American Steamship Company", the "National Tube Works", and the "Troy and Greenfield Railroad" divided his leisure between gentleman farming and the aggressive politics of business. After a successful mercantile career, James Madison Beebe retired in 1866 to combine directorships in the Boston and Albany Railroad and the Webster Bank. From *Nat. Cyclo.,* vol. XIV, p. 66. Son of the first nativeborn Methodist minister in the United States, Hon. Enoch Redington Mudge became one of Boston's leading merchants, manufacturers, and cultured gentlemen; and David Dunlay Stockpole enjoyed a similar reputation as a merchant. After serving an apprenticeship with West Indian merchants, Charles Octavius Whitmore rapidly built a business with his sons Charles and William, holding, after his retirement, the presidency of the Market National Bank.

41   See Chapter V post; *11th National Board of Trade, 1880,* p. 27.

42   *14th Boston Board of Trade, 1868,* pp. 6, 9-11.

43   *14th Boston Board of Trade, 1868,* pp. 60, 100-01; *1st National Board of Trade, 1868,* pp. 256-60; *5th National Board of Trade, 1872,* pp. 21, 30; *10th National Board of Trade, 1879,* pp. 4-7; *2nd National Board of Trade, 1869,* pp. 11-12.

44   *5th National Board of Trade, 1872,* p. 31; *8th National Board of Trade, 1876,* pp. 209-10.

45   See Chapter V post; *10th Boston Board of Trade, 1864,* pp. 14-15; *17th Boston Board of Trade, 1871,* p. 85; *1st National Board of Trade, 1868,* p. 6.

46   *6th National Board of Trade, 1876,* pp. 10-11, 45, 57-64; *42nd Philadelphia Board of Trade, 1875,* pp. 14-15.

47   *10th National Board of Trade, 1879,* p. 4.

48   *4th National Board of Trade, 1871,* p. vi; *Cincinnati Trade, 1868,* p. 7; and Chapter V post.

49   *9th Boston Board of Trade, 1863,* p. 8; *25th Cincinnati Trade, 1873,* p. 43; *19th New York Chamber of Commerce, 1877,* p. 63; *St. Louis Trade, 1870,* p. 12.

50 *20th Philadelphia Board of Trade, 1853,* pp. 13-14. *9th Boston Board of Trade, 1863,* pp. 26, 89—Bostonians were especially sensitive on this point since the city bore one-third of the state's taxes, and its merchants were on first call in state and nation; *St. Louis Trade, 1874,* p. 12, in this instance the city fathers regarded themselves guardians of the state and regional interests.

51 *20th Philadelphia Board of Trade, 1853,* pp. 20-21; and Chapters V and VI post; *Cincinnati Trade, 1866,* p. 8.

52 *22nd Philadelphia Board of Trade, 1855,* p. 7; *Adjourned National Board of Trade, 1874,* pp. 17-18.

53 *37th Philadelphia Board of Trade, 1865,* p. 91; *Adjourned National Board of Trade, 1874,* p. 19 et seq.

54 *37th Philadelphia Board of Trade, 1865,* p. 91; *12th N. Y. Chamber of Commerce, 1870,* pp. 19-27; *20th N. Y. Chamber of Commerce, 1877,* p. 56; *7th National Board of Trade, 1875,* p. 69; *1st National Board of Trade, 1868,* p. 5.

55 *4th National Board of Trade, 1871,* p. 18; *7th National Board of Trade, 1875,* pp. 67-69.

56 *16th N. Y. Chamber of Commerce, 1874,* pp. 87-99; *19th N. Y. Chamber of Commerce, 1877,* p. 70.

Chapter II: THE BOSTON, PHILADELPHIA, NORTH-WESTERN ALLIANCE

1 *12th Boston Board of Trade, 1866,* pp. 18-21.

2 *33rd Philadelphia Board of Trade, 1866,* pp. 14-15.

3 *8th New York Chamber of Commerce, 1866,* pp. 3, 14-15.

4 Sir F.W.A. Bruce to Earl Russell, Washington, April 17, 1865. *F.O. 5* Vol. 1017 IV No. 241, *Public Record Office, London.* These records are on file in bound photostats in the Manuscript Division of the Library of Congress. For the British Business reaction to Lincoln's death see Thomas M. Widley to Wm. H. Seward, U.S. Consulate Liverpool, May 17, 1865, *American Consular Letters, Liverpool,* Vol. 31, No. 486 (1865); for the interpretations of American regulations in Southern ports in favor of Northern ports see Consul Archibald to J.H. Burnley, Feb. 22, 1865, *F. O. 5,* Vol. 1016 No. 158, *Public Record Office, London.*

5 Edward McPherson, *The Political History of the United States during the Period of Reconstruction.* (Washington, 1880). Hereinafter cited—*Pol. Hist.* This is a part of the speech made

during the storm that arose over the Second Freedman's Bureau Bill.

6 Claude G. Bowers, *The Tragic Era* (New York, 1929) p. 109 et passim.

7 New York *Herald*, Nov. 28, 1865.

8 Sumner and Sherman were jointly interested in a speculative venture to bring Germans into the country for settlement.

9 Richard N. Current, *Old Thad Stevens, A Story of Ambition* (Madison, 1942) pp. 158-175.

10 Alphonse Bertram Miller, *Thaddeus Stevens* (New York, 1939) pp. 219-21.

11 Charles Janeway Stille, *Northern Interest and Southern Independence* (Philadelphia, 1863) pp. 12, 22, 39; *33rd Philadelphia Board of Trade, 1866,* p. 10.

12 *29th Philadelphia Board of Trade, 1862,* p. 6; Richard Hofstadler, "The Tariff Issue and the Civil War", *American Historical Review* 44, No. 1 (Oct. 1938) pp. 50-56; Thomas M. Pitkin, "Western Republicans and the Tariff in 1860", *Mississippi Valley Historical Review XXVII* (1940-41) p. 401, 420. See also the answer to Thomas P. Kettell's *Southern Wealth and Northern Profits* (New York, 1860)—Samuel Powell, Notes on "Southern Wealth and Northern Profits" (Philadelphia, 1861) pp. 9-10, 21; Erastus B. Bigelow, *The Tariff Question Considered in Regard to the Policy of England and the Interest of the United States* (Boston, 1862) pp. 3, 39, 64, 71-75; Cf. Robert R. Russel, *Economic Aspects of Southern Sectionalism, 1840-1861* (Urbana, 1922) pp. 229-230.

13 *33rd Philadelphia Board of Trade, 1866,* pp. 13-19. The Railroad Interest also was clamoring against the protective iron duties. *29th Philadelphia Board of Trade, 1862,* p. 11; *5th New York Chamber of Commerce, 1862.*

14 *30th Philadelphia Board of Trade, 1863,* p. 10; *31st Philadelphia Board of Trade, 1864,* p. 11; *32nd Philadelphia Board of Trade, 1865,* p. 12; *7th New York Chamber of Commerce, 1865,* Jan. 19, 1865, Feb. 2, 1865; *12th Boston Board of Trade, 1866,* p. 11.

15 Bostonians also figured that no bankrupt bill should be passed unless its provisions corresponded to the insolvent laws of Massachusetts.

16 Walter S. Griffith, Chairman of the New York Chambers Committee of Arbitration put it thus: "The Southern States are largely in debt to the Merchants of New York, and this Chamber, as representing such creditor interest, cannot view without concern,

the enactment of postponement of legislation having reference t
the sequestration of property for the purpose of discharging such in
debtedness".

17   *7th New York Chamber of Commerce, 1865,* pp. 69-70
for the letter to Lincoln on Confiscation, pp. 72-73; for the memoria
to the New York Chamber, pp. 83-84; for the Chamber debate an
Special report, pp. 102-149-160; for further relief efforts of th
Chamber in Savannah, *8th New York Chamber of Commerce
1866,* pp. 2-3; for final action on the confiscation issue, *8th Nev
York Chamber of Commerce 1866; 33rd Boston Board of Trade
1866,* p. 18; the question of cotton owned by British M.P.'s an
Liverpool merchants seized in Savannah by federal authorities
see Mr. Burnley to Earl Russell (No. 55) Jan. 24, 1865, (No. 90
Feb. 7, 1865, (No. 95) Feb. 10, 1868, *F.O. 115* Vol. 437, *Publi
Record Office, London;* on the banking situation in Savannah se
miscellany *The Bankers' Magazine and Statistical Register,* N.S
XIV No. 8, Feb. 1865, p. 667.

18   Daniel Lord, *The Effect of Secession Upon the Commercia
Relations between the North and South, and upon each Sectio*
(London, 1861), pp. 7-8, 16-17, 20, 26-27, 55-56; Stephen Colwell
The Five Cotton States and New York (Philadelphia, 1861), pp
24-29, 53-59.

19   *Commercial and Financial Chronicle,* Aug. 28, 1909 and
Oct. 15, 1910; Frank L. Mott, *A History of American Magazine*
III, 1865-1885 (Cambridge, 1938) p. 46; *The New Internationa
Year Book,* 1910, p. 203. Dana was born Aug. 26, 1829, in Utica
New York. Graduated from Yale 1851. Practiced law in Utica
1853-1859. In 1859 moved to New York City because of wife'
health and bought *Hunts Merchants Magazine,* in which he ex
pressed free trade sentiments. Wishing to provide a dynamic busi
ness journal that would be a living force in the daily life of th
Business world, Dana, in July of 1865 began the *Chronicle* modele
on the London *Economist.* Dana published the *Chronicle* unti
his death in 1910.

20   *Commercial and Financial Chronicle,* July 1, 1865. "Th
President's Policy" and "Industrial Rehabilitation of the South."

21   *Commercial and Financial Chronicle,* Aug. 26, 1865. "South
ern Reconstruction and the National Commerce" and "The Re
vival of Southern Manufacturers". Dana thought that the Recon
struction of the South was in this category. Dana was not intereste
in the ideal way of Southern Reconstruction but the practical wa

to get the region back into normal production and consumption with the rest of the nation.

22 *Commercial and Financial Chronicle*, Sept. 2, 1865. "The Southern States A Desirable Point for Emigrants—Colonization of the South".

23 Claude G. Bowers, *op. cit.*, p. 86.

24 Herbert Ronald Ferleger, *David A. Wells and the American Revenue System, 1865-1870*, (New York, 1942) passim.

25 The original version of this situation was that Wells established confidence abroad and got Lincoln's nod for the job by the publication of his pamphlet *"Our Burden and Our Strength"*, *D.A.B. XIX*, pp. 637-38. This version is refuted by H.R. Ferleger, *op. cit.*, pp. 17-22.

26 Wells was born in Springfield, Massachusetts. At this time of his appointment he was a resident of New York State.

27 Hugh McCulloch, *Men and Measures . . .* , p. 239. The Secretary of the Commission, E.B. Eliot was also from Massachusetts.

28 *D.A.B. III*, 487-9; Charles H. Levermore "Henry C. Carey and His Social System", *Political Science Quarterly I*, No. 4 (Dec. 1890) pp. 553-582. "Upon the course of economic discussion and political action in the United States, Carey exercised an influence more than commensurate with either his learning or ability. Many since Hamilton had spun the threads for an American protective system, but Carey wove the fabric".

29 H.R. Ferleger, *op. cit.*, 28-29.

30 Harold Francis Williamson, *Edward Atkinson, the Biography of an American Liberal, 1827-1905* (Boston, 1934) pp. 57-63; *The National Cyclopedia of American Biography*, IX, p. 416. Hereinafter cited, *National Cyclopedia*. Atkinson was chairman of the Cotton Spinners of New England, organized to secure the best interests of the cotton manufacturers. He was also a member of the Board of Directors of the Boston Board of Trade.

31 Report of the United States Revenue Commission on Cotton as a Source of National Revenue, Special Report No. 3, House Executive Document No. 34, *39th Congress 1st Session* 1865-66.

32 Wells to Thomas H. Dudley, Nov. 8, 1865, cited in H.R. Ferleger, *op. cit.*, p. 59.

33 See note 31. The Testimony of Atkinson, Grey, Frothingham, Lowell, Nourse, Amory, Dwight, Batchelder; *7th New York Chamber of Commerce, 1865, Part II*. Trade Reports, "Iron". A more significant statement is to be found in Special Report

No. 10 by Stephen Colwell entitled "Report upon the Relation of Foreign Trade to Domestic Industry and Internal Revenue" in the non-official governmental document series compilation—David A. Wells, Stephen Colwell, and Samuel Hayes, *Reports of a Commission Appointed for a Revision of the Revenue System of the United States* 1865-66 (Washington, 1866) pp. 276, 278, 281-283. Colwell openly attacked the concentration of foreign capital in New York City as dangerous to the future development of the American economy.

34   London *Economist,* April 15, 1865 and Nov. 18, 1865 "Conditions and Prospects of Cotton"; Leland H. Jenks, *The Migration of British Capital to 1875* (New York, 1938) p. 260 et passim.

35   Note 31 supra, especially the testimony of Edward L. Atkinson and E. H. Derby.

36   Wells to Stevens Feb. 2, 1866, cited in Ferleger, *op. cit.* p. 79.

37   W. L. Trenholm, *The Centennial Address before the Charleston Chamber of Commerce,* 11th of February, 1884 (Charleston, S.C., 1884) pp. 32-37.

38   George W. Smith, *Generative Forces of Union Propaganda,* MSS. Thesis, The University of Wisconsin 1939, pp. 435-449. Henry C. Carey also had strong views on industrial colonization of the South.

39   R. G. Albion, *Square Riggers on Schedule,* (Princeton, 1938) p. 6.

40   See *Bureau of Refugees, Freedmen, and Abandoned Land, Letter Books,* 1865, No. 83, Sept. 12, 1865; No. 146, July 16, 1865; No. 27, Sept. 26, 1865; No. 38, Sept. 27, 1865; No. 48, Oct. 1, 1865; Especially Brev. Maj. Genl. A. Baird from Maj. Woodhua Oct. 21, 1865, and R. V. Richardson, Treas. of Cotton Planters Assn., New York City from Major Woodhua Nov. 11, 1865; Wm. H. Seward from Vice Consul Wm. Long, 30 Sept. 1865, *American Consular Letters, Liverpool,* Vol. 32, No. 540.

41   *William King to Maj. General O.O. Howard,* Savannah, Georgia, 30 May, 1865. This letter, with the original planters' plan and the revisions after King's New England Conference (to be found in the appendix), were located in the Freedmen Bureau MSS., War Department archives, The National Archives, Washington, D.C. See also *Bureau of Refugee, Freedmen and Abandoned Lands, Letter Books,* No. 20, June 15, 1865. On the transcript of the New England copy of King's plan Adj. Gen. M.

Woodhua wrote "In my opinion a worse form of Slavery than the old one".

42   London *Economist,* November 18, 1865.

43   Sir S. Morton Peto, Bart., M.P. for Bristol, *The Resources and Prospects of America Ascertained during a Visit to the States in Autumn of 1865* (London, 1866) pp. 344-346; Leland H. Jenks, *op. cit.,* pp. 255-259; *D.N.B.* Vol. 45, pp. 86-88. Peto came to America to try to straighten out the James McHenry-Atlantic and Great Western Railroad—Erie Railroad fiasco, one of the most daring gambles in securities—juggling the international money market—that has ever been known. While Peto was here, he also looked over the possibilities of the American government liquidating its foreign held securities, and found them good.

44   John A. Andrew to Charles Sumner, Nov. 21, 1865, cited in Henry Greenleaf Pearson, *The Life of John A. Andrew,* 2 vols. (Boston, 1904) II, pp. 273-74. Andrew regretted the Bureau's want of independence and suggested that "Hereafter the Bureau ought to control and command the local military and not be subordinate to the military". He also thought that the Bureau needed a strong man with power. See also New York *Daily Tribune,* Feb. 22, 1866, citing a letter from the Washington Correspondent of the *Cincinnati Commercial* dated Feb. 12, 1865 for O.O. Howard's responsibility at this point.

45   *D.A.B.* Vol. XVIII, p. 567; S.M. Peto, *op. cit.,* p. 344; *Nat. Cyclopedia* XIII, pp. 416-17; Boston *Journal,* Nov. 28, 1865; *Daily Evening Voice,* Nov. 29, 1865; Boston *Daily Advertiser,* Nov. 28, 1865; New York *Journal of Commerce,* Nov. 28, 1865; New York *Herald,* Nov. 29, 1865; *12th Boston Board of Trade,* 1866, pp. 56-58; The Boston *Advertiser* is the only one of the above references that carries Tobey's speech full text. See Chapter I for an estimate of Tobey. *The Daily Evening Voice* was the official organ of the Workingmen's Assembly of Boston and vicinity. The paper was pro-Johnson up to this time. *The Voice* approved in principle Tobey's plan; but suggested that, instead of Northern capitalists, the Southern States should issue their credit to the old planters and the Negro population would then prove to be a blessing.

46   "National Cotton Convention", memorial of Mr. A. Penfield of the Treasury Department to the New York Chamber of Commerce, Washington, D.C., Nov. 9, 1865, *The Banker's Magazine,* N.S. XV, No. 5 (Dec. 1865) p. 481; Edward Atkinson to O.O. Howard, Oct. 12, 1865, *Bureau of Refugees, Freedmen, and*

Abandoned Lands, Letter Books, letters received, 1865, No. 30; *8th New York Chamber of Commerce,* 1866, pp. 60-61, for Penfield's letter of Nov. 9, 1865; p. 67 for the letter of the Boston Board on the Tobey Idea; 100 for the second Penfield letter dated Washington, D.C. Jan. 31, 1866.

47   A.B. Miller, *op. cit.,* p. 295; R.N. Current, *op. cit.,* p. 223; Claude G. Bowers, *op. cit.,* p. 91 et passim; F.W.A. Bruce to the Earl of Clarendon, Washington, Dec. 12, 1865, *F.O.* vol. 1021, II, No. 500, *Public Record Office,* London; Benjamin B. Kendrick, *The Journal of the Joint Committee of Fifteen on Reconstruction* (Columbia University Studies in History, Economics, and Public Law, Vol. 62, New York, 1914) p. 175; for the Journal itself see Journal of the Joint Committee on Reconstruction, *39th Congress,* 1st Session appointed pursuant to the concurrent Resolution of December 13, 1865, Senate Document No. 711, *63rd Congress, 3rd Session.*

48   Andrew to the Officer in charge of the Commissary Department to the Freedmen's Bureau in Louisiana, Nov. 1865 and Andrew to W. L. Burt, January 21, 1866, in Pearson, *op. cit.,* pp. 268-69; A. Delmor, "Security for Capital", *Debows Review,* rev. series (January-June 1866) Art. X. The Company was organized as follows: John A. Andrew, President; Frank E. Howe, Vice President and General Agent, North; L. W. Winchester, Treasurer; M. N. Wesewell, General Agent, South. There were but thirty-five shares in the company at $1,000.00 per share.

49   *The Daily Evening Bulletin,* Nov. 30, 1865, "Protection to American Industry". Frederick Fraley and other leaders of Philadelphia's Board of Trade were forced to organize against the League. New York papers and other sources failed to reveal the details of the "League's" Organization. *The Evening Post* carried the League's pamphlets—see Nov. 28, 1865, Tract No. 11, "Revenue and Protection". W. C. Bryant's biographies are useless for this organization immediately after the war. Dr. Martin of the Division of Manuscript of the Library of Congress told this writer that his researches revealed that this organization was financed in part by British capital.

50   *8th New York Chamber of Commerce,* 1866, p. 64. For the letter of Conway dated December 14, 1865 and for the resolution of the Chamber approving the mission.

51   London *Economist,* Jan. 27, 1866, citing the *Commercial and Financial Chronicle.* Cotton seemed about to succeed petroleum, as petroleum succeeded mining, as the speculation of the hour.

For a history of the phenomenal development of petroleum as a speculative craze in Pennsylvania see S. M. Peto, *op. cit.,* pp. 191-206.

52 Henry W. Lord to Hon. W. H. Seward, U. S. Consulate, Manchester Jan. 27, 1866, *American Consular Letters, Manchester,* Vol. 2, No. 63.

53 F. H. Norse to Hon. Wm. H. Seward, U. S. Consulate, London, Feb. 2, 1866. *American Consular Letters, London,* Vol. 36, No. 357.

54 *8th New York Chamber of Commerce,* 1866, p. 70.

55 *D. A. B.* XIV, pp. 45-6; George Wilson, *Portrait Gallery of the Chamber of Commerce of the State of New York,* (1890) p. 60; *Catalogue of Portraits in the Chamber of Commerce of the State of New York* (New York, 1924) p. 88—hereafter cited *Catalogue of Portraits.* See Chapter I.

56 *D. A. B.* IX, pp. 279-281; Oliver Otis Howard, *Autobiography of Oliver Otis Howard, Major General United States Army,* 2 Vols. (New York—1907) II pp. 280-282. There has been some question as to how much Howard was implicated in the framing of the Second Freedmen's Bureau bill—*Journal of Commerce,* Feb. 23, 1866 "Trap for the President; *Cincinnati Commercial,* Feb. 24, 1866 citing the *Philadelphia Press; New York Evening Post, Feb. 24, 1866.* However Howard's activities in this matter are revealed beyond question by the following: Maj. Gen. O. O. Howard to Robert L. Murray, Washington, Jan. 24, 1866 giving his endorsement of the western association idea of flooding Congress with petitions favoring the new Bureau; Maj. Gen. O. O. Howard to Hon. Lyman Trumbull, Washington, Jan. 13, 1866 and the Washington Office to Bt. Maj. Genl. Swayne, Washington, Jan. 20, 1866, excluding Texas and adding Louisiana and Alabama to Florida, Mississippi and Arkansas as states with large tracts of public land upon which Negroes might be settled. See also circular letter 528 to Asst. Com's. of Ala., Miss., Ark., La., and Fla., Washington, July 9, 1866, *Bureau of Refugees, Freedmen, and Abandoned Lands, Letter Books* (letters sent) 1866.

57 Paul Skeels Pierce, *The Freedmen's Bureau, A Chapter in the History of Reconstruction* (State University of Iowa Studies in Sociology, Economics, Politics and History, Vol. III, No. 1), *Bulletin of the State University of Iowa,* new series, No. 74 (March, 1904) pp. 55-74; George Fort Milton, *The Age of Hate, Andrew Johnson and the Radicals* (New York, 1930) pp. 285-90; Howard K. Beale, *The Critical Year, A Study of Andrew Johnson and*

Reconstruction (New York, 1930) pp. 80-90; Claude Bowers, *op. cit.*, pp. 101-103; Ewarts B. Green, "Some Aspects of Politics in the Middle West, 1860-1872", *Proceedings of the State Historical Society of Wisconsin* at its 59th Annual meeting (Madison, 1912) pp. 60-76; Lewis Ethan Ellis, "A History of the Chicago Delegation in Congress, 1853-1925", Illinois State Historical Society *Transactions,* Vol. 37 (1930) pp. 76-78.

58   Frederick W. A. Bruce to the Right Honorable the Earl of Clarendon K. G., Washington, Feb. 20, 1866, *F. O.* 5.

59   R. B. Hayes to S. Birchard, Washington Feb. 28, 1866, cited in Charles Richard Williams, ed., *Diary and Letters of Rutherford Birchard Hayes* 5 vols., (Columbus, 1924) III 1865-1881, p. 18. Johnson vetoed the Bureau bill on Feb. 19, 1866; *National Intelligencer,* Feb. 20, 1866; *Journal of Commerce,* Feb. 21, 1866.

60   Boston *Daily Advertiser,* Feb. 26, 1866; *Daily Evening Voice,* Feb. 21, 1866. "With such a party (Radicals sic) the interests of the workingmen are identified."

61   *New York Daily Tribune,* Feb. 20, 1866; "If three million bales of cotton are made this year—and we judge that there will be—the Freedmen's Bureau will have given us at least one third of it, worth not less than $100,000 in gold". *The Daily Morning Chronicle,* Feb. 23, 1866 (citing the *New York Tribune*).

62   *Nation,* March, 1866.

63   New York *Evening Post,* Feb. 23, 1866. Bryant advised that Congress revise the bill to meet Johnson's objections.

64   New York *Morning Herald,* Feb. 21, 1866, "The Freedmen's Bureau in a commercial financial point of view"; *ibid.,* Feb. 23, 1866. E. D. Morgan, New York Senator, was said to have changed his vote on the bribe of the Collectorship of New York port. Doolittle was to have a "mountain of patronage"; and Cowan was to have a Cabinet post.

65   *World,* Feb. 21, 1866. The reaction of the British Press was quite revealing. The *Morning Star,* March 8, 1866 and the *Daily Telegraph* March 8, 1866 were anti-radical. The *Daily News,* March 9, 1866 was neutral. But the *London Morning Herald, Morning Post, Morning Advertiser* and *Times* for March 8, 1866 and the *Times* and *Standard* for March 9, 1866 were strongly pro-Johnson. The *Standard* termed Radicalism a system of proscription, confiscation and military colonization. On the other hand Johnson wanted the Southern states to legislate for their own people, "taking care that they shall not, under the guise of necessary measures for the organization and enforcement of industry, revive a modified

system of slavery". His aim is a restored union purged of Slavery; that of the radicals, a Northern Republic with a Southern Poland held in subjection by Negro bayonets and ruled by Negro ballots. Hon. Wm. H. Seward from Thomas H. Dudley, U. S. Consulate Liverpool, March 9, 1866, *American Consular Letters, Liverpool,* Vol. 33, No. 615.

66 George E. Baker, ed., *The Works of William H. Seward,* Vol. V, pp. 529-540. The Chamber of Commerce men were well represented among the organizers of this meeting, viz.: Opdyke, E. D. Morgan, Wm. E. Dodge, Moses H. Grennell, A. A. Low (President of the Chamber), and several others. The meeting was held at Cooper Union, New York *Morning Herald,* Feb. 23, 1866.

67 *Cincinnati Commercial,* Feb. 24, 1866 citing the *Philadelphia Press; Journal of Commerce,* Feb. 23, 1866 citing the *Daily Morning Chronicle* under the caption "trap for the President".

68 Edward L. Pierce, *Memoir and Letters of Charles Sumner,* Vol. IV, 1860-1874 (Boston, 1894) pp. 307-308. Charles Sumner to W. W. Story, Dec. 16, 1866.

69 New York *Daily Tribune,* Feb. 27, 1866. Governor Cox to General George B. Wright, Chairman of the Union Central Committee, Columbus, Ohio, Washington, Feb. 27, 1866.

70 Edward McPherson, *A Political Manual of 1867* (Washington, D. C., 1867). This speech was delivered Sept. 8, 1866. By that time a new Bureau bill had passed over his veto.

71 George Fort Milton, *op. cit.,* p. 289.

72 *Commercial and Financial Chronicle,* Feb. 17, 1866—"The Production and Taxation of Cotton", and "The Importance of the Reorganization of the South"; the latter article also appeared in Dana's *Merchant's Magazine and Commercial Review,* LIV, No. III (March, 1866) p. 169. The *Economist,* Feb. 17, 1866, under the title "The proposed tax on the export of American cotton" simply reproduces the tax provisions without comment, but editorialized under the caption "The Report of the American Commission on Revenue".

73 H. K. Beale, *op. cit.,* p. 82. As late as Feb. 17, 1866 there was some hope of Johnson signing the Bureau bill. His decision to veto the bill, like that of Senator Dixon, Doolittle, E. D. Morgan, Norton and Van Winkle to sustain the veto after previously voting for the bill, can be explained only by the fact that the Bureau's double entendre was revealed by the Wells' report.

74 Maj. Gen. O. O. Howard to Hon. T. D. Elliot, M. C. & Chrm. of Comm. on Freedmen Affairs, War Dept., B. R. F. & A. L.

Wash., April 8, 1866, *Bureau of Refugees, Freedmen, and Abandoned Lands, Letter Books* (letters sent) 1866.

75 Andrew Johnson to the House of Representatives—In compliance with the resolution of the House of Representatives of the 21st Instant, I transmit herewith a report from the Secretary of War with accompanying papers in reference to the operations of the Bureau of Refugees, Freedmen, and Abandoned Land, Washington, D. C., May 25, 1866, War Dept. B, of R. F. & A. L., May 21, 1866, Circular No. 4, *H. of R. M. S. S. Box 11, Bundle 40,* No. 7.

76 Congressional Globe, *39th Congress, 1st Session,* pp. 2473-2474.

77 Sir S. M. Peto, *op. cit.,* pp. 373-74. "It is curious that those who contend the most vigorously in America for a duty upon cotton, are those who contend the most vigorously for the removal of every duty on native manufactures as injurious to native industry".

78 Congressional Globe, *39th Congress, 1st Session,* pp. 2473-2474.

79 *9th N. Y. Chamber of Commerce* 1867, pp. 12-15. "Memorial to Congress for the abolition of the tax on cotton". See also page 26 for Hon. E. D. Morgan's letter telling of the disposition of the memorial after it reached him. See also Sir Samuel Morton Peto, *op. cit.,* p. 371.

80 H. R. Ferleger, *op. cit.,* pp. 83-91; "The Southern Cotton Trade and the Excise Laws", Department of Agriculture, *Debows Review,* II (Nov. 1866) p. 527; "The New Era of Southern Manufacturers" Art. VII, *Debows Review* III (Jan. 1867), pp. 56-57.

81 Congressional Globe, *39th Congress, 1st Session,* pp. 2871-2874.

82 Howard K. Beale, *op. cit.,* p. 278; Sir Samuel M. Peto, *op. cit.,* p. 399.

83 Note 12 supra.

84 *9th New York Chamber of Commerce,* 1867, p. 12—for the Philadelphia Board's Memorial, pp. 29-30; for the Chamber's memorial and debate thereon, July 6, 1866, pp. 60-61; for the same Feb. 7, 1867. Opdyke's memorial had not been endorsed by the executive committee and the mid-summer heat had reduced the attending membership of the Chamber.

85 Herbert R. Ferleger, *op. cit.,* pp. 144-149; Howard K. Beale, *op. cit.,* pp. 279-285, 291-292; Alphonse B. Miller, *op. cit.,* pp. 384; Caroline Hazard, Ed. *Rowland Gibson Hazard, Economics and Politics 1846-1885* (Boston, 1889) pp. 299-301, passim.

86   For the complete Wool story, especially the Middle-western extravagance, see *9th New York Chamber of Commerce 1867,* Part II, Trade Reports, pp. 94-97 "Annual Report of the Wool Trade of the United States for the Year 1866". Succeeding reports of the Chamber offer an excellent discussion of the controversy over the reciprocity treaty with Canada.

87   London *Economist,* Sept. 29, 1866.

88   *Commercial and Financial Chronicle,* June 2, 1866; *Merchants' Magazine and Commercial Review LIV,* No. VI, June 1866 "The Past and Future Cotton Supply"—the article is the same in both journals, *Commercial and Financial Chronicle,* Sept. 29, 1866, "Treasury Regulations for Collecting the Cotton Tax", *Commercial and Financial Chronicle,* Nov. 24, 1866, "The Cotton Tax and the Industries of the North".

Chapter III: THE FAMINE YEAR AND AFTER

1   "Industrial Association of Mississippi", *Debows Review,* vol. 5, no. 5 (January, 1868) p. 82. James E. Yeatman to Senator Henderson January 23, 1867, in *Charleston Daily Courier,* February 6, 1867.

2   *Message* of Governor Charles J. Jenkins to the Georgia Legislature, November 1, 1866. Jenkins sounded a sad note: "The planting interest in Georgia can never again be what it has been. Few, if any, will be able to prosecute it on as large a scale as some have done in the past. But agriculture must continue to be the chief industrial pursuit of the state". *Annual Report* of the Cincinnati Chamber of Commerce and Merchants' Exchange for the Commercial Year ending August 31, 1867. (Cincinnati, 1867), Trade Reports—"Cotton". Robert Somers, *The Southern States Since the War, 1870-71* (London, 1871) p. 280.

3   George H. Morgan, *Annual Statement* of the Trade and Commerce of St. Louis for the year 1866, reported to the Union Merchants Exchange (St. Louis, 1867), pp. 10-11. A committee appointed by the Exchange collected from the citizens generally money and supplies to the amount of $12,780.50 "which were sent free of charge, and, no doubt, did much good".

4   *Message No. 1,* of His Excellency, Governor J. L. Orr, with accompanying documents, November, 1866. These messages are so cited because they were published in pamphlet form, and

are filed as such in the document division of the Wisconsin Historical Society Library.

5   Note 1 supra; *Charleston Daily Courier,* May 8, 1867
"Capital for the South"; Henry G. Pearson, *The Life of John A*
Andrew II (Boston, 1904) p. 314. In the circular of the "Land
Agency" announcing the suspending of business was this comment
"Every Northern man engaged in planting has lost his entire
investment; many their entire fortunes. We do not report one
instance of success amongst those who went through our agency
and from whom commissions are due. Not one has escaped without
the loss of his entire capital invested, and nearly all have returned
North and abandoned everything, while the two or three who
remain promise no better. These purchasers are now suffering
without exception, from the peculiar trials of their new position
but more than all from the terrible and ruinous seasons of the
past two years."

6   *Charleston Daily Courier,* February 5, 1867.

7   "Famine in the South", *Harpers' Weekly,* March 23, 1867
p. 179 et seq.

8   *Southern Opinion,* June 15, 1867.

9   See note 5 supra; *Debows Review,* n.s. III (January-June
1867) p. 315, "Department of Miscellany". The law was approved
December 15, 1866.

10   See Chapter II supra; *10th N. Y. Chamber of Commerce*
1867-8, p. 3 et passim. The Macon Board had asked the previous
month for a loan of food until the crops were gathered.

11   George H. Morgan, *St. Louis Trade,* 1867, pp. 8-11. In this
instance $28,283.66 was collected, and food and clothing were
purchased. The supplies were forwarded free of charge. The Exchange also helped the Howard association of New Orleans in
their fight against yellow fever with $1,000 of its own funds and
$18,391.50 collected by its committee.

12   *Annual Report* of the Board of Trade and Merchants
Exchange, of the Commerce and Trade of Louisville for the year
ending March 31, 1867 (Louisville, 1867) p. 12.

13   Brown's office was located at 61 Wall Street.

14   *True Index,* May 4, 1867.

15   *The Examiner,* May 2, 1868; Colonel J. W. De Forest, "The
Condition of the Poor Whites", *Putnams Magazine* N. S. I (June,
1868) p. 704 et passim.

16   Charleston *Daily Courier,* March 13, 1867; *The Abingdon*
Virginian, October 28, 1870.

17 Hon. T. D. Elliot—from War Department, Bureau of Refugees, Freedmen and Abandoned Lands, Washington, January 9, 1868, in *Freedmens Bureau Letter Books,* (Letters Sent) Vol. 3, 1867. See also for actions of Bureau on Southern destitution, Letters number 91, 104, 111, 119, and 147. These books and all other records of the Bureau are in the War Dept. division of the National Archives, Washington, D. C.

18 See Chapter II supra; and *13th Boston Board of Trade,* 1867, pp. 17-18; *34th Philadelphia Board of Trade,* 1867, p. 17. The effort all along had been designed to block operation of statutes of limitation in the Southern states, and prevent passage of bankruptcy legislation by Congress which would benefit the Southern states. The merchants thought that Congress should either suspend the Southern "Stay Laws" or open the federal courts in the South to a smaller class of interstate-citizenship suits.

19 *Proceedings of the National Commercial Convention, Held in Boston,* February, 1868 (Boston, 1868) pp. 106-110, 117. A full discussion of this meeting follows in Chapter V.

20 The *Proceedings of the National Chamber of Commerce* all through the '70's give a clear picture of this reaction. Nevertheless the South remained optimistic: note *Minutes of the Proceedings* of the Commercial Convention held in the city of Memphis, Tennessee, May, 1869 (Memphis, 1869) passim; continuous water line communications between the Mississippi and the Atlantic, memorial of the Louisville and Cincinnati Commercial Conventions to the Congress of the United States on opening of a complete system of continuous water communications between the Mississippi River and the Atlantic Ocean (Richmond, 1873).

21 C. Vann Woodward, *Tom Watson, Agrarian Rebel* (New York, 1938) p. 53; Hon. Edward McPherson, *A Political Manual for 1867* (Washington, D. C., 1867) pp. 15-17. Andrew Johnson made these observations in an interview with Charles G. Halpine March 5, 1867. Johnson revealed clearly his class consciousness with the remark: "We have all read history, and is it not certain that of all aristocracies, that of mere wealth is the most odious, rapacious and tyrannical? It goes for the last dollar the poor and helpless have got; and with such a vast machine as this government under its control, that dollar will be fetched. It is an aristocracy that can see in the people only a prey for extortion."

22 *10th N. Y. Chamber of Commerce* 1867-68, pp. 22-23; and Chapter IV post.

23   *The Commercial and Financial Chronicle,* December 28 1867, p. 807. "The impoverishment of the South, by persistence in this tax, tends directly to deprive us of the commercial advan tages Emancipation was said to promise. Many anticipated tha the freeing of the Negroes would elevate them in the scale o civilization, and result in their becoming large consumers of North ern manufactures." "The Cotton Tax", *Debow's Review,* III, n.s (June, 1867) pp. 561-3. The article is a reprint from the *Alabam Republic,* written by Pierce Burton, A Freedmen's Bureau agent Burton observed: "Congress has now given Freedmen the ballot while it takes away much of their bread and bacon."

24   Charleston *Daily Courier,* October 19, 1866.

25   *14th Boston Board of Trade,* 1868. Special Report "On th Proposed Repeal of the Cotton Tax", Appendix-report on Indi "Surat" cotton—William H. Thompson, dated Boston, Decembe 20, 1867, and A. D. Lockwood, dated Lewiston, Maine, Decembe 23, 1867. "The Distress of the Cotton trade and the Future Cotto Supply", *Economist* (London) November 6, 1869 and "Importatio and Consumption of Cotton in 1866", January 5, 1867.

26   The Macarthy gin was said to be superior to all others The ancient "Churka" gin was a rude framework with two roller of teakwood, fluted lengthwise by five or six grooves, which revolve near contact. Drawing the cotton between these rollers freed i of seed. Before the Civil War 20 persons, using this two thousand year old gin, could clean 100 lbs. of cotton a day.

27   No. 25 was the average number of the manufactures of th American mills. Number as used by the cotton manufacturer meant so many skeins, or hanks, of 840 yards each to one pound In England, Lockwood found manufacturers spinning all number from 16 to 60 with "Surat" successfully. The answer was that th machines had been adapted to work short staple dirty cotton Lockwood found also that the Egyptian and South American cotto was nearly as long as American, had a good color, was quite a clean as a good grade of American middling, and possessed as goo spinning qualities as American uplands. He found this situatio very common in English textile manufacturing districts.

28   For numbers ranging from 30 down, the raw cotton pric was cheaper than that.

29   These goods named are such as are used by the best shir makers.

30   Members of the Committee were E. R. Mudge, George L Ward, Edward Atkinson, C. W. Freeland, and C. O. Wetmore

ee also on this point Herbert R. Ferleger, *David A. Wells and
he American Revenue System* 1865-1870 (New York, 1942) pp.
09-110.

31   Added to the demand for repeal by the Secretary of the
Treasury, the Commissioner of Internal Revenue, and the Commis-
ioner of Agriculture was that of the Southern states: for that of
he Alabama Constitutional Convention see *House Miscellaneous
Documents, No. 52,* Nov. 27, 1867, *40th Congress, 1st Session,* vol.
1; for that of the Tennessee Legislature, House Executive Documents No. 1, December 2, 1867, *40th Congress, 1st Session,* vol. 1;
or that of the Georgia Convention, *House Miscellaneous Documents, No. 29,* Jan. 16, 1868, *40th Congress, 2nd Session,* vol. 2.
10th New York Chamber of Commerce, 1867-68, p. 27. The Board
of Trade of Macon, Georgia, asked the New York Chamber to
press Congress for repeal, and was referred to the Chamber's
memorial presented by their Senator, Hon. E. D. Morgan. See also
Louisville Board of Trade, 1867, p. 28; House of Representatives
MSS. *40th Congress,* Box 14, Bundle 54.

32   George P. Sanger, Ed., *Statutes at Large, Treaties, and
Proclamations of the United States of America,* XV (Boston, 1868)
citing *40th Congress, 2nd Session,* Chapter V. "Be it enacted . . .
that all cotton grown in the United States after the year 1867
shall be exempt from internal tax; and cotton imported from foreign
countries on and after Nov. 1, 1868, shall be exempt from duty."

Textile manufacturers protected themselves for a while with the
following "Joint resolution" of July 14, 1870:

> Joint resolution to construe the act of March 31, 1868—
> . . . That the act of March 31, 1868, Chapter 41, shall be
> held and construed not to prohibit the drawback provided for
> by section 6 of the act of July 30, 1866, Chapter 184, of as
> many cents per pound of cotton cloth, yarn, thread or knit
> articles, manufactured exclusively from cotton and exported
> prior to May 1, 1869, as shall have been assessed of raw cotton.
> George P. Sanger, *Stats. At Large,* XVI, no. 112.

Around 1872 a movement was begun at the South to get a
refund of the Cotton Tax. See—House Miscellaneous Documents,
no. 18, *42nd Congress, 2nd Session,* V, for a resolution by the
Tennessee Legislature for a refund of the tax for 1865, '66, and '67.
For the efforts of the New Orleans Chamber of Commerce for
refund and the negative reaction of the Northeastern Business
Community, see *19th Boston Board of Trade,* 1873, Special Reports;

39th Philadelphia Board of Trade, 1872, p. 10; *14th New York Chamber of Commerce,* 1871-2, p. 56.

33   Charles Sumner to John Bright, May 27, 1867, Edward L. Pierce, *Memoir and Letters of Charles Sumner,* IV, 1860-1874 (Boston, 1894) p. 319: Claude G. Bowers, *The Tragic Era* (New York, 1929) p. 198; William Best Hesseltine, *The South in American History* (New York, 1943) pp. 521, 530, 543.

34   See Chapter II, supra.

35   *House of Representatives MSS., 40th Congress,* Box 21 (Unnumbered Bundle) Freedmen's Affairs. This bundle contained appeals by Bureau agents to O. O. Howard and Hon. Thomas D. Elliot of the House Committee on Freedmen's Affairs for some effort to stave off the discontinuance of the Bureau's efforts after December 31, 1868. The appeals came from as far west as Huntsville, Texas, and from Mississippi, North Carolina, Virginia, and Kentucky. There were some letters in the bundle to Thaddeus Stevens. See especially Petition of L. E. Dudley and others of Virginia praying for the continuance of the Freedmen's Bureau in that State, Dec. 7, 1868. The letter was dated Rooms Republican State Central Executive Committee, Richmond, Virginia, November 3, 1868.

36   Bureau of Refugees, Freedmen, and Abandoned Land, *Letter Books* (Letters Sent) IV, 1867-8, War Department MSS., the National Archives.

37   Senators and Representatives went to Congress from these states in 1870.

38   Caroline A. Lloyd, *Henry Damorest Lloyd,* 1847-1903, 2 vols. (New York, 1912) I, pp. 24-28 et passim. Some of the members were Alfred Pell, Robert B. Minturn, Carl Schurz, Ex-governor Jacob D. Cox of Ohio, Horace White of the Chicago *Tribune,* David A. Wells, Edward Atkinson, E. L. Godkin, William Lloyd Garrison, and Samuel J. Tilden.

39   *36th Philadelphia Board of Trade,* 1869, p. 23.

40   Chapter II supra.

41   Edward Atkinson, *On the Collection of Revenue* (read before the American Social Science Association in Boston, January, 1867) (Boston, 1867).

42   Herbert R. Ferleger, *op. cit.,* 165-182 for the legislative history of this tariff controversy.

43   David A. Wells was unable to get over the revisions he contemplated. Professor Frank Taussig has said that the bill of '67, even in its amended form, would have been a step in the right

irection. The bill would have introduced the idea of looking at ariff rates soberly and destroyed the later tendency of the solid halanx of manufacturers to regard the Civil War tariff rates as he sine qua non of protection. See note 40 supra; Merle Fainsod nd Lincoln Gordon, *Government and the American Economy* New York, 1941) pp. 85-89; Frank W. Taussig and H. D. Vhite, *Some Aspects of the Tariff Question, an Examination of the)evelopment of American Industries Under Protection (Harvard Iconomic Studies, Vol. XII) (Cambridge, 1934) Part III and IV.*

44   Henry C. Carey, *Reconstruction: Industrial, Financial and Political—Letters to the Hon. Henry Wilson, Senator from Massa-husetts* (Philadelphia, 1867). This series of seven open letters were vritten between August 20, 1867, and mid-September of the same ear.

45   See Chapter II supra.

46   "Commercial Policy of England 1st and 2nd Quarter", *1merican Consul Letters, London,* vol. 34, no. 677 (Aug. 10, 1866); state Department MSS., The National Archives, Washington, D.C.

47   Wm. H. Seward, Secretary of State, from Thomas H.)udley, U. S. Consulate (Liverpool), March 5, 1867, in *American Consul Letters, Liverpool,* vol. 35, no. 762 (1867). Dudley is known o have intensely disliked the English because their antagonistic ttitude toward the Northern cause during the War persisted, in he face of their need of the American market, after the War. efferson Davis' appearance from Canada on the Liverpool Ex-hange in the late summer of 1868 and the merchants' reaction onfirmed this view. See Wm. H. Seward from T. H. Dudley, etc., Aug. 12, 1868, *American Consul Letters, Liverpool,* vol. 37, no. 898 1868). See also the statistics in Hon. Wm. H. Seward, Sec'y of tate from F. H. Morse, U. S. Consulate, London, January 22, 868, *American Consul Letters, London,* vol. 37, no. 464, "Report f the Commerce of the United States with Foreign Countries".

48   Hon. Hamilton Fish, Sec. of State, from Thomas Dudley, J. S. Consulate, Liverpool, June 19, 1869, *American Consul Letters, .iverpool,* vol. 39, no. 980. Reports continue through this period o show depression in Europe, especially in the textile districts. "here was much hope in America that English operatives would mmigrate to that country.

49   Hon. Hamilton Fish, Sec. of State, from F. H. Morse, U. S. Consulate, London, May 8, 1869, *American Consul Letters, London,* ol. 38, no. 515 (1869); Hon. Hamilton Fish, Sec. of State, from '. H. Morse, U. S. Consul Gen. London, June 17, 1869, *American*

Consul Letters, London, vol. 38, no. 702. "In the new series of forms", wrote Morse, "I shall require the shipper to state in his affidavit whether or not the goods are sent on consignment for sale or account of foreign owners, and this affidavit will be sworn to."

50   A letter to the New York *Tribune,* May 21, 1869, indicated that the city was swarming with foreign agents, a few of whom received orders amounting to from one to four million dollars annually. The average salary of an agent was $1,500 and up. Office and desk space ran a few hundred dollars yearly. The agent took out a commercial brokers license of $25 per year. He paid no taxes on sales or otherwise, and though he did a large business "he (did) not contribute one copper to the support of the Government." It was suggested by "De facto" that, in any consideration of the revision of the revenue, these agents might be taxed $5,000 per year.

51   Hon. Asst. Sec. of State from Adam Badeau, U. S. Consl. Gen., London, 24th, Feb., 1877, *American Consul Letters, London* vol. 45, no. 706 (1877).

52   Hon. Asst. Sec. of State from Adam Badeau, U. S. Consl. Gen., London, March 21, 1874, *American Consul Letters, London* vol. 42, no. 413; Hon. Asst. Sec. of State from Adam Badeau, U. S. Conslt., Gen., Nov. 15, 1875, *American Consul Letters, London,* vol. 44, no. 576 (1876); Hon. Asst. Sec. of State from Adam Badeau, U. S. Conslt. Gen., Nov. 10, 1877, *American Consul Letters, London,* vol. 46, no. 786 (1878) (Printed) "Summary of Trade with the United States in 1876".

53   Hon. Asst. Sec. of State from Adam Badeau, U. S. Conslt Gen., London, 12th, Dec., 1877, *American Consul Letters, London* vol. 46, no. 798 (1877). The articles cited above were from the London *Standard* and *Times,* Oct. 10, 1877; Hon. Frederick W Seward, Asst. Sec. of State from Lucius Fairchild, U. S. Consulate Liverpool, Sept. 28, 1877, *American Consul Letters, Liverpool* vol. 45, nos. 325-26 (1878); Edwin Guthrie, *The Cotton Trade Its Condition and Prospects.* (To the Economic Section of the British Association for the Advancement of Science at its meeting held at South Port, Sept. 20, 1883) (Manchester, 1883) pp. 10-11 14-21; *21st N. Y. Chamber of Commerce, 1878,* Part II, Trade Reports—"Annual Review of the New York Drygoods Trade, 1878" p. 112; *22nd N. Y. Chamber of Commerce, 1879,* Part II, Trade Reports—"Annual Review of the New York Drygoods Trade, 1879"

54 *Reports from Commissioners, Inspectors, and Others,* 1886, 25 vols., (*Parliamentary Papers, House of Commons, 1886,* vol. 22) citing vol. 10 (c. 4715-1), "Second Report of the Royal Commission Appointed to inquire into the Depression of Trade and Industry", Appendix, Part II, *The United States,* pp. 372-390. In the summary report from British consuls in America may be found the following: "The manufacturing interest clustering around Philadelphia and sheltered by the tariff are exceptionally situated, and continue very active. They are supplanting British manufactures, both on the Atlantic and Pacific Coast, aided, of course, by the general fall in wages". At another point William Lane Booker, Her Britannic Majesty's Consul General located New York City, observed: "The cause of our not having been able to increase the trade is to be found in the vast strides that have been made in the manufacturing industries of the United States, fostered, as they have been, by high, and in some instances, prohibitory duties. . . . The Americans claim that their products have an advantage in their freshness of invention and adaptation, . . . and for that reason, the fact of an article being of American manufacture is a voucher for its superiority."

Chapter IV : CREATING THE SELLERS' MARKET

1 W. L. Trenholm, Esq., "Portions of an Address delivered at the 3rd Anniversary of the Charleston Board of Trade", *Hunt's Merchants Magazine and Commercial Review,* 61 (July-Dec. 1869) p. 10.

2 Charleston *Daily Courier,* Feb. 21, 1867; for a scheme for white settlers in British Guiana, see W. M. Price to Sir Frederick Bruce (British Minister to the U. S.) Scottsville, Va., May 26, 1865, in *F. O.* 5, vol. 1019-11, *Public Record Office, London.* This reference comes from the MSS. of the British Ministry to the United States. Photostating these papers was supervised by Miss Fisher, a Negro woman, who was, before the War, in charge of the London Office of the Division of Manuscripts of the Library of Congress, and who is author of the work on "Slave Manifest".

3 "Petition of Augustus Gideon and 150 others (Negroes of Georgia and Alabama) praying for aid to remove to Liberia", *House of Representatives MSS, 40th Congress,* Box 21 (Unnumbered bundle).

4 Mr. Carlisle to Mr. Burnley, Jan. 28, 1865, in F. O. 5, vol. 1014, *Public Record Office*, London. Carlisle said that Andrew Johnson and the administration were in favor of the scheme.

5 *First Annual Message* of his Excellency, Franklin J. Moses, Jr., Governor of South Carolina, to the General Assembly at the Regular Session of 1872-3.

6 *Message* of the Governor C. J. Madison Wills, of Louisiana to the General Assembly held in the city of New Orleans, commencing June 28, 1867.

7 "Report of Carl Schurz on the States of South Carolina, Georgia, Alabama, Mississippi, and Louisiana", Senate Executive Document, no. 2, *39th Congress, 1st Session;* Oscar Zerchner, "The Legal Status of the Agricultural Laborer in the South", *Political Science Quarterly*, LV, no. 3 (Sept., 1940) p. 412.

8 Charleston *Daily Courier,* Feb. 21, 1867.

9 *Ibid.,* Feb. 7, 1867.

10 "Emigration A New Phase", *Hunt's Merchant Magazine and Commercial Review 62* (January-June, 1870) pp. 115-18; "Industrial Association of Mississippi", *Debows Review,* vol. V, n.s. (January, 1868) p. 82.

11 *Southern Opinion,* Sept. 5, 1868, "Why is it done"; The Freedman's Bureau also was bringing Negroes from the Northeast to work in the South, "Report of Consul Donahoe at New Orleans", *Parliamentary Papers,* 1867, vol. 67, p. 280; E. Franklin Frazier, *The Negro Family in the United States* (Chicago, 1939) p. 447. Frazier records that "Negro mechanics outnumbered the white, at the close of the Civil War, five to one". See also, Sidney Andrews, *The South Since the War as shown by 14 Weeks of Travel and Observation in Georgia and the Carolinas, 1865* (Boston, 1866) p. 225. Andrews found that whites in the post war South not only did not work, but did not know how to work. Most of the artisans he saw were Negroes. Cf. *Southern Opinion,* June 15, 1867. "The Negroes of the South today are sober, industrious, honest and polite, and it gives us pleasure to bear testimony to their good conduct and deportment since their emancipation. We wish them well . . . "

12 *Southern Opinion,* October 26, 1867. "What Should be Done".

13 *Report* of the Commissioner of Agriculture for the Year 1879 (Washington, 1880) p. 152.

14 *Ibid.,* p. 147. Statistics on the percentage of decrease in the value of farm land show for Virginia 27%, North Carolina 30%, South Carolina 60%, Georgia 55%, Florida 55%, Alabama

60%, Mississippi 55%, Louisiana 70%, Texas 28%, Tennessee, 18%.

15 *Southern Opinion,* July 27, 1867.

16 Chapter II supra.

17 *Texas Constitution,* 1815, Art. 1, sec. 15, extended *1866; Alabama Constitution, 1818,* Art. 1, sec. 18 and *1865,* Art. 1, Sec. 22. Practically all such provisions ran "no person shall be imprisoned for debt", and were usually to be found in the Bills of Rights of the new constitution.

18 *North Carolina Code, 1883,* Ch. 4 (Citing acts 1866-7).

19 *Alabama Constitution, 1867,* Art. 14, secs. 1-7. These provisions, exempting $1,000 in property, did not become operative until July, 1868. *The North Alabamian,* Dec. 7, 1866, "Exemption laws"—This writer called the provisions class legislation designed to protect the well-to-do against the honest claims of the poor.

20 *Message No. 1* of His Excellency Governor J. L. Orr with accompanying documents, November, 1866; see also *Message* of Governor J. W. Throckmorton to the Legislature of Texas, 1866.

21 *Mississippi Constitution,* 1868, Art. 1, sec. 11; *Georgia Constitution 1868,* Art. 1, secs. 18-19; *South Carolina Constitution,* 1868, Art. 1, sec. 20; *North Carolina Constitution,* 1868, Art. 1, sec. 16. Some of these include in their provisions a statement on "contracts" to distinguish the kind of debt, and a few actually state the extent to which real and personal property must be surrendered.

22 *The Abingdon Virginia,* Oct. 28, 1870, citing new constitutional exemption of $2,000; Virginia Code 1887, Title 54, Sec. 3630 citing acts 1869-70, Ch. 54; *Message* of His Excellency Governor Harrison Reed to the Legislature of Florida in Extra Session June 9, 1869; *North Carolina Code* 1883, Ch. 4 (citing acts 1866-7, $500 exempt); *Message* of Robert K. Scott, Governor of South Carolina with accompanying documents submitted to the general Assembly of South Carolina at the Regular Session Nov. 1869—Homestead $1,000 with its procedure and $500 in personal property for each family head; *Message* with accompanying documents of His Excellency Rufus B. Bullock, Governor of Georgia, to the General Assembly, read July 24, 1868—$2,000, gold value, in real estate and $1,000 in personal property exempt.

23 *The Abingdon Virginian,* Oct. 28, 1870, "Save Your Homestead"; *Southern Recorder,* March 23, 1869—see "Ordinary Office" advertisement in all of the Southern press for this period.

24 *Message* from His Excellency Governor Bullock, transmitting Reports of the Public Institutions, Aug. 15, 1870. Knowing Gov-

ernor Bullock's political situation, it may be presumed that the rescue of the planters had proved a boomerang.

25   Note 73 supra. It was Scott's idea that farmer and laborer were especially subject to the whim of the landlord who was "enjoying in comfort the munificent bounty of the State".

26   *Third Annual Message* of Governor Harrison Reed to the Legislature of Florida, Jan. 5, 1871.

27   Macon *Daily Telegraph,* April 1, 1866.

28   *First Annual Message* of His Excellency Franklin J. Moses, Jr., Governor of South Carolina . . . 1872-3; General Jno. A. Wagner, "European Immigration", *Debows Review,* n.s. III (Jan.-June, 1867) p. 525.

29   *Southern Recorder,* May 11, 1866.

30   *Message* of David P. Lewis, Governor of Alabama to the General Assembly, Nov. 17, 1873.

31   *Message* of the Governor of Louisiana to the General Assembly held in the city of New Orleans . . . Jan. 28, 1867.

32   "American Land Co. and Agency", *Debows Review,* n.s. I (Jan.-June, 1866) "ads". Chartered by New York State, the company was located no. 194, Broadway, New York City.

33   William B. Hesseltine, "Economic Factors in the Abandonment of Reconstruction", *Mississippi Valley Historical Review* 22 (1935) pp. 191-210; "Southern Immigration", *Little's Living Age* 95 (1867) pp. 679-81.

34   *Nation,* April 14, 1870.

35   Charles F. Fleischman, "Our Exhausted Lands", *Debows Review* n.s. III (Jan.-June, 1867) p. 539.

36   *Report* of the Commissioner of the General Land Office to the Secretary of the Interior for the Year 1869 (Washington, 1878). The Land Office was prepared to offer settlers, under government regulations, 80 acres at the fee of 10 or 11 cents per acre; Robert Somers, *op. cit.,* p. 22, on the situation in Virginia; Mr. Acting Consul Bennett reported that only one third of the land of Georgia cultivated before the War, was under cultivation in 1868. *Parliamentary Papers* LX, 1868, p. 69.

37   *Laws of the State of Mississippi passed at a Called Session of the Mississippi Legislature,* held in Jackson, Oct., 1866—Feb. 1867.

38   *Debows Review,* n.s. V (Jan., 1868) p. 82.

39   *Daily South Carolinian,* Feb. 13, 1869.

40   *Southern Recorder,* Jan. 19, 1869.

41   *Southern Recorder,* April 13, 1869.

42   *Debows Review,* n.s. VII (July-Dec., 1869) pp. 699-701; *The Commercial and Financial Chronicle,* Oct. 6, 1866.

43   "Report of Mr. Acting-Consul Bennett on the Trade and Commerce of Savannah for 1868", *Parliamentary Papers* 60, 1868-69.

44   *The Knoxville Weekly Tribune,* June 1, 1884.

45   "Report of Mr. Consul Credland at Mobile for 1878", *Parliamentary Papers* 70, 1878-79, pp. 693-703. Congress had granted these lands to the railroad. The settlement was one of the busiest and favorite stations of the railroad.

46   *Nation,* April 14, 1870; for Charles Sumner's resolution and discussion against the trade see *Congressional Globe,* 39th Congress, 2nd Session, p. 483 (Jan. 16, 1867).

47   *Annual Message* of His Excellency Governor Wm. Pitt Kellogg to the General Assembly of Louisiana, Session of 1874 at New Orleans; *The Southwestern Advocate,* Dec., 1873. The state was in the throes of the bitter McEnery fight.

48   *Message* of Governor Edmund J. Davis to the Twelfth Legislature, April 28, 1870; see also the appeal in the Belton *Weekly Journal,* Nov. 5, 1870.

49   *Parliamentary Papers,* 1867, vol. 67, pp. 280, 385.

50   *Parliamentary Papers,* 1869, vol. 60, p. 247.

51   *Parliamentary Papers,* 1875, vol. 75, p. 459.

52   Robert Somers, *op. cit.,* p. 70.

53   *Parliamentary Papers,* 1875, vol. 75. Donahoe had been transferred to Baltimore. See Appendix A.

54   The system was borrowed from New York.

55   *The Richmond Whig and Advertiser,* Feb. 28, 1873, "Population, the Power of a Nation".

56   *The Jeffersonian Republican,* Dec. 22, 1880.

57   *Parliamentary Papers 1880,* vol. 73, pp. 352-353.

58   G. S. Callender, "The Early Transportation and Banking Enterprises of the States in Relation to the Growth of Corporations", *The Quarterly Journal of Economics* XVI no. I (November, 1902) pp. 111-162.

59   *Message No. 1* of His Excellency Governor J. L. Orr . . . Nov. 1866. On the situation in Georgia, see the "Report of Acting Consul Bennett".

60   *Message* of Jonathan Worth, Governor of North Carolina to the Called Session of the General Assembly, 1866. Worth admitted he knew little or nothing about banking and only made the suggestion as an attempt to get a bad situation straightened out.

61   Mr. J. J. Davis, "Report of the Committee on Banking and Currency Accompanying Bill H.R. 109 Authorizing National Banks to make loans on Real Estate", *46th Congress* 2nd Session, House of Representatives report No. 180—Series 1934.

62   Somers, *op. cit.,* p. 240.

63   Somers, *op. cit.,* p. 79, and Acting Consul Bennett's Report, note 59 supra. *Hunt's Merchants' Magazine and Commercial Review* carried regularly among its miscellany statements on southern firms like R. T. Wilson & Co., Commission Merchants and Bankers of Memphis, and the "Georgia Railroad and Banking Co." The insurance companies also performed banking functions.

64   *Ibid.,* p. 45 and "Report of Mr. Consul Walker at Charleston", *Parliamentary Papers* 60, 1868-9. "Report of Mr. Consul Lynn at Galveston", *Parliamentary Papers* 60, 1869, pp. 229-236. The "1st National" of Galveston and the "National Bank of Texas" were located in Galveston. Houston and San Antonio also had national banks. Of the private banks, of which Lynn submits a list, Galveston had 5, Houston 2 (one being an insurance company), Austin 2, San Antonio 3, and 12 others scattered about the State.

65   Charleston *Daily Courier,* Oct. 25, 1866, "To the Planters of South Carolina". Governor's (F. H. Pierpont's) *Message,* Richmond, Dec., 1866).

66   *The True Index,* Jan. 26, 1867. Somers, *op. cit., passim.* The banks charged from 18 to 24 per cent. See also John A. Pritchett "On the Policy of Usury Laws", *Debows Review,* n.s. VII (July-Dec., 1869) p. 655.

67   *Southern Recorder,* March 13, 1866. Alfred Johns "Report of the Committee of Agriculture of the Industrial Association of Mississippi, *Debows Review* n.s. V (Jan., 1868) 82; Oscar Zeichner, "The Transition from Slave to Free Agricultural Labor in the Southern States", *Agricultural History* XII, no. 1 (Jan., 1939) 22-32.

68   *Va. Code,* 1887, C. CXLI s. 2972, 2496 (citing act of 1858) and c. CX x. 2474-2498 (citing acts 1869-70 s. 2475); *N. C. Code* 1883 c. 41 (citing acts 1869-70 all improved property subject to lien) s. 1799 (citing acts 1866-7 c. I sl. On crops in favor of those making advances).

69   Somers, *op. cit.,* 240. This is undoubtedly the source of the Ku Klux Klan's proscription of Jews. As early as 1863 an English merchant observed that there were more Jews in Charleston than in Palestine. These Jews were in the trading business even then;

they dealt in the highly profitable wholesale merchandise and grocery business. Richard Bently, *Two Months in the Cotton Confederate States* (London, 1863) pp. 125-127; Edward King, *The Southern States of North America* . . . (London, 1875) p. 274. "The shrewd Hebrew, who has entered into the commerce of the South in such a manner as to preclude Gentile competition . . ."

70   *Debows Review,* n.s. VIII (Jan.-Sept., 1870) 187-8, "Agricultural Department".

71   The Greenville *Enterprise,* Feb. 21, 1872.

72   See Generally *Parliamentary Papers* 1873, vol. 64, R 191 et passim.

73   "Report of Mr. Consul Credland at Mobile", *Parliamentary Papers,* 1875, vol. 75, pp. 428-429. "Planters and farmers at last begin to see the necessity of diversifying their crops, for this plan makes them independent of the western states for food and keeps money in the state."

74   "Report of Mr. Consul de Fonblanque at New Orleans", *Parliamentary Papers,* 1875, vol. 75, pp. 435-459.

75   *Inaugural Message* of James L. Kemper, Governor of Virginia to the General Assembly, Jan. 1, 1874. Virginia had had three times the amount of currency before the War that she was allotted in the '70's. *Enterprise and Mountaineer,* Oct. 8, 1873.

76   *Annual Message* and Accompanying Documents of the Governor of Virginia to the General Assembly, Dec. 2, 1874.

77   *Belton Journal,* Jan. 16, 1879. Yet the idea was current in Texas that the national money policy had hurt business in the State. *Belton Journal,* Jan. 31, 1878—clipped from Houston Telegram, "Does Contraction Contract?"

78   *Enterprise and Mountaineer,* Nov. 26, 1873.

79   *S. C. Gen. Stats. and Code,* 1882 C. LXXI s. 1888. cf. *The Greenville Enterprise,* March 19, 1873, for early provision.

80   *N. C. Acts,* 1876-7 c. 2535 1.

81   *Alabama Constitution* 1895, Art. XIV, s. 1-7.

82   *Va. Code* 1887, title 54, s. 3653.

83   *Miss. Rev. Code* 1880 c. 45 s. 1244—given in Appendix C.

84   *Rev. Civ. Stats. of Texas,* 1895 title XLII c. 1. S. 2395-2402 (citing acts Aug. 15, 1870 & April 24, 1874), and Art. 2399 (citing Constitution) 1876, Art. 11, 5, 9) "Public Property of Counties, cities and town exempt from force sale". See also Appendix C.

85   *The Richmond Whig and Advertiser,* March 11, 1873. The farmers of Virginia had voted for a return to 6% interest rates, but the town element had voted against it. The farm element argued

that it increased their debt burden and made farm land a drug on the market. *The Richmond Whig and Advertiser,* Jan. 28, 1873, "Letters from the People". This writer, commenting on the Governor's message, as to the prosperity and increase in land values, pointed out that such was not the case in the Henrico County section. The farmers were poorer there than any time since the War. They could not sell their land. Money was not invested in land, but stayed in the cities among brokers and bankers where 2½ to 5% interest per month could be taken.

86   *Inaugural Address* of Governor Adelbert Ames to the Mississippi Legislature, Thursday, Jan. 22, 1874.

87   *Annual Message* of Governor J. M. Stone to the Legislature of Mississippi session of 1878.

88   *Biennial Message* of Governor Robert Lowry to the Legislature of Mississippi on Jan. 9, 1884.

89   Mr. M. R. Cooper, of Adams Run, Colleton County, S. C. *Report* of the Committee on Agriculture and Forestry on the condition of Cotton Growers in the United States, *Senate Report* no. 986, Part I, *53 Congress, 3rd Session.*

90   *Message* of Johnson Hagood, Governor of the State of South Carolina, to the general assembly delivered Wednesday, Nov. 23, 1881.

Chapter V: WESTWARD THE STAR OF EMPIRE TAKES ITS WAY

1   Chapter III supra.

2   *Thirty-Fifth Annual Report of the Philadelphia Board of Trade, Prepared for the Executive Council and Presented to the Association February 5, 1868* (Philadelphia, 1868) pp. 32-35.

3   Frederick Jackson Turner, *The United States, 1830-1850* (New York, 1935) p. 323; Henry Clyde Hubbart, "Pro-Southern Influences in the Free West, 1840-1865" *Mississippi Valley Historical Review* XX (1933-34) pp. 45-62; Avery Odelle Craven, *The Coming of the Civil War* (New York, 1942) p. 206, passim on the pivotal importance of the Baltimore convention of 1844; William E. Dodd, "The Fight for the Northwest, 1860" *American Historical Review* XVI No. 4 (July 1911) pp. 774-778; Ollinger Crenshaw, "The Speakership Contest of 1859-1860" *Mississippi Valley Historical Review* XXIX No. 3 (December, 1942) pp. 323-338.

4   Thomas M. Pitkin, "Western Republicans and the Tariff
n 1860" *Mississippi Valley Historical Review* XXVII (1940-41)
p. 401-420; F. W. Taussig and H. D. White, *Some Aspects of the
Tariff Question: an Examination of the Development of American
ndustries under Protection* (Harvard Economic Studies Vol. XII)
Cambridge 1931] pp. 301-315; Chester W. Wright, *Wool Growing
nd the Tariff* (Boston, 1910) pp. 139-152.

5   Philip Sheldon Foner, *Business and Slavery; The New York
Merchants and the Irrepressible Conflict* (Chapel Hill, 1941) p. 6;
Robert Greenholgh Albion, *Square-Riggers on Schedule; The New
York Sailing Packets to England, France, and the Cotton Ports.*
Princeton, 1938) pp. 50-52, 73-76; Robert G. Albion and Jennie
Barnes Pope, *The Rise of New York Port* (New York, 1939) pp.
5-121, at 105.

6   Frederick Jackson Turner, "Greater New England in the
middle of the 19th Century" *Proceedings of the American Antiquarian Society* XXIX (October 15, 1919) p. 238. *20th Philadelphia Board of Trade,* 1853 pp. 12-21. As early as 1853 Philadelphians, in the face of New York competition, sensed the connection
between foreign and domestic commerce; and not only rejoiced
over the completion of the Pennsylvania Railroad to Pittsburgh, but,
n the request of the Cincinnati Chamber of Commerce, memorial-
zed Congress to improve the Ohio-Mississippi waterway. *28th
Philadelphia Board of Trade,* 1861 pp. 25-87: In October of 1860,
at the invitation of the Pennsylvania Railroad, Board members
pent three weeks visiting Cleveland, Chicago, Milwaukee, St.
oseph, St. Louis, Louisville, Lexington, and Cincinnati, and re-
urned warmed by the successful contacts. Realizing that they had
he shortest direct route to the west, Board members were urged
o see to it that trade did not go thence through "other hands".
863 (*30th Philadelphia Board of Trade* 1863, pp. 24-25) found
Philadelphia merchants quite jubilant over the "Southwest Trade"
pened by the successes of Lincoln's Legions. *Annual Report of the
Chamber of Commerce of the State of New York for the Year 1859*
New York, 1859) p. 12; *9th N. Y. Chamber of Commerce 1866-
7,* pp. 79-85. In an effort to show that the foreign commerce of
New York loomed large in the National total, exports 37%—imports
5% and still growing, the secretary of the New York Chamber ob-
erved that "This must continue to be the case as long as New York
urnishes to the consumer and producer of the west, ample facili-
ies for the transportation of merchandise and produce to and from
he mouth of the Hudson". By 1866 Elliot C. Cowdin, during his

remarks on the Paris Exposition to be held the following year
voiced the dominant attitude thus: "This broad belt of country
some 2,500 miles wide at its northern limit, between these two
rods (placing the rods on the map), one you will observe, lying
upon the Allegheny and the other upon the Rocky mountains, in
the valley of the Mississippi. In the comparison you see that all
the valleys of the Atlantic slope do not amount to much. It is the
largest, and in all respects the richest valley upon the globe, and a
very few decades more will suffice to concentrate there the wealth
and the population, and the power of the Republic. From it New
York must draw that commerce which will make her the largest
and most significant city upon the globe."

7   *6th N. Y. Chamber of Commerce* 1864, pp. 28, 30-31; *Boston
Board of Trade, 1864, Tenth Annual Report of the Government
Presented to the Board at the Annual Meeting, on the 13th of
January, 1864* (Boston, 1864) pp. 25-32. According to Lorenzo
Sabine, Boston's Board's great secretary, fourteen Senators and eight
members of the House of Representatives were in attendance at Chi
cago, among whom were Senators Charles Sumner and Henry Wil
son, and seven Massachusetts congressmen.

8   Isaac N. Arnold to John Austin Stevens, Jr., Washington
March 4, 1863.

9   Honorable Sidney P. Ingraham, Jr., member of the Chamber
and of the State Legislature, kept the Chamber informed on these
matters. See Special Meeting of the Chamber February 18, 1864.

10   *31st Philadelphia Board of Trade 1864* p. 9.

11   Taylor himself proposed three Pacific railroad lines, north
middle, and south.

12   Chapter II supra.

13   *Boston Board of Trade,* 1866 p. 15.

14   *Ibid.,* pp. 24-41; John F. Beaty, Sec., *8th Annual Statement
of the Trade and Commerce of Chicago for the year ending March
31, 1866.* Reported to the Chicago Board of Trade (Chicago
1866) p. 9.

15   In the St. Louis Delegation was Hon. H. T. Blow, member
of Congress, as was Hon. William A. Howard, of the Michigan
delegation. Hamilton Hill of Boston's entertainment committee
arranged visits to the navy yard, the Athenaeum; constant open
house at the "Union" Club, trips to the suburbs of Brookline
and Watertown, concerts at the Music Hall, trips to the Lowell
Mills and to Lawrence, a banquet at Faneuil Hall, excursions in
the harbor to Fort Warren, and finally a banquet at the Revere

house, ending with E. O. Stannard of St. Louis proposing three cheers for the Boston mayor and business men and the singing of 'Auld Lang Syne". Whether such efforts were successful or through the lack of imagination, this pattern of entertainment was to be repeated by every Board or Chamber inviting their fellow businessmen as guests.

16 *Proceedings of the Commercial Convention held in Detroit, July 11, 12, 13, 14, 1865* (Detroit, 1865) p. 3 et passim; *33rd Philadelphia Board of Trade,* 1866 p. 15, and appendix pp. 1-12; *12th Boston Board of Trade 1866* pp. 41-51, 58; *5th Boston Board of Trade,* 1859, pp. 30-31; *8th N. Y. Chamber of Commerce 1866,* pp. 35, 66-67; *26th Philadelphia Board of Trade,* 1859, pp. 46-47; *8th Chicago Board of Trade,* 1866, p. 9.

17 Aspinall further advocated the modification, not the voiding, of the reciprocal trade treaty with Canada, the improvement of the St. Lawrence waterway, a ship canal around the American side of Niagara, and a uniform decimal system of weights and measures.

18 Walbridge was the inveterate delegate from New York to most of these gatherings. Honorable Hannibal Hamlin of Maine, Liconln's first Vice President, was elected Vice President-at-large, as was Honorable Charles Walker of Illinois; each state represented also had a Vice President. William Lacy of New York, Ray Hadlock of Michigan, and Adam Brown of Canada were elected secretaries. The rules of procedure of the House of Representatives were adopted, as at Chicago two years previously, as the rules of the convention. The Canadians had the good sense to participate in the discussion, but refrained from voting.

19 The English Board of Trade, established in its *present* form by an order of the council in 1786, has the formal title, "Committee of the Privy Council for Trade". Though it exercises its jurisdiction in Scotland as well as England, it has lost some of its functions to the Ministry of Transport and Labor. However it controls patents, weights and measures, foreshores belonging to the Crown, Administration of Laws relating to wrecks, to copyrights, to companies and bankruptcy, to gas undertakings, and to merchant shipping. The Board also publishes statistical and other information on commercial subjects, relating to Great Britain and other countries. *Encyclopaedia Britannica, X.*

20 *12th Boston Board of Trade,* 1866 p. 59; *8th N. Y. Chamber of Commerce,* 1866, pp. 66-67.

21 *14th Boston Board of Trade,* 1868, p. 116.

22   *10th N. Y. Chamber of Commerce,* 1867-68, pp. 18, 28
18th Boston Board of Trade, 1868, p. 59. Prominent Boards of
Trade and Chambers of Commerce had asked, in the spring of
1867, the New York Produce Exchange to issue a call for the national commercial convention and suggested Cleveland, Ohio, as
the place of meeting. The idea failed. Then the Detroit Board
started the movement again in October, 1867. Detroit merchants
reminded Boston of her mandate in 1865 and suggested Boston
as the meeting place.

23   *34th Philadelphia Board of Trade* 1867, p. 14.

24   *33rd Philadelphia Board of Trade,* 1866, p. 18; *34th Philadelphia Board of Trade,* 1867, pp. 15, 126-127; *11th Boston Board
of Trade,* 1865, pp. 32-36; *24th Boston Board of Trade,* 1876, pp.
19-20.

25   "The Report of Mr. Acting Consul Bennett on the trade
and commerce of Savannah", *Parliamentary Papers,* 1868-69, Vol.
60, p. 237; "Report of Mr. Consul Walker on the trade and commerce of North and South Carolina", *Parliamentary Papers,* 1868-
69, Vol. 60, p. 56; Somers, *Op. Cit.,* pp. 14, 171. Cornelius Attwood
Boston's Board's secretary in 1878 commented on the problem
thus: "Upon the reopening of the southern ports to trade, steam
lines were established from this port, as well as from New York
and a prosperous business was transacted at the outset. But the
South replenished their exhausted supplies, the demand was greatly
diminished, the steamers were also brought into competition with
the railroads which had been constructed and, as a consequence
serious losses were made. Some lines from here as well as New
York sunk nearly their entire capital, and all the lines from
this port were discontinued. At the present we have one line of
steamers in the Savannah trade."

26   *Chicago Tribune,* November 30, 1865. "Boston and the
West—What's the matter with Boston."

27   *13th Boston Board of Trade,* 1867, p. 32, Charles G. Nazro
was making his inaugural address as the Board's new president
January 9, 1867.

28   The roads involved were: (1) "The Red Line", via Albany,
Buffalo, and Toledo to Chicago; "The Blue Line", via Albany,
Suspension Bridge, and Detroit to Chicago; and the "White Line",
via Albany, Buffalo, and Cleveland to Cincinnati and St. Louis.
14th Boston Board of Trade, 1868, pp. 27-28.

29   *15th Boston Board of Trade,* 1869, p. 20. The appeal went out to the railroads that they make their east-west rates conform 'with those ruling in cities with which we are in direct competition".

30   *22nd Boston Board of Trade* 1876, pp. 10-11; *24th Boston Board of Trade* 1878, p. 25.

31   Note 6 supra.

32   *32nd Philadelphia Board of Trade,* 1865, p. 27. The merchants claimed to feel that Congress owed this boon to east Tennessee because of its loyalty during the war; and besides it was a sound military measure.

33   *37th Philadelphia Board of Trade* 1870, pp. 72-73-74.

34   *34th Philadelphia Board of Trade* 1867, pp. 32-35.

35   Note 33 supra.

36   *35th Philadelphia Board of Trade,* 1868, pp. 10-11. On the address of Samuel V. Merrick the Executive Council extended the operation of the law as George H. Morgan had suggested. By the wholesale dealers license tax, imported goods to Philadelphia through New York, directly or indirectly, amounted to $50,000,000 per year.

37   *14th Boston Board of Trade,* 1868, pp. 72-73, 100-101.

38   The purposes of the meeting were: The improvement of our inland and interior means of transportation; the adoption of a uniform system for the measurement of grain; the adjustment of the currency question in a manner which will reconcile conflicting sectional views, while at the same time promoting the welfare of the whole country; the restoration of the foreign commerce of the country from its present depressed condition; and the organization of a National Chamber of Commerce. W. M. Egan, President of Chicago's Board of Trade expressed a common idea when he said, "The perfecting of the organization has been left with the Boston Board of Trade, which is sufficient assurance that in all its parts it will be thorough and complete, *10th Chicago Board of Trade,* 1868, p. 11.

39   *Proceedings of the National Commercial Convention held in Boston,* February, 1868 (Boston, 1868) p. 27; *35th Philadelphia Board of Trade* 1868, pp. 21-34. *10th N. Y. Chamber of Commerce,* 1868, pp. 39-40. The states represented were New York, Pennsylvania, Illinois, Virginia, Ohio, Missouri, Wisconsin, Maine, California, Delaware, Massachusetts, Minnesota, Iowa, and Kentucky.

40   They were in order "3rd: the relief of our manufacturing and other great producing interest by reducing the burden of taxation; 6th: the speedy construction of the Northern Pacific Rail-

road; 8th: the Agriculture and manufactures of the country and the promotion and protection of these great national interests."

41   New England and the West clashed here. Boston's Nazro and Cincinnati's Covington took opposite positions. Covington was doubtless for it because of Cincinnati's anticipated trouble with Kentucky when she would begin her railroad southward.

42   So important is this statement as a part of the economic fiction of the new era that it is produced here in full. Under "Agriculture and Manufactures" the theory ran: "Resolved, that the natural market of agriculture is the home market, and that all the interest of this great and growing country should be so arranged as to harmonize, and that in a revision of the Tariff laws the duties should be so adjusted as to keep the balance of trade in favor of this country and at the same time afford the greatest protection to domestic labor and production by placing upon those articles in which labor constitutes the greatest proportion of cost the highest duties; thus encouraging the importation of the laborer instead of the completed fruits of his labor." The Philadelphia Board was supported in this move by the Commercial Exchange of Philadelphia and the Pittsburgh Board of Trade.

43   *15th Boston Board of Trade* 1869, p. 49; *36th Philadelphia Board of Trade* 1869, pp. 13-15; *11th N. Y. Chamber of Commerce* 1869, p. 60; *Proceedings of the First Meeting of the National Board of Trade held in Philadelphia* June 3 to 7, 1868 (Boston, 1868) pp. 30-38, 146-161, 181-183 and post index 1-7; *Proceedings of the First Annual Meeting of the National Board of Trade Held in Cincinnati,* December, 1868 (Boston 1869), pp. 250-60. Hereinafter cited as *National Board of Trade* (date).

44   *3rd National Board of Trade* 1871, pp. 27-36; *38th Philadelphia Board of Trade* 1871, pp. 16-17. The act provided that (Section 32) carriers into the interior must carry government custom inspectors at the carrier's expense. Boutwell (article 11 of Secretary of Treasury regulations) ruled that nothing but bonded goods could be carried in the railroad car for that purpose. Philadelphians found that Boutwell failed to inform custom authorities of the Bond put up by the Camden and Amboy railroad between New York and Philadelphia. Boutwell also, by a strict reading of Section 32 of his regulations on transshipment, ruled that the ferry trip from New York to Amboy was a violation of the law and thus could not be done without double bond. These regulations served to make the law inoperative.

The law may be found in *Revised Statutes of the United States ssed at the 1st session of the 43rd Congress* (with an appendix) d Edition (Washington 1878), title XXXIV collection of duties, hapter 7. Sec. 997, citing acts of 14 July, 1870 c. 255, s. 33, v. 16, 271.

45   *4th National Board of Trade,* 1871, pp. 231-235; *5th Na-onal Board of Trade* 1872, pp. 20-21; *7th National Board of rade,* 1875, pp. 211-213; *8th National Board* 1876, p. 10; *9th ational Board of Trade* 1877, pp. 104-117; *40th Philadelphia oard of Trade,* 1873, p. 15; *17th Boston Board of Trade 1871,* p. 78, 89, 90.

46   *38th Philadelphia Board of Trade* 1871, p. 12; *42nd Phila-elphia Board of Trade* 1875, pp. 89-91.

47   *11th N. Y. Chamber of Commerce* 1869, Part II, 58-59; 5th *N. Y. Chamber of Commerce* 1873, Part II, pp. 79, 96-105; 1st *N. Y. Chamber of Commerce* 1880, pp. 101-106; and Chapter I, post.

48   Edward King, *Op. Cit.,* p. 58. "The receipts from custom t New Orleans for 1872 were very much diminished by large ipments of goods in bond to the interior cities of Memphis, Nash-lle, Louisville, Cincinnati, Cairo, St. Louis, Chicago, etc., the uties on which were collected at those respectively"; *24th Boston oard of Trade* 1878, pp. 19-20. Cornelius Attwood, Boston's cretary observed: "I see no prospect of any resumption of our ade with the South. It was an important business for this port. ut the South now produces largely what was formerly sent to them, nd import direct their coffee and fruit; and the West supplies em with ice, wooden ware, furniture, fish, and the leading articles f merchandise which was sent from here. In New York the busi-ess has also changed to some extent, though while the steam lines ave been sustained in a measure to the different ports, the results ave been disastrous, and in a majority of cases the entire cost of e steamers has been sunk. I think that with the exception of erhaps a line to Galveston, every line has sustained a loss." Villiam F. Switzler, Chief of the Bureau of Statistics, Treasury Department, *Report on the Internal Commerce of the United tates,* submitted December 20, 1886, Part II of Commerce and Iavigation (Washington, 1886), pp. 679-681. Charles A. Sindall, ecretary of the Southern Railway and Steamship Association of tlanta, Georgia, "The development of the traffic between the outhern states and the northern and northwestern states." Sindall lso records the falling off of the coastwise trade from the eastern

seaboard to the South. Sindall observed, "The growth of busine[ss] from west to south and southeast has been of a much more marke[d] character than that from the eastern cities to the same territory . . [that] the rapid development of the South has been most profitable [to] western manufacturers." Sindall said that prior to the late 1870[s] eastern cities furnished the South with all of her furniture, agricu[l]tural implements, and goods of like character. Since that da[te] the West became so developed that fully 75 per cent of the furn[i]ture, farm tools and machinery used in the South was furnished [by] the West. Paints, oils, boots and shoes, and groceries were furnishe[d] from that quarter.

Chapter VI: IRON SLUICE GATES

1   See Chapter II supra.

2   The *Charleston Courier*, Monday, July 2, 1866, "Procee[d]ings" of a Railroad Convention held at Atlanta, Georgia, June 1[9-]20, 1866.

3   "Railroad Progress in the South", *Hunt's Merchant's Mage[?]zine* V:57 (Sept., 1867), pp. 174-177. See also Henry M. Flin[t] *The Railroads of the United States; Their History and Statisti[cs]* (Philadelphia, 1868), pp. 43-52, for trunk lines to the West an[d] South from the Northeastern cities.

4   Fairfax Harrison, *A History of the Legal Development [of] the Railroad system of the Southern Railway Company* (Washing[?]ton, D. C., 1901), pp. 15-18. (1st) Charleston to Memphis, opene[d] in 1857 (755 miles) with five lines; (2nd) Alexandria to Mobil[e] and New Orleans, opened in 1861 and 1870, respectively (121[?] miles) with eleven lines; (3rd) Louisville to Charleston, opene[d] 1859 (782 miles) with 14 lines operative in 1881.

5   *Ibid.*, pp. 19-21. Reference here is to such examples as th[e] Central Railroad and Banking Co. of Georgia, the Virginia Centra[l] and the Louisville and Nashville. See also Carl Russell Fish, *Th[e] Restoration of the Southern Railroads* (University of Wisconsi[n] *Studies* in the Social Sciences and History No. 2) (Madison, 1919[?] and Eva Swantner, *Northern Control of Southern Railroads durin[g] the Civil War.* (MSS Thesis in the University of Wisconsin, Ja[n.] 4, 1939) ; Samuel M. Derrick, *Centennial History of South Carolin[a] Railroad* (Columbia, 1930), Chap. XV.

6   H. W. Scholter (Asst. Treas.), *The Growth and Develop[?]ment of the Pennsylvania Railroad Company: A Review of [I?]*

Charter and Annual Reports, 1846-1926 (Dec., 1927), p. 151. The
investments were as follows:

Alexandria and Fredericksburg Railroad Stock	$ 31,600.00
Alexandria and Washington Railroad Stock	63,724.00
Southern Railroad Security Company	783,734.33
Richmond and Danville Railroad Stock and Bonds of the Atlanta and Richmond Airline Railroads with Collateral	1,164,997.00
Western Railroad of Alabama and Central Railroad of Georgia	600,000.00
Total	$2,704,055.33

The Pennsylvania Railroad, by an investment of $1,300,000, also
controlled a line of railroads from Cairo, Illinois, to New Orleans.
This investment proved profitable and allowed control for "commercial purposes" the whole line of railroad between the two points.
Bonds were held in the Mississippi Central (from Cairo to Canton,
Mississippi) and the New Orleans, Jackson, and Great Northern
(from Canton to New Orleans). The two were combined to form
the Chicago, St. Louis, and New Orleans Railroads Company,
which, when it defaulted its bond interest payments in 1876, was
reorganized and in 1882 was leased for 400 years to the Illinois
Central Railroad Company, becoming the latter's mainline between
Cairo and New Orleans.

7   *Organization and Charter of the Southern Railway Security
Company* (Dec. 4, 1871), pp. 4-5.

8   C. K. Brown, "The Southern Railway Security Company,
An Early Instance of the Holding Company", *The North Carolina
Historical Review*, VI: No. 2 (April, 1929), p. 160.

9   *Ibid.,* p. 159. The organization was as follows:

George W. Coss   *President*
(President of Pittsburgh, Fort Wayne,
and Chicago Railroad)
B. F. Newcomer   *Vice-President and Treasurer*
(Baltimore)

Directors

Thomas A. Scott	J. D. Cameron, Philadelphia
W. T. Walters, Baltimore	Daniel James, Liverpool
H. B. Plant, Augusta	R. T. Wilson, of the East
M. K. Jessup, New York	Tennessee, Virginia and
D. Willis James, New York	Georgia Railroad

10 H. W. Schalter, *op. cit.*, pp. 86, 110. The Pennsylvania Railroad controlled the Alexandria and Washington and Alexandria and Fredericksburg, running from Washington, D. C. to Quantico, Virginia, and had through traffic arrangements with the Richmond, Fredericksburg, and Potomac Railroad to Richmond.

11 Richmond Terminal Company and the Atlantic Coastline Company.

12 William Z. Ripley, Ph.D. Ed., *Railway Problems* (Boston, 1902), pp. 98-104. Statement by Mr. Powers, afterward Commissioner for the Southern Railway and Steamship Company.

13 William Z. Ripley, *op. cit.*, p. 99. There was an attempted agreement in 1873 between the roads centering in Atlanta, viz., the Central and Georgia, Western and Atlantic, and the Atlanta and Charleston Airline. These agreed to share the freight in cotton, with the accounts being kept by the Superintendent of the Western & Atlantic. The accounts resulting from this agreement which covered only the cotton season of 1873, were eventually settled after some delay and dispute. Southern road representatives also met in Macon, Georgia, in December of 1874, and in an adjourned meeting in January of 1875 where agreements were drawn up and provisional division of business between competitive points was agreed upon. Several other meetings of similar character were held in 1875.

14 "The New Southern Railway Programme", *The Railway World*, 4: Vol. 1 (October 23, 1875), p. 692. Mr. Fink was elected at the Atlanta meeting on October 6. The experiment of operating rival lines as parts of a single system without effecting complete consolidation was believed at the time to be the solution of the Southern Railway Problem. Fink originated the plan of action and accepted the post of General Commissioner, for six months, only to complete the organization and set it in motion.

15 The Commissioner General operated by the circular letter method. These letters have been collected in 24 volumes and constitute the chief source on the Association.

16   Joseph Nimmo, Jr., Chief of the Bureau of Statistics, *Report on the Internal Commerce of the United States*, Treasury Department, submitted December 1, 1879 (Washington, 1879), p. 86. "The changes in the course of southern commerce have resulted from the construction of railroads throughout the Southern states, the main trunk lines of which are directly tributary to the commercial interest of St. Louis, Louisville, and Cincinnati."

17   Nimmo, *Internal Commerce* 1881, p. 174 et passim; George R. Leighton, *America's Growing Pains, the Romance, Comedy and Tragedy of Five Great Cities* (New York, 1939) pp. 49-100. "Louisville, Kentucky, an American Museum Piece." The town was originally settled by English, Irish, Scotch and African stocks with an addition of Germans around 1860. This population base remained largely fixed since the great immigration waves did not touch the city. We have it on the authority of Debow that 50,000 transients visited Louisville each year from down river.

18   J. Stoddard Johnston Ed. *Memorial History of Louisville from its First Settlement to the year 1896* (New York, 1896) p. 104; see generally, Charles Henry Ambler, *A History of Transportation in the Ohio Valley* (Glendale, 1932), p. 265, passim.

19   Kincaid A. Herr, *The Louisville and Nashville Railroad 1850-1942* (Louisville, 1942) p. 1; John Leeds Kerr, *The Story of a Southern Carrier: the Louisville and Nashville* (New York, 1933) p. 6 passim; Thomas D. Clark, *The Beginning of the L & N: The Development of the Louisville and Nashville Railroad and its Memphis Branches from 1836 to 1860* (Louisville, 1933) pp. 16-17.

20   *Charter of the Louisville and Nashville Railroad Company with Amendment to 1869, together with the General Railroad Laws of the States of Kentucky and Tennessee;* James F. Tanner, *The Louisville and Nashville Railroad to 1868* (Unpublished Master's Thesis, the University of Indiana, 1933) ; Thomas D. Clark, *op. cit.*, pp. 22-23; (4th sic) *Report of the Railroad Commission of Kentucky to November 30, 1883* (Property of the State of Kentucky, Frankfort, 1884), pp. 174-180: The Louisville and Nashville was incorporated by Legislative act of March 5, 1850, under its name. The authorized capital stock was $3,000,000 at $100 per share, with the understanding that capitalization might be increased $1,000,000 (Act of 1859). The Road was given power to build to the Kentucky line, and Tennessee by act of December 15, 1851, to connect not only anywhere on the Mississippi, but specifically at Memphis in the direction of Louisville. Acts of 1854, 1856, 1864, 1868, the Road had privileges of a Land Company; the right to

extend any branch and purchase and hold any road; to acquire land for stone quarries, coal, and timber reserves; by majority vote of Board of Directors may acquire interest in, unite or consolidate with any railroad company or companies chartered by the laws of another state, etc.

21   "The Chicago, Indianapolis, and Louisville, Railroad Company", *The Monon Outlook*, 1: No. 4 (October, 1939), p. 445; Charles E. Fisher, "The Early Railroads of Kentucky", *The Railway and Locomotive Historical Society Bulletin*, No. 5, pp. 7-15. John Leeds Kerr, *op. cit.*, pp. 12-13.

22   Thomas D. Clark, *op. cit.*, pp. 27-28. "By an act of the Louisville city council, the city subscribed $1,000,000 to the capital stock of the company. This was to be paid over a period of thirty years, the paid in capital to bear six per cent per annum. The capital for this subscription was raised by taxation, and the stock of the company distributed pro rata as tax receipts", pp. 23-24. The Road, as chartered, was due more to the influence of the citizens of Louisville than to the various counties and the state.

23   E. Merton Coulter, "Effects of Secession Upon the Commerce of the Mississippi Valley", *Miss. Valley Hist. Rev.* III (1916) pp. 284-285; Charles R. Wilson, "Cincinnati, a Southern Outport in 1860-1861?", *Miss. Valley Hist. Rev.* XXIV (1937-8) pp. 473-482; R. S. Cotterill, "The Louisville and Nashville Railroad, 1861-1865", *American Historical Review* (Reprint) XXIX, No. 4 (July, 1924) pp. 700-715; George R. Leighton, *op. cit.*, p. 64.

24   E. Merton Coulter, *The Civil War and Readjustment in Kentucky* (Chapel Hill, 1926), pp. 239-245.

25   Kincaid Herr, *op. cit.*, p. 22. *Tennessee Commissioners on the Louisville and Nashville Railroad, 1865,* "Settlement with the Louisville and Nashville Railroad Company", Report of A. J Fletcher, Sec'y of State, S. W. Hatchett, Comptroller, Thos. H Caldwell, Att'y Gen'l, and A. W. Hawkins, Commissioner of Roads *Annual Report* of the President and Directors of the Louisville and Nashville Railroad Company commencing on the 1st of July, 1865 and ending on the 30th of June 1866 (Louisville, 1866) pp. 7-8.

26   John W. Clark and Bro. Ed., "Annual Review of the Trade and Commerce of Louisville for the Year Ending March 31, 1866" *Supplement to the Louisville Letter Sheet Price-Current* (Louisville 1866) p. 7 et passim; Young E. Allison, *The City of Louisville and a Glimpse of Kentucky* (Louisville, 1887) p. 4; J. Stoddard John ston, *op. cit.*, p. 249. "In 1862 the present Board of Trade wa organized by leading merchants, manufacturers and business mer

of Louisville who had become convinced that it was necessary for their mutual protection."

27   Edward King, *The Southern States of North America: Journey through Louisiana, Texas, Indian Territory, Missouri, Arkansas, Mississippi, Alabama, Georgia, Florida, South Carolina, Kentucky, Tennessee, Virginia, West Virginia, and Maryland* (London, 1875) pp. 708-709.

28   E. Merton Coulter, *op. cit.*, p. 354; George R. Leighton, *op. cit.*, p. 58 et passim; M. Joblin and Co. Comp., *Louisville Past and Present: Its Industrial History as Exhibited in the Life Labors of Its Leading Men* (Louisville, 1875), II, p. 333; *First Annual Report of the Louisville Board of Trade for the Year Ending December 31, 1879* (Louisville, 1880).

29   Thomas W. Herringshaw, *Herringshaw's Encyclopedia of American Biography of the 19th Century* (Chicago, 1905) p. 689; M. Joblin and Co., *op. cit.*, p. 83; Lewis Collins, *Collins' Historical Sketches of Kentucky* (History of Kentucky, revised by Richard H. Collins) (Louisville, 1924) II, p. 395.

30   E. Polk Johnson, *A History of Kentucky and Kentuckians; the Leaders and Representative Men in Commerce, Industry, and Modern Activities* (Chicago, 1912) II, p. 805; Josiah Stoddard Johnston, *op. cit.*, II, p. 325; *First Annual Report of the Louisville Board of Trade for the Year Ending December 31, 1879* (Louisville, 1880).

31   *First Annual Report of the Louisville Board of Trade for the Year Ending December 31, 1879* (Louisville, 1880). Young E. Allison, *The City of Louisville and a Glimpse of Kentucky* (published under the direction of the Committee on Industrial and Commercial Improvement of the Louisville Board of Trade, 1887) (Louisville, 1887), p. 144.

32   Johnston, *op. cit.*, II, p. 655; John W. Clark & Bro., *op. cit.*, Wicks was also Director of the Merchants National Bank, Southern Mutual Life Insurance Company, and President of the Louisville Cotton Exchange.

33   John W. Clark and Bro., *Louisville Trade 1866* (Louisville, 1866); *First Annual Report of the Louisville Board of Trade for the Year Ending December 31, 1879* (Louisville, 1880). Father and son have the positions of members of finance committee and executive, respectively, by these records. S. J. Clark Publishing Company, *History of Kentucky, the Blue Grass State* (Chicago and Louisville, 1928) IV, pp. 316-319. The Robinsons were reputed to have one of the largest hardware houses in the South. Johnston, *op. cit.*,

p. 653; *Louisville Fifty Years Ago:* A souvenir issued on the occasion of the Louisville Board of Trade luncheon on March 9 in honor of firms that have been in business fifty years or more, 1873-1923 (Louisville, 1923).

34   *Who Was Who in America,* I, 1897-1942 (Chicago, 1942) p. 266.

35   S. J. Clark Pub. Co., *op. cit.,* III, pp. 5-9; Y. E. Allison, *op. cit.,* p. 72.

36   Johnston, *op. cit.,* II, p. 945.

37   *First Louisville Board of Trade, 1879* (Louisville, 1880); *The National Encyclopedia of American Biography,* XVI, p. 28; S. J. Clark Pub. Co., *op. cit.,* III, pp. 828-831.

38   Johnston, *op. cit.,* II, p. 637.

39   *Ibid.,* pp. 972-3. No listing of Louisville's commercial great would be complete without mention of John B. McFenan, capitalist and stock breeder; John T. Gathright, saddler; Bennett H. Young of the L & N; Samuel L. Avery, farm implements and banking; John P. Morton, publishing house; James S. Lithgow, capitalist; Governor Helm, of the L & N as was E. D. Standiford; George D. Prentice and Henry Watterson; and finally C. Bamberger and Nathan Bloom, whose house had "the largest trade in jeans done in the world".

40   *Annual Report* of the Board of Trade and Merchants Exchange of the Commerce and Trade of Louisville, for the Year Ending March 31, 1867 (Louisville, 1867) p. 11.

41   Annual Report of the President and Directors of the Louisville and Nashville Railroad commencing on the 1st of July, 1869 and ending on the 30th of June, 1870 (Louisville, 1870) pp. 7-9, 22; *Annual Report* of the Board of Trade and Merchants Exchange of the Commerce and Trade of Louisville, for the Year Ending March 31, 1869 (Louisville, 1869) pp. 7, 12-13, 18, 60-63. Colonel Blount on April 7, appeared before the Board for backing of a scheme to push the L and N connection through to Pensacola, Florida. Though freight rates and facilities for handling, storing, receiving, and forwarding cotton had improved and increased, the anticipated direct trade in the staple had not been fully realized. However, the auctioning of cotton in the Louisville market was established March 23, 1866, and with the growth of cotton factories in the city, the merchants looked forward to its becoming a leading market.

42   The Board instructed Kentucky senators and representatives to seek for reduction of taxes on tobacco and liquors and hoped to

have the same success here as they had in initiating the move for the abolition of the cotton tax; on July 23, 1869, sent a telegram to the President asking him to sign the bill. The Board also asked for government action in removing obstructions from the Mississippi and its tributaries before the National Board of Trade and took a strong stand for the making of Louisville an internal port of entry. Nimmo, *Internal Commerce 1879*, Appendix No. 14. Information furnished by Mr. C. H. Pope of Louisville in regard to the transportation, commercial, and manufacturing interest of that city, in reply to inquiries addressed to him by the Chief of the Bureau of Statistics, June 30, 1879, p. 125. "It is probable that in 1869, or shortly thereafter, her (Louisville's) purely distributative commerce attained a maximum; . . . these exports attained a maximum in 1869 and 1872 when their amount via Louisville, Nashville, and Great Southern Railroad was 228,000,000 pounds for the year ending June 30, 1872.

43 John L. Kerr, *op. cit.*, p. 37 et passim; Kincaid Herr, *op. cit.*, pp. 27-31.

44 Raymond B. Nixon, *Henry W. Grady, Spokesman of the New South* (New York, 1943) pp. 167-68. The Bureau of Railroad Economics, Washington D. C. has in its file (No. 15213) an undated typed transcript from the *Graphic* entitled "Mr. H. Victor Newcomb—The Great L & N Railroad Combination". Internal evidence shows that the article was written around 1880. The author is unknown.

45 *Ibid.*, H. D. Newcomb, born in Massachusetts had come to Louisville early in life and crowned a successful career as a wholesale grocer with aiding Guthrie in building the L & N. H. Victor was born in Louisville in 1844. After completing his education, H. V. traveled in Europe, where, with his passion for finance, he devoted himself in London and the continent to the study of commercial methods and operations and the investigation of English financial institutions. It was shortly after his return that he discovered that his father was in serious difficulties.

46 Raymond B. Nixon, *op. cit.*, pp. 169, 171-72, 182, 185-86. The notion was current that to purchase control in the *Atlanta Constitution*, Grady lent his pen both to Newcomb's railway scheme and the candidacy of Justice Stephen J. Field, brother of Cyrus Field. Newcomb encouraged a loan from Cyrus Field of $20,000 and showed Grady how it could be paid back by playing L & N stock in the New York market.

47   For the broad scope of this program see "The Louisville &
Nashville . . .", *The Railway World* 4: Vol. VL (January 31, 1880)
pp. 105-106; and Editorial Comment (Feb. 21, 1880) p. 172;
Charles Mohn, *The Lands of the L & N Railroad in Alabama as
Homesteads for the Settlers* (Roberts & San Printers, 1884); "The
Louisville and Nashville", *The Railway World* 4: Vol. VI (January
24, 1880) p. 74. For the liberal charter grants of authority to the
L & N by Kentucky for this expansion see cited supra *Report* of the
Railroad Commission of Kentucky to November 30, 1883 (Property
of the State of Kentucky), Frankfort (1884) pp. 174-180. "Legis-
lative History of the L & N Railroad Company and Roads in its
System."

48   "The Louisville and Nashville", *The Railway World* 4: Vol.
V (April 19, 1879) p. 370 for the purchase of the Tennessee Division of the St. Louis and Southeastern (July 5, 1879); p. 638 for
the refusal of the directorate to allow the sale of 18,000 shares of
L & N stock owned by the city of Louisville; "The Louisville and
Nashville, and the Louisville, New Albany and Chicago" (Dec. 27,
1879) p. 1233 for the purchase of a controlling interest in the latter
company in the title by such "friends" of the L & N as Mr. Standiford, President of the L & N, R. S. Veech, Hon. Isaac Caldwell,
and their New York associates, John Jacob Astor, William Astor,
Robert L. Kennedy, Henry F. Vaile, and Samuel Sloan; footnote
46 for the purchase and/or control of the South and North Alabama; Mobile and Montgomery; Montgomery and Eufaula; Nashville, Chattanooga and St. Louis; St. Louis and Southeastern;
Owensboro and Nashville; Cumberland and Ohio; Cecilia Branch;
Western of Alabama; Central of Georgia; Western and Atlantic;
Macon and Brunswick. The total mileage of this combination was
3,572;—"Southeastern Connections", *The Railway World* 4: Vol. 6
(April 10, 1880) p. 345, and (April 17, 1880) pp. 368-369; "The
Southern Railroad Trouble—End of the Southern Railroad War",
The Commercial and Financial Chronicle, V:31 (Aug. 21, 1880)
p. 191, and (Aug. 28, 1880) p. 2117; (Dec. 11, 1880) p. 1188
for the determination to extend the L & N into Arkansas and Texas
by a syndicate which had chosen Texarkana as the terminus. For
the impact of the new L & N scheme on New Orleans after the
purchase of the New Orleans and Mobile Railroad, see Nimmo,
Internal Commerce 1880, pp. 100-102, Appendix No. 4, "Information in Regard to the Commercial and Transportation Interest of
New Orleans, furnished by Henry G. Hester Esq., Secretary of the
National Cotton Exchange under the date of November 6, 1870,

in reply to *inquiries* addressed to him by the Chief of the Bureau of Statistics". For an interesting sidelight on the L & N in politics, which came as a result of these combinations and controls, see the pamphlet, Jere Baxter, *Louisville and Nashville Monopoly: Its Methods and Purposes Exposed.* (The reply of Jere Baxter to Milton H. Smith.) This pamphlet is not dated but internal evidence reveals that 1893 is its probable date. This pamphlet deals with Tennessee, but there is some indication that the Alabama situation was equally as interesting—Reprint from the *Mobile Register,* Sept. 3, 1913.

49 In 1880 the mines of Alabama were paying in freight to the L & N $350,000 per year. For an example of aid to settlement by the L & N, see "Report of Mr. Consul Credland at Mobile for 1878", *Parliamentary Papers,* vol. 70, 1878-79, pp. 693-703. John G. Cullman, an influential German, bought 300,000 acres thirty-three miles south of Decatur and settled 600 German families thereon. The town was called "Cullman" and was one of the L & N's best stations.

50 Nimmo, *Internal Commerce 1879,* Appendix 14, p. 133. "Now in sending out solicitors for cotton shipments, many houses being both cotton factors and wholesale grocers, add to the duties of such solicitors, the duties of selling groceries. And it is true, in fact, that, throughout the entire South, cotton and groceries move through the same channels, but in opposite directions, so that very largely cotton goes where groceries come from."

51 *Ibid.,* p. 126. Order of distributive trade in importance: leaf tobacco, groceries and provisions, dry goods and clothing, whisky, distilled and malt liquors, hardware (including bar iron and steel), drugs, seeds and agricultural implements, wood and willow ware, caps and hats, boots and shoes, queens-ware, bagging, machinery, cotton, horses and mules.

52 First *Annual Report* of the Louisville Board of Trade for the Year Ending December 31, 1879 (Louisville, 1880) pp. 47-49. Board members suggested that a new line be built to tap the Texas area and thus create an airline from New York to Austin, Texas, which would be the shortest and quickest link to the Southern Pacific Railroad.

53 *Ibid.,* p. 50. Merchants agreed that if they intended to outstrip New Orleans and Memphis as a cotton depot, they must be more liberal in their credit policy to southern planters and storekeepers. See also, Second *Annual Report* of the Louisville Board of Trade for the Year Ending December 1880 (Louisville,

1880) p. 45, for an unsatisfactory conference by members of the Board with General E. V. Alexander of the L & N relative to the adjustments of freight rates to induce larger shipments of cotton to Louisville. The city handled only from 360 to 400,000 bales per year, of which only about 25,000 bales stopped for handling and reshipment. The remainder was in transshipment from other cotton markets, one-half of which being governed by Louisville bagging.

54 Nimmo, *Internal Commerce 1879*, Appendix 14, p. 126, and Nimmo, *Internal Commerce 1880*, Appendix 6, p. 160. There were in Louisville nearly 7,000 business houses of all kinds and sizes and about 700 manufacturing establishments, both with a volume of sales from $160 to $200 million. Louisville merchant capitalists found that the South was "essentially a market for cheap goods. Quality and finish there (could) be largely sacrificed, provided strength and cheapness (were) retained. In some classes of goods the sole requisite is the latter one. There (was) however (then) some disposition . . . to require quality in manufactured goods, though this tendency (was) not always accompanied by a corresponding willingness to pay a fair price for the requirement."

55 See note 53 supra. April 5, 1879, was the first meeting of the new Board.

56 J. M. Elstner & Co., *The Industries of St. Louis: Her Advantages, Resources, Facilities, and Commercial Relations as a Center of Trade and Manufacture, Together with a Delineation of Representative Industrial and Commercial Establishments* (St. Louis, 1885) pp. 10-23; George H. Morgan, *Annual Statement* of the Trade and Commerce of St. Louis for the Year, 1865 (Reported to the Union Merchants Exchange) (St. Louis, 1865) p. 5 "cut off from the Southern trade which had always sought a market in St. Louis; the trade of the Northwest diverted to other cities on account of the disturbed state of our affairs; the trade of our own state completely prostrated; it is not to be wondered at that the commercial interest of our city suffered deeply."

57 Edward King, *op. cit.*, p. 219. "The 100,000 freedmen have never constituted a troublesome element in the state; no political exigencies have impeded immigration or checked the investment of capital".

58 L. U. Reavis, *A Change of the National Empire: Or Arguments in Favor of the Removal of the National Capital from Washington City to the Mississippi Valley* (St. Louis, 1869) pp. 5-6. After citing figures Reavis states that "it is easy to be seen that the great preponderance of political power will soon be far removed

from the Atlantic slope" for it was plain that "the cohesive power of nationality demands that the ruling power of the nation be located in the midst of its material power".

59 Howard L. Conrad, *op. cit.*, V, pp. 594-98; Letter to the author with illustrated pamphlet from Eugene L. Johnson, Vice-President, the Shapleigh Hardware Company. Mr. Johnson's company acquired all of the assets of the Simmons Hardware Company July 1, 1940, on the surrender of the charter. Interestingly enough A. F. Shapleigh, founder of the Shapleigh Hardware Co., was a contemporary of E. C. Simmons and also built a great company. Mr. Simmons was director of the St. Louis National Bank, the National Bank of Commerce, The St. Louis Trust Co., and the Boatmen's Bank.

60 Howard L. Conrad, *op. cit.*, VI, pp. 53-54.

61 *Ibid.*, I, pp. 30-32.

62 Howard L. Conrad, *op. cit.*, II, p. 469. Fisk did not remain in St. Louis, but later went to New Jersey where he was prohibition candidate for Governor in 1886 and Presidential candidate on the same ticket in 1888. The now famous Negro College in Nashville, Tennessee, bears his name.

63 *Ibid.*, p. 39. Cobb came from a Whig family opposed to secession.

64 Howard L. Conrad, *op. cit.*, III, pp. 59-60.

65 James Cox, *Old and New St. Louis, A Concise History of the Metropolis of the West and Southwest, with a Review of its Present Greatness and Immediate Prospects, with a Biographical Appendix* (St. Louis, 1889) p. 322.

66 Howard L. Conrad, *op. cit.*, V, pp. 305-306.

67 Howard L. Conrad, *op. cit.*, V, p. 545.

68 James Cox, *op. cit.*, p. 310.

69 Howard L. Conrad, *op. cit.*, III, p. 509.

70 James Cox, *op. cit.*, pp. 175-76.

71 *National Cyclopedia of American Biography*, IV, p. 501. Bain was also president of the National Miller's Association. No account of the post-war capitalists of St. Louis would be complete without mention of John Wahl of Hesse Dormstadt, commission merchant, early large-scale lead dealer, insurance man and President of the Merchants Exchange. The same may be said of William J. Lemp, also of the important German element of the city, Union veteran, with interstate icehouse and brewing interests as far as Texas and international brewing interests in Mexico, South America, Hawaii, and Australia. Frank Gaiennie, Confederate veteran

from New Orleans, was public impresario extraordinary for the city and president of its Merchants Exchange as well as Vice-President of the National Board of Trade. See respectively Howard L. Conrad, *op. cit.*, VI, p. 310; *National Cyclopedia of American Biography*, XII, p. 36, and James Cox, *op. cit.*, p. 168.

72   George H. Morgan, *St. Louis Trade 1867* (St. Louis, 1868) pp. 7-12; George H. Morgan, *St. Louis Trade 1866* (St. Louis, 1867) pp. 10-78. The great famine in the South, the revival of the New Orleans cotton market, with prices rising as high as in the New York market, and treasury restrictions on removing cotton in bond all served to hurt the St. Louis market.

73   George H. Morgan, *op. cit.*, p. 540. "These organizations, sometimes designated as Boards of Trade, chambers of commerce, merchant's exchanges, grain exchanges, and produce exchanges, are organized to handle in the quickest and most economical manner the various commodities, to inculcate just and equitable principles of trade, to establish and maintain uniformity in commercial usages, and to acquire and disseminate valuable business information for their guidance as well as for their customers." The Merchant's Exchange was successor to the old St. Louis Chamber of Commerce organized in 1834 and chartered 1837. See also George H. Morgan, *St. Louis Trade 1868* (St. Louis, 1869) pp. 7-8; George H. Morgan, *St. Louis Trade 1869* (St. Louis, 1870) pp. 7, 11, 66, 75, and 78. It is interesting to note that the St. Louis grocers abandoned the pre-war method and now sold for cash and short credits at small profits. St. Louis was distributing, at this time in the Valley, dry goods, boots and shoes, queens-ware, groceries and other wholesales, manufactures (out of the combination of Missouri Iron and Illinois Coal to supply its seven furnaces in the production of good rail iron) and minerals.

74   George H. Morgan, *op. cit.*, p. 225. "The Merchants Exchange of St. Louis, while primarily a trading body, keeps close touch with all movements of a financial or commercial character affecting the interest of the city, states, or nation. Being careful and conservative in the consideration of all public questions, its opinions are given due consideration by legislative bodies and assist in securing the enactment of proper laws for the safe conduct of business."

75   Edward King, *op. cit.*, p. 230. This writer is indebted to this source for the full sketch that follows. As early as 1868 George H. Morgan began to carry the torch for a new Exchange building.

76   L. U. Reavis, *op. cit.*, p. 55; George H. Morgan, *St. Louis Trade 1869* (St. Louis, 1870) p. 10.

77   Edward King, *op. cit.*, p. 270.

78   *Ibid.*, pp. 233-34. There were over 550 disasters on the River and its tributaries and the annual destruction of property was enormous. For the lack of cooperation of New Orleans port authorities and shippers, see George H. Morgan, *St. Louis Trade 1870* (St. Louis, 1871) p. 26.

79   *Corporate History of the Missouri Pacific Railway Company and the St. Louis, Iron Mountain and Southern Railway Company and their Constituent Lines, showing mileage constructed by each, with dates of completion; also a brief outline of mileage operated under outright leases and trackage rights agreements, compiled pursuant to and in accordance with valuation order No. 20,* Interstate Commerce Commission, dated May 13, 1915 (December 31, 1915) pp. 62-113.

80   Howard L. Conrad, *op. cit.*, I, pp. 30-32.

81   George H. Morgan, *St. Louis Trade 1870* (St. Louis, 1871) pp. 14, 68. Thos. G. Meyer, Esq., Treasury of the St. Louis Cotton Factory was one of the leaders in making St. Louis a great inland cotton market, and listed the unfinished condition of the railroads south as a key factor preventing it. Others were no compress, no facilities for storing, and the St. Louis laws against storing cotton in certain parts of the town which discouraged insurance firms from underwriting crops protection.

82   Nimmo, *Internal Commerce 1879, Appendix 14,* p. 125. St. Louis had, before the Iron Mountain scheme, a Texas feeder in the Missouri, Kansas, and Texas Railway.

83   George H. Morgan, *St. Louis Trade, 1871* (St. Louis, 1872) p. 19. Hon. A. W. Mitchell, President of the St. Louis Cotton Association, was very optimistic about all of this.

84   George H. Morgan, *St. Louis Trade 1872* (St. Louis, 1873) pp. 7, 80; George H. Morgan, *St. Louis Trade 1873* (St. Louis, 1874) pp. 10-11, 80. Even though the panic hit the city broadside, merchant activity southward did not slack and cotton business boomed.

85   Allen held his interest in the road until 1880 when he sold it to Jay Gould for $2,000,000 cash. Allen also fathered Missouri's plan of state aid to railroads, and as a state senator was strong for internal improvements. Intensely interested in the city, Allen rebuilt the famous Southern Hotel and sponsored its street railways. He also endowed in St. Louis' Washington University, a professor-

ship in mining and metallurgy. Allen put up a fight for the control of his road in 1877-78. See pamphlet Thomas Allen, *To the Stockholders and Bondholders of the St. Louis, Iron Mountain and Southern Railway Company* (St. Louis, Oct. 20, 1877) for Allen's answer to the firm of S. G. and G. C. Ward, attorneys for Baring Brothers and Co. who wished to force the road into receivership. For the court's position, denying the motion, see *The Case of the Union Trust Company against the St. Louis, Iron Mountain and Southern Railway.* Important decision by Justice Miller, concurred in by Judge Dillon. The application for the appointment of a receiver denied (1878).

86   George H. Morgan, *St. Louis Trade 1874* (St. Louis, 1875) pp. 12, 59; *1875* (St. Louis, 1876) p. 90; *1876* (St. Louis, 1877) pp. 24, 65; *1877* (St. Louis, 1878) p. 59; *1878* (St. Louis, 1879) pp. 61-62; *1879* (St. Louis, 1880) pp. 12, 23, 101; *1880* (St. Louis, 1881) p. 82; Edward King, *op. cit.,* pp. 231-232. Mr. C. W. Simmons, secretary of the St. Louis Cotton Exchange listed the advantages of the St. Louis cotton market as follows:

"1st   From the fact that she is in a direct line from Arkansas and Texas to the East and Liverpool.

2nd   As the country merchants control the cotton they save exchange by shipping to where they buy.

3rd   St. Louis is the best point from which the planters and merchants can draw their supplies.

4th   St. Louis is above the yellow fever line, and the trade can be conducted the year round.

5th   The Cotton produced by the above states is of best quality, thus making our market desirable for both spinners and buyers.

6th   Our market, under its system of warehousing, can and does handle cotton cheaper than other markets.

7th   Our railroad facilities are better than any other cotton market.

8th   Our purchasers are North, East, Liverpool, and home."

Nimmo, *Internal Commerce 1879,* Appendix No. 6, p. 86.

87   Nimmo, *Internal Commerce 1879,* Appendix No. 14, pp. 133, 141-142. "This railroad, built largely by St. Louis capital, and operated entirely in the interest of St. Louis and against all interest opposed to St. Louis . . ." always "pursued a policy of enmity towards the Memphis and Little Rock, and Memphis and Louisville roads, sometimes refusing entirely to take freights from

hese sources and at all times giving preference in transportation to
$t. Louis merchandise." Stockholders of Allen's road finally bought
:ontrol of the Memphis and Little Rock: See *Railway World* 4:
Vol. 6 (Oct. 9, 1880) p. 972, and 4: Vol. 6, (Dec. 11, 1880) p. 1186.

88   Nimmo, *Internal Commerce,* 1879, p. 87.

89   Nimmo, *Internal Commerce 1881,* Appendix No. 3, p. 171.

90   William Smith, *Annual Review of the Commerce of Cincinnati, for the Commercial Year Ending August 31, 1864, reported
to the Chamber of Commerce by . . . Superintendent of the Merchants Exchange* (Cincinnati, 1864) pp. 22-23; hereinafter cited
viz., William Smith, *Cincinnati Trade, 1865,* pp. 5-6.

91   William Smith, *Cincinnati Trade, 1865,* p. 23. Cotton fell
off in the Cincinnati market in 1865. New York received most of
it from the Atlantic and Gulf cities after close of hostilities. Prices
spiraled downward with frequent fluctuations, and the business remained unsettled, unprofitable and dangerous to those engaged in it.

92   William Smith, *Cincinnati Trade, 1866,* pp. 23, 41, 46.

93   *Ibid.,* p. 8.

94   William Smith, *Cincinnati Trade, 1867,* pp. 6-7.

95   William Smith, *Cincinnati Trade, 1868,* p. 6.

96   William Smith, *Cincinnati Trade, 1867,* p. 7; and footnote
93 supra for the city merchant's reaction to the National Board
of Trade's meeting in Cincinnati. Note also, *Cincinnati Trade,
1869,* p. 6. The merchants sponsored Prof. Cleveland Abbe and his
weather report charts for the Ohio Valley and the Midwest. This
was a distinct innovation useful to the trading process.

97   See Chapter II supra.

98   Nimmo, *Internal Commerce, 1881,* Appendix No. 3. Information furnished by Mr. Sidney D. Maxwell, Superintendent of the
Cincinnati Chamber of Commerce, in regard to the commercial,
transportation, and industrial interest of that city in reply to inquiries addressed to him by the Chief of the Bureau of Statistics,
pp. 62-64. Mr. Maxwell's rather extensive collection of manuscripts are in the possession of his daughter, Mrs. Lewis Earle Lea,
353 Thrall Ave., Cincinnati, Ohio. Letters by this writer and by
Harlow Lindley of the Ohio State Archaeological and Historical
Society failed to secure their release to a competent library agency
or their use. Maxwell's long tenure as secretary of the merchants
organization and his friendship with leading Ohio enterpreneurs
makes this collection one of the most valuable in the business history
of the period.

99   Charles G. Hall, Ed., *The Cincinnati Southern Railway, A History* (Cincinnati, 1902) pp. 27-30. For the impact of railroads on Cincinnati's northwest trade. "Three lines of railroad now reached the eastern seaboard, putting the West in direct communication with New York, Philadelphia, and Baltimore; and traffic that had heretofore gone through Cincinnati, coming from Pittsburgh via the river, was now lost."

100   *Ibid.*, pp. 30-32. To break up this obvious discrimination "the Cincinnati Board of Trade kept a special representative at Louisville for the purpose of seeing that the transfer of shipments was not unnecessarily held back."

101   E. A. Ferguson, *Founding of the Cincinnati Southern Railway, with an autobiographical sketch* (Cincinnati, 1905) p. 126 et passim. The Cincinnati merchant community, in the immediate post war years, awoke to realization that the East-West rail lines were discriminating against the city in the matter of rates to the extent of practically destroying her participation in that trade—see *Cincinnati Trade 1868*, p. 7; *1869*, p. 7. See generally Ellis Merton Coulter, *The Cincinnati Southern Railroad and the Struggle for Southern Commerce, 1865-1872* (Chicago, 1922) passim.

102   Samuel H. Goodin, *Plan for the Construction of the Direct Railroad South, Connecting Cincinnati with the Southern System of Railroads (1868); Cincinnati Southern Railway: The Ferguson Railway Act, Views of the Press. Address of Committees, Action of Board of Trade and Chamber of Commerce, Record of the Case and Opinion of the Superior Court of Cincinnati and the Supreme Court of Ohio thereon* (Cincinnati, 1872) passim. Ford, *History of Hamilton County Ohio* (Cleveland, 1881) pp. 214-215.

103   E. A. Ferguson, *op. cit.*, passim; Charles G. Hall, *op. cit.*, pp. 47-48. Born in New York, Nov. 6, 1826; 1830 moved to Cincinnati with his parents. Educated in public schools and read law, history, political economy and classics with Henry Snow. May term 1848 admitted to bar. Married 1851 Agnes Moore, granddaughter of Adam Moore, early pioneer and leading merchant of Cincinnati. 1852 elected city solicitor. 1853-61 retained by commissioner of Hamilton county as legal advisor and participated in important street and steam railway cases. 1859 elected one of three State Senators of Hamilton County for 1860-1861. 1861 drew up act with General George B. McClellan under which was organized the Ohio volunteer force. 1861 retained by Cincinnati Gas, Light and Coke Company, and held it for thirty-three years. May 4,

1869, in his forty-second year, drafted the Cincinnati Southern Railroad Act.

104 *Laws of Ohio, Kentucky, and Tennessee Authorizing the Construction of the Cincinnati Southern Railway* (Cincinnati, 1881) pp. 1-9. For follow-up legislation in the matter see *Report of the House Judiciary Committee on House Bill No. 254* (John M. Fleming, Chairman) Nov. 30, 1869, declaring the spirit and letter of the Ferguson act unconstitutional. However, see *J. Bryant Walker, Solicitor, etc., Plaintiff, Against the City of Cincinnati, Trustee of the Cincinnati Southern Railway, et al., Defendants, Superior Court of Cincinnati* (26007) and footnote 101 supra.

105 Charles G. Hall, *op. cit.*, pp. 35, 45-48.

106 See note 102 supra.

107 Joseph Fletcher Brenson, Ed., *Biographical Cyclopedia and Portrait Gallery of Distinguished Men, with an Historical Sketch of the State of Ohio* (Cincinnati, 1879) pp. 92-93. Born in Kentucky Nov. 4, 1812; educated for a merchant, Bishop came to Cincinnati in 1848 and eventually built a $5,000,000 per year wholesale grocery business. He was in time common councillor and mayor of Cincinnati during the secession crisis, member of Ohio's Constitutional Convention, President of the Baltimore Commercial Convention 1871, College Trustee and Churchman, and Governor of Ohio 1877. Early agitator and subscriber to the Southern Railway Scheme, he largely handled the job of securing the Kentucky and Tennessee charters for the road.

108 George Wilson, Comp., *Portrait Gallery of the Chamber of Commerce of the State of New York: Catalogue and Biographical Sketches* (New York, 1890) pp. 76-83. Sherman was land speculator, investor in manufacturing schemes, and counsellor and director of many railroads, among which was the Pittsburgh, Fort Wayne, and Chicago. See also *D. A. B.* XVII, pp. 84-88.

109 Charles Theodore Greve, *Centennial History of Cincinnati and Representative Citizens*, II (Chicago, 1864) p. 126.

110 S. J. Clock Publishing Co., *Cincinnati, the Queen City Pictorial and Biographical* (Deluxe Supplement) II, (Cincinnati, n.d.) p. 245.

111 Charles Theodore Greve, *op. cit.*, II, pp. 57-60, 721.

112 *The Cincinnati Commercial Tribune*, January 16, 1898. Gano was interested in manufacturing, the Canal Elevator Co., Westinghouse Airbrake Co., Card Electric Motor Co., Economy Fuel and Steam Heating Co., and the Atlas Mining Co. Gano was also interested in insurance. He worked to extend the trade

relations of the city to South America and especially to the Southern states.

113   S. B. Nelson & Co., *History of Cincinnati and Hamilton County, Ohio* (Cincinnati, 1894) pp. 440½, 944. This man, as was most of the others in this chapter, was selected from the delegate list of the National Board of Trade.

114   *The Cincinnati Enquirer*, February 8, 1893; *The Commercial Gazette*, February 8, 1893; *The Cincinnati Times Star*, February 7, 1893.

115   Charles G. Hall, *op. cit.*, p. 36 et passim.

116   Edward King, *op. cit.*, pp. 530-535. In 1860 there were a number of furnaces worked in Dyestone Belt and excellent ore was produced. As an example of Post-war activity the case of General John T. Wilder of Ohio who noted possibilities while serving under Rosecrans (1863) is well taken. He returned with capital of $1,000,000 and opened Roane Iron Company and purchased a government built railmill in Chattanooga. Tunneling the Cumberland Mountain for coal, Wilder, by 1868, began to manufacture pig iron cheaper than it could be made elsewhere in the United States. It is also interesting that both President Lincoln and General Burnsides had considered building a line in the territory used by the Cincinnati schemers as a war measure. Surveys were made but time did not permit the completion of the project.

117   E. A. Ferguson, *op. cit.*, p. 67; R. Biggs, "The Cincinnati Southern Railway: A Municipal Enterprise", East Tennessee Historical Society *Publications*, VII (1935) pp. 81-102.

118   *Cincinnati Southern Railway: Memorial of Trustees and Speech of Hon. John C. Breckenridge to the General Assembly of Kentucky, and Proceedings of the Lexington Railroad Convention* (1871). Breckenridge, in his speech on January 25, 1870, claims he was not in the pay of the trustees, but spoke because East Kentucky was the widest part of the State with no Southern connection and the scheme would bring in capital and labor; thus the state would prosper.

119   *Cincinnati Trade, 1870*, pp. 6-8, 66; *Cincinnati Trade, 1871*, pp. 34, 54; *Cincinnati Trade, 1872*, pp. 24-29, 64.

120   *Cincinnati Trade, 1873*, pp. 42, 58-59, 81. These reports end Aug. 31, and hence a boom year is recorded for the city. All branches of trade prospered, and direct shipments of cotton to Eastern spinners, and Canada, and Europe was constant.

121   W. A. Gunn, *Surveys for the Cincinnati Southern Railway: Preliminary Report of the Chief Engineer* (March, 1873).

122 *Cincinnati Trade, 1874,* pp. 35-37, 58-59, 85.

123 Charles G. Hall, *op. cit.,* pp. 39-40. The final payment by the bank was made in May, 1875.

124 "Cincinnati Railway Projects", *Railway World,* 4: Vol. 1, (May 29, 1875) p. 343.

125 *The Cincinnati Commercial,* Jan. 30, 1876; Cincinnati Southern Railway (Petition) (Cincinnati, February, 1876) for Passage of Bates Bill authorizing the loan; *Cincinnati Trade 1876,* pp. 56-58, 88.

126 *Cincinnati Trade 1877,* pp. 56-57, 90. The rate war was still in full swing and the cotton trade was falling off.

127 "Railway Projects: Cincinnati Southern", *Railway World* 4: Vol. 2 (Oct. 7, 1876) p. 653.

128 *Cincinnati Trade, 1878,* pp. 28-29, 63-64, 98; *Cincinnati Trade, 1879,* pp. 64-65, 98-99. During the fight a race to push the road to Boyce Station to connect with the Western and Atlantic road six miles from Chattanooga before the court could act was successful. This effort proved needless.

129 Nimmo, *Internal Commerce, 1879,* p. 88; Nimmo, *Internal Commerce, 1881,* Appendix No. 3, pp. 63-64, 123-124; J. B. Killebrew, Commissioner, *Valuable Farms and Timbered Lands for Sale in the State of Tennessee, Registered in the Office of Bureau of Immigration* (Nashville, 1880).

130 "Completion of the Cincinnati Southern", *Railway World:* Vol. 6 (March 20, 1880) p. 270; E. A. Ferguson, *op. cit.,* p. 125; *The Cincinnati Commercial,* March 12, 1880—March 14, 1880— March 18, 1880—March 19, 1880; *Cincinnati Trade, 1880,* pp. 3-4; Cincinnati Trade List, *A Brief History of the Inaugural Excursion and Banquet Celebrating the Opening of the Cincinnati Southern Railway Connecting Cincinnati and Chattanooga, March 18, 1880* (Cincinnati, 1880); *Brief History of the Inaugural Excursion and Banquet, March 18, 1880* (Cincinnati, 1880); *Cincinnati Southern Railroad Banquet, Letters March 18, 1880* (Manuscripts) Ohio Philosophical and Historical Society.

Chapter VII: KNIGHTS OF THE BAG

1 Edgar White, "The Merchants of Yesterday", *The Sample Case* 50: No. 5 (May, 1917) pp. 339-40; William H. Baldwin, *Travelling Salesmen . . .* an address delivered before the Boston Young Men's Christian Union, November 22, 1874; Alexander

Strong MSS. A. C. 3798, Manuscript Division, The Library of Congress; L. P. Brackett, *The Commercial Travelers' Guide Book* (N. Y., 1871) p. 24.

2 L. P. Brackett, *op. cit.,* p. 24. It is interesting to note that agents for costly books or clocks were first in the field and usually sold very small orders, often at retail. Note also the nature of the orders in the pre-war South as revealed by the letters of Alexander Strong's agent, R. M. Beardeu in the Strong MSS. cited supra.

3 Edgar White, *Loc. Cit.*, p. 340. These collectors traveled in two-wheeled carts and stored the firm's collections in sacks in the cart, for there were no banks. In the Missouri area the barter of country foodstuffs was not acceptable in paying the local dealer's debt to the city merchants. Only the staples, tobacco, corn, and wheat were acceptable at the store for purpose of credit. However, before the Civil War the city collector was safe without a guard. During and after the War this was not so. The collector also made out an elaborate report to the firm on the local situation, crops, etc. This became a definite requirement of all agents in the field after the war, and their reports, then, constitute an untouched source of our history.

4 Edward P. Briggs, *Fifty Years on the Road,* the autobiography of a traveling salesman, (Philadelphia, 1911).

5 Charles H. Smith, "Introducing Another Grand Veteran of the Road", (J. Aaron of Pittsburgh, one of the first in New York State in the early '60's), *The Sample Case,* 63: No. 1, (July, 1923), p. 18; George F. Massey, "64 Years on the Road"—" 'Uncle Charlie' Terry still a 'live one' at the age of 87." *The Sample Case,* 63: No. 2, (August, 1923), pp. 13, 31, 32. Terry was a representative of the Aetna Insurance Company in Illinois and Missouri.

6 L. P. Brackett, *op. cit.,* p. 25 et passim.

7 L. P. Brackett, *op. cit.,* p. 26. The cities involved in this early period were San Francisco, Cincinnati, Chicago, St. Louis, Louisville, Memphis, New Orleans, Mobile, Charleston and Wilmington. These cities' jobbers supplied the back country merchants by using commercial travellers. The absence of railroad facilities forced many a traveller to make the country circuits on horseback.

8 Edward P. Briggs, *op. cit.,* pp. 48-49.

9 Frank Haitheax, "Reminiscences of an Old Time 'Drummer' ", *The Sample Case,* 74: No. 8, (May, 1929), p. 21. Recalling happy days selling in southern territory; James H. Canfield, "What I Think of Commercial Travellers", *The Sample Case,* 8: No. 3, (Sept., 1895), p. 11. This president of Ohio State University runs

a comparison of the agent of 1895 with his knowledge of them thirty years before when he was a railroad worker in Kansas, Iowa, and Minnesota; George L. Marshall, *O'er Rail and Crossties with Gripsack* (N. Y., 1891), p. 207 et passim for a clever description of a woman drummer. Edgar White, *Loc. Cit.*, pp. 339-340.

10 L. P. Brackett, *op. cit.*, p. 45 et passim; William H. Baldwin, *op. cit.*, passim.

11 James H. Canfield, *Loc. Cit.*, p. 11.

12 Nimmo, *Internal Commerce 1881*, Appendix No. 24, p. 208. The daily expenses of a travelling salesman were as follows:

Hotel Bill	$2.00
Railroad Fare	1.50
Bus and Porterage	.75
Postage and Telegrams	.25
Salary	5.00
per diem	$9.50

When heavy trunks were carried the expense would average from $1.00 to $2.00 per day greater.

13 *Ibid.*, p. 208; Frank Haitheax, *Loc. Cit.*, p. 21.

14 George F. Massey, *op. cit.*, p. 32; George M. Hayes, *Twenty Years on the Road* (Philadelphia, no date). (Internal evidence indicates written around 1880) Passim.

15 George L. Marshall, *op. cit.*, pp. 54-55. The classification above was given by a veteran in the calling to a reporter of the *Macon Telegraph*.

16 "Commercial Travelers and Taxes on Them", *Dunn and Bradstreets*, February 26, 1881: This source lists the following organizations with date and place of origin: Commercial Travelers Association of the State of New York (Syracuse, 1872); Michigan Commercial Travelers Association (Detroit, 1874); Merchants and Salesmen's Association (Philadelphia, 1874); Mercantile Benefit Association (New York, 1877-82); New England Commercial Travelers Association (Boston, 1877); The Northwestern Association (Chicago, 1875); Western Commercial Travelers Association (St. Louis, 1877). By 1880 these organizations had a total membership of 11,477. The Syracuse organization was the largest with 2,625 members; and the Chicago organization stood next with 2,500 members. Yet it was estimated that all these agencies represented not more than 12% of the Commercial Travelers in America.

17   A. S. Dodd, President, et al., *Descriptive Handbook and Abstract of the Advantages, Privileges, and Franchises of the Commercial Travelers National Association.* (New York, 1872), pp. 4-5. This handbook was issued from the general office, of this the first organization in the field, 944 Broadway between 22nd and 23rd Streets, New York. Certificates of membership were also to be had from the branch offices in Philadelphia, Baltimore, Cincinnati, Chicago, St. Louis, Louisville, Kentucky, New Orleans, Indianapolis, Peoria, Quincy, Bridgeport, Conn. This organization boasted special ticket rates for 30,000 miles of rail and water; more baggage free—150 to 200 lbs. instead of the usual 80 to 100 lbs; reduced rates in 1000 hotels; and a one-half rate arrangement with Western Union. The License-law-on-drummers-fight was wide open at the inauguration of this organization and they pledged to fight for abrogation. L. P. Brackett, *op. cit.,* Tables. This writer, in his Travelers' Guidebook, shows the type of information available to the average salesman. The tables run as follows:

    I. Towns on Railroads (400 folk or more)—Population in 1870 —Number and Kind of Stores and Manufacturers

   II. Towns Off Railroads (600 folk or more)—Population in 1870—Number and Kinds of Stores and Manufacturers

  III. Postoffices, Cities, and Villages having express or money order office

  IV. Rates of Postage to Europe, North and South America, and the British Colonies, 1871, and Domestic Postage

   V. Tariff of the United States for 1871

  VI. New Table of Stamp Duties, 1871

 VII. List of Best Hotels for Commercial Traveler's Accommodation with Board Price per Day

VIII. List of Leading Booksellers and Publishers to Guide Commercial Travelers in Selecting Reading Matter

  IX. Table of Population, Valuation of Real and Personal Estate, Capital Invested in Manufactures, Trade, and Commerce in each State and Length and Cost of Railroads in 1870

   X. Table of Principal Cities of the United States with a Population of 1000, showing Population in 1870, Value of Real and Personal Property, Capital Invested in Manufactures, and Amount of Annual Product for 1870.

George L. Marshall, *op. cit.,* pp. 121-123, "Salesmen and the Railroads". Here is registered a complaint against the roads.

18   T. Edgar Harvey, Ed. and Comp., *Commercial History of the State of Ohio,* (Columbus, 1916)—Issued by Columbus Council No. 1, United Commercial Travelers of America.

19   Nimmo, *Internal Commerce,* 1881, Appendix No. 23. "Statement prepared by Mr. F. B. Thurber, of the House of H. K. and F. B. Thurber and Co., of New York, in regard to the policy of conducting trade through the agency of commercial travelers", pp. 205-6; "Statement in regard to the employment of commercial travelers, by Mr. E. C. Simmons, President of the Simmons Hardware Co., of St. Louis," pp. 212-13. There is an interesting difference of opinion here as to the value of these agents which rested on a two-fold basis. The Thurbers were against "Travelers" because the grocery business sold on close margins and successful western competition by use of these agents was being felt in the east. Hence, the Thurbers favored sales in the New York house and by trade circulars. Simmons, like all hardware merchants sold on wide margins and enjoyed the business success that all Middle Western merchants were having at the South by the operation of their agents in the southern towns and back country.

20   See chapter III, supra.

21   Edward P. Briggs, *op. cit.,* p. 30 et passim.
Significantly Briggs observes, "The country, of course, was poor and it was necessary to extend very long credits to almost every buyer."

22   *Ibid.,* p. 34. "It was customary to take in payment notes running from four to eight months. The notes were generally timed so as to run until their crops were ready for the market. The chief money crop was cotton and the customer was sometimes carried from one year to the next. The notes were discounted and in cases when they were not paid when due we had to send our check to take up the note."

23   See Chapter V supra.

24   L. P. Brackett, *op. cit.,* p. 26. "The competition in most classes of goods is now so active, that the wholesale prices of goods in St. Louis, Chicago, or Cincinnati are not, if freight be included, materially higher than the same line of goods in the great Atlantic cities." This author attributes the fall of retail prices in the interior to the competition of commercial travellers. However, he concedes that improved transportation was a minor factor.

25   Nimmo, *Internal Commerce,* 1881, Appendix No. 26, pp. 212-13. The Simmons House's greatest trade strength was in the

upper Mississippi Valley to the East, and Missouri, Kansas, Arkansas, and Texas on the West.

26   *Ibid.*, p. 212. Simmons stated that 19/20 of their trade was carried over railroads because of the quickness of distribution afforded. "Merchants", he said, "will buy goods from points where they will reach them quickest. Take, for instance, Corsicana, Texas. The all rail rate from St. Louis is $1.25 to $1.50 per 100 pounds, and from New York by Morgan line it is but 50 to 75 cents per 100 pounds; still, on account of the quicker transportation, the merchants buy more of their goods in St. Louis and ship by rail."

27   *Ibid.*, 213. "Throughout the states south of the Ohio and east of the Mississippi River, viz., Kentucky, Tennessee, Mississippi, Alabama, Georgia, Louisiana, and some little in North Carolina, we meet the competition of Louisville and Cincinnati merchants and also a very vigorous competition from New York."

28   Thomas D. Clark, *Pills, Petticoats, and Plows: the Southern Country Store 1865-1915* (Indianapolis, 1944), pp. 109-123; *Belton Journal,* (Texas) January 2, 1879—note the ads in this paper asking for agents to sell inventions for Sherman and Co. in Marshall, Michigan; goods of La Bell Manufacturing Co. in Chicago; and household articles for the New York Manufacturing Co. in New York. Obviously any man in Belton, Texas, could apply.

29   Edward P. Briggs, *op. cit.*, pp. 48-49.

30   Gerard Corl Henderson, *The Position of the Foreign Corporation in American Constitutional Law* . . . (Cambridge, 1918); 8 Wall. 168, 81; Bernard C. Gavit, *The Commerce Clause of the United States Constitution* (Bloomington, 1932), Chapter XII passim.

31   Eugene W. Hilgard, "Report on the Cotton Production in the United States" *10th Census, House of Representatives Miscellaneous Document 42, Part 6, 47 Congress, 2nd Session.* See Part III of Individual State Reports. Life Insurance Companies boomed in the South for the first time after the War.

32   Paul v. Virginia, 75 U. S. 168; 19 Law ed. 357, 1868. "Foreign" as used here means a firm incorporated in another state.

33   This was a common occurrence; i.e. in *The Daily Constitutionalist,* March 19, 1866, one Joseph E. Marshall was agent for the following companies: Home Insurance Co., (N. Y.); Security Insurance Co., (N. Y.); Manhattan Ins. Co., (N. Y.); Atlantic Ins. Co., (Brooklyn); Springfield Ins. Co., (Massachusetts); and Insurance Co., (Valley of Va.).

34 Governor Robert K. Scott of South Carolina spoke out
gainst these insurance companies in 1869 and in 1871 suggested
axing their premiums. See also the Charleston *Daily Courier,* Feb-
uary 5, 1867, and Somers, *op. cit.,* 264, "The Planters Co." The
roblem waxed serious because many of these companies were in
he commercial banking business and southern investment in them
vas heavy. In Memphis alone $73,000,000 was the capital invested
n "foreign" life insurance companies, and $41,000,000 in fire com-
anies. Governor Warmoth noted the same trend in Louisiana and
alled for protective legislation, *Governor's* (H. C. Warmoth)
Message, 1871, State of Louisiana. North Carolina proved very
olerant of insurance company's activity—Doc. No. 1, Governor's
Tod R. Caldwell) *Message,* Nov. 20, 1871, and "Report of William
I. Finch, Delegate to the National Insurance Convention", Doc.
No. 13 of *Executive and Legislative Documents laid before the
General Assembly of North Carolina,* Session 1871-72. The Con-
ention, sitting in New York City, Oct. 18-30, 1871, had convened
ust before the fall session of the Southern legislatures to forestall
he rising tide of restrictive legislation. They, like the merchants
t the same time, asked for free trade in insurance, aid in squeezing
ut British insurance firms in the American market, and their own
eneral usefulness.

Yet these companies had forced all kinds of settlements, often
ecause of the suspicion of intentional burnings of gin houses and
omes for cash. On the other hand, bankruptcy, often real or
eigned, overtook the firms and policy holders were victimized;
rms refused to deposit state securities, often become worthless by
epreciation, with proper authorities; firms used brokers to secure,
nstead of agents to issue policies; firms claimed "situs" in a neigh-
oring southern state to evade the law; and finally the northern
rms connived with the old planters to help throw out the Radical
Rascals"—See 5th *Annual Message* of Governor Harrison Reed
. . of Florida, Jan. 4, 1872, *Inaugural Address* of Governor D. H.
Chamberlain delivered before the General Assembly of South Caro-
na Dec. 1, 1879; *Message* of His Excellency Governor S. D.
McEnery to the General Assembly of the State of Louisiana, 1886;
Message of J. S. Hogg, Governor of Texas to the Twenty-Second
egislature, Jan. 21, 1891. Dates of these citations show how per-
stent the problem of insurance companies was in the South.

35 *Proceedings* of the 2nd Annual Meeting of the National
oard of Trade held in Richmond, Dec., 1869, pp. 340-346,
Abstract of State Laws Relating to Non-Resident Traders and

Peddlers." The laws of the various states are listed as operative in codes, digest, and statutes at the following dates: Virginia, 1866-67; West Virginia, 1866; Texas, 1866; Tennessee, 1868; South Carolina, 1864; North Carolina, 1863; Missouri, 1865; Maryland, 1868; Louisiana, 1850; Kentucky, 1860; Kansas, 1867; Georgia, 1868; Florida, 1847; Arkansas, 1858; Alabama, 1859-60 (repealed, 1867).

36   Edward P. Briggs, *op. cit.,* p. 48. It is significant that around 1869-70 the border cities and states repealed their license laws when their merchants began to send salesmen out on a large scale; L. P. Brackett, *op. cit.,* p. 39— The city ordinance of St. Louis Art. XIII paragraph 13-14-15 was so amended June 4, 1869.

37   Note 34 *Supra,* pp. 32-47.

38   Maryland v. Ward of New Jersey.

39   The reference is to Paul v. Virginia.

40   The memorial is to be found in the Convention *Proceedings* Jan. 20, 1870, pp. 347-48.

41   *Proceedings* of the Third Annual Meeting of the National Board of Trade held in Buffalo, December, 1870 (Boston, 1871) pp. 88-106.

42   The Bill provided for free flow of goods between all the states and territories; forbade the imposition of any kind of tax on the distribution of goods and the imposition by states or territories of any obstructions to trade whatsoever.

43   Note 40 supra, pp. 309-310; George H. Parmele and M. P. Wiles, *Law Reports Annotated,* Vol. 60 (Rochester, N. Y., 1929) Annotation, pp. 994-1039 at 996 citing Ward v. Maryland, 79 U. S. 418 (1871) 20 Law Ed. 449-453. Justice Clifford delivered the opinion. It is interesting to note that Justice Bradley, while citing with favor Clifford's opinion in the former's treatment of Robbins v. Taxing District, 120 U. S. 489 (1887) 30 Law Ed. 694—on the same issue of salesmen, Bradley invoked Interstate Commerce to kill the license law.

44   Edward P. Briggs, *op. cit.,* pp. 48-49. The activity of the salesman throws light on the practice. He was arrested once in Memphis on suspicion of offering to sell and was taken to the police station where he had to deposit $50 bond to appear the next morning. On the charge of the officer he pleaded "not guilty" and the prosecution could not prove its case. However, Briggs remarked, "While I was not guilty in this specific instance, for I had sold no goods in the store where I had been arrested, I had nevertheless sold to another party the previous day and had drawn through them $100 on my New York house for travelling expenses.

peaking of the laws of Savannah, Charleston, and Baltimore, Briggs observed, "In these towns I never took out any license and always escaped arrest." See also George M. Hayes, *op. cit.*, chap. 7 passim for an interesting experience in this same connection in Richmond, Va.

45 Nimmo, *Internal Commerce,* 1881, appendix 25, pp. 210-11. The average number of travelers per year in Arkansas is at least 75, and they spend an average of not less than $7 per day making 3,325 per day, which absolutely supports the hotels and livery tables."

46 *Ibid.,* pp. 211-12. By 1881 Colorado, Connecticut, Florida, Illinois, Indiana, Iowa, Kansas, New York, Ohio, Rhode Island, Vermont, West Virginia, Wisconsin and the Territories of Arizona, Dakota, Idaho, Indiana, Utah, and Washington had observed the Supreme Court admonition against license taxes. Alabama levied no tax, but empowered municipalities to do so; thus Mobile levied a trifling one. While Arkansas levied no tax, Little Rock collected 25 per quarter, and the same held true in many Georgia cities, although the state did not tax. Mississippi levied no state tax and its courts ruled that not even municipalities could be so empowered. South Carolina had some moderate municipal taxes and Tennessee had none save in Memphis. Louisiana openly collected a direct tax of $25 per month; New Orleans, $10 per week or $50 per year, and Baton Rouge, $25 per year. The state of Maryland continued to offer food for constitutional thought by taxing residents and non-residents the same; her levy ranged from $12.75 to $150 per year. North Carolina had a municipal tax in Wilmington and a state tax of $100 per year which exempted from any other license on trading in the state. Texas required a tax of $200 per year for which the travelers might represent any number of firms and any merchant or firm could send any number of travelers by paying the same as a merchant tax. Finally, Virginia exacted an annual tax of $100.

47 Chapter VI ante.

Bibliography

I. GOVERNMENT DOCUMENTS — THE UNITED STATES

A. Manuscripts

Legislative

1. House of Representatives
   a. 39th Congress
      1. Box 4, Bundle 12, Sundry Documents on Reconstruc tion and other Matters.
      2. Box 11, Bundle 40, Relating to the Establishing c the Freedmen's Bureau.
      3. Box 12, Bundle 47, Report of Blair Investigation and on Freedmen's Affairs.
      4. Box 18, Bundle 76, Senate Reports—Commerce an Navigation; Copies of State Department Letters Colored Troops to be Employed in Construction c Railroads; Bankrupt Act; Amendments to the Con stitution.
      5. Box 24, Petitions on the Use of Public Lands.
   b. 40th Congress
      1. Box 1, Bundle 1, Colored Troops, Reorganizatio and Colonization.
      2. Box 8, Bundle 25, Secretary of War's Report, Recon struction.
      3. Box 14, Bundle 54, Tax on Cotton; Government c Rebel States; Union League.
      4. Box 21, Freedmen's Affairs.

Legislative: The House of Representatives

1. Davis, J. J., "Report of the Committee on Banking and Cur rency Accompanying Bill H.R. 109 Authorizing Nationa Banks to make Loans on Real Estate" House of Representa tives Report No. 180 series 1934. *46th Congress, 2nd* Session
2. Hilgard, Eugene W., "Report on the Cotton Production i the United States", House Miscellaneous Document No. 4 part 6. *47th Congress, 2nd* Session.
3. "Memorial for the Repeal of the Cotton Tax", House Mis cellaneous Document No. 52, November 27, 1867, *40t* Congress, *1st* Session.

4. "Memorial for the Repeal of the Cotton Tax". House Executive Document No. 1, December 2, 1867, *40th* Congress, *1st* Session.

5. "Memorial for the Repeal of the Cotton Tax", House Miscellaneous Document No. 29, January 16, 1868, *40th* Congress, *2nd* Session.

6. "Repeal of Cotton Tax", House Miscellaneous Document No. 18, *42nd* Congress, *2nd* Session.

The Senate

1. "Journal of the Joint Committee on Reconstruction", *39th* Congress, *1st* Session. Appointed pursuant to the Concurrent Resolution of December 13, 1865", Senate Document No. 711, *63rd* Congress, *3rd* Session.

2. "Report of the Committee on Agriculture and Forestry on the Condition of Cotton Growers in the United States", Senate Report No. 986, *53rd* Congress, *3rd* Session.

3. "Report of Carl Schurz on the States of South Carolina, Georgia, Alabama, Mississippi and Louisiana", Senate Executive Document No. 2, *39th* Congress, *1st* Session.

General

1. *The Statutes at Large of the United States* . . . 1789-1873. 17 Vols. Little Brown (Later Little Brown and Company), Boston, 1845-1873.

2. *Congressional Globe, 1834-1873.* Blair and Rives (et al.) Editors and Publishers (Washington, 1834-1873).

3. Revised Statutes of the United States passed at the *first* session of the *43rd* Congress (with appendix) 2nd edition (Washington, 1878).

The United States

Executive: The Department of State

Consul Letters received—*London*

1. London, Vol. 36 Jan., 1866
2. London, Vol. 36 Feb., 1866
3. London, Vol. 37 Jan., 1868
4. London, Vol. 38 Jan., 1869
5. London, Vol. 38 May, 1869
6. London, Vol. 38 June, 1869
7. London, Vol. 42 March, 1874

8. London, Vol. 42 May, 1874
9. London, Vol. 44 Oct., 1875
10. London, Vol. 45 Aug., 1876
11. London, Vol. 45 Feb., 1877
12. London, Vol. 46 June, 1878
13. London, Vol. 46 Nov., 1879

Manchester

1. Manchester, Vol. 2, Jan., 1862-Nov., 1869

Liverpool

1. Liverpool, Vol. 31 Jan., 1865
2. Liverpool, Vol. 31, May, 1865
3. Liverpool, Vol. 32 July, 1865
4. Liverpool, Vol. 32 Sept., 1865
5. Liverpool, Vol. 33 Jan., 1865
6. Liverpool, Vol. 33 March, 1866
7. Liverpool, Vol. 34 April, 1866
8. Liverpool, Vol. 34 May, 1866
9. Liverpool, Vol. 35 Jan., 1867
10. Liverpool, Vol. 37 April, 1868
11. Liverpool, Vol. 38 Jan., 1869
12. Liverpool, Vol. 39 June, 1869
13. Liverpool, Vol. 45 Sept., 1876

The United States—Executive

The Bureau of Refugees, Freedmen and Abandoned Lands
MSS. War Department Archives, The National Archives
Washington, D. C.
Records of the Nine Special Agencies, MSS., Treasury
Archives, The National Archives, Washington, D. C.
*Corporate History of the Missouri Pacific Railway Company
and the St. Louis, Iron Mountain and Southern Railway Company and their Constituent Lines,* showing mileage constructed
by each, with dates of completions; also a brief outline of mileage operated under outright leases and trackage rights agreements, compiled pursuant to and in accordance with Valuation Order No. 20, Interstate Commerce Commission dated
May 13, 1915 (December 31, 1915).

Report of the Commissioner of Agriculture for the Year 1879 (Washington, 1880).

Statistical Abstract of the United States No. I, 1878 (Prepared by the Chief of the Bureau of Statistics of the Treasury Department) (Washington, 1879).

Wells, David A., Stephen Colwell and Samuel Haynes, *Report of a Commission appointed for a Revision of the Revenue System of the United States, 1865-1866.* (Washington, 1866).

Wilson, Joseph S., Commissioner, *Report of the Commissioner of the General Land Office to the Secretary of the Interior for the Year 1869* (Washington, 1878).

Nimmo, Joseph, Jr., Chief of the Bureau of Statistics, Treasury Department, *Report on the Internal Commerce of the United States,* submitted December, 1879 (Washington, 1879).

Nimmo, Joseph, Jr., Chief of the Bureau of Statistics, Treasury Department, *Report on the Internal Commerce of the United States,* submitted December, 1880 (Washington, 1880).

Nimmo, Joseph, Jr., Chief of the Bureau of Statistics, Treasury Department, *Report on the Internal Commerce of the United States,* submitted December, 1881 (Washington, 1881).

Switzler, William F., Chief of the Bureau of Statistics, Treasury Department, *Report on the Internal Commerce of the United States,* submitted December, 1886 (Washington, 1886).

Judicial

1. Paul v. Virginia, 75 United States 168; 19 Law Ed. 357 (1868).

British

MSS.

1. Foreign Office: Exchange of Instructions and Messages Between the Foreign Office and the British Minister in Washington, F. O. Vol. 1014-1020, 1063, 1068. Public Record Office, London. (Bound photostats of these are to be found in the Division of Rolls and Manuscripts, The Library of Congress.)

Published Documents

House of Commons: Accounts and Papers, Commercial Reports *The Reports of Her Majesty's Consuls—The United States* 1865, Vol. 53—1875, Vol. 75, 1879, Vol. 70.

Reports from Commissioners, Inspectors, and Others: 1886
25 Vols: at Vol. 10, C.4715-1. Second Report of the Royal
Commission Appointed to Inquire into the Depression of Trade
and Industry; Appendix, Part II—The United States, House
of Commons, Vol. 22, 1886.

State

(The messages were published in this form by the several state
and they are so collected by the Historical Society of the State of
Wisconsin)

Alabama

1. *Message* of Robert M. Patton, Governor of Alabama with
   accompanying documents. House of Representatives, January
   16, 1866 (Montgomery, 1866).
2. *Message* of David P. Lewis, Governor of Alabama to the
   General Assembly on November 17, 1873 (Montgomery,
   1873).
3. A. J. Walker, *The Revised Code of Alabama* adopted by Act
   of the General Assembly, Approved 19th February, 1867,
   and published in Pursuance thereof (Montgomery, 1867).
4. Robert C. Brickell, Peter Hamilton, and John P. Tellman,
   The Code of Alabama, adopted by Act of the General Assembly approved February 28, 1887, with such Statutes of 1886-
   87, Required to be Therein and Decisions of the Supreme
   Court, 2 vols. (Nashville, 1887)

Florida

1. *8th Annual Message* of Governor Harrison Reed of Florida,
   January 4, 1872.
2. *Annual Message* of His Excellency Governor Harrison Reed
   to the Legislature of Florida, January 7, 1869, with accompanying Documents (Tallahassee, 1869).
3. *Message* of His Excellency Governor Harrison Reed to the
   Legislature of Florida in Extra Session, June 9, 1869 (Tallahassee, 1869).
4. *Third Annual Message* of Governor Harrison Reed, January
   5, 1871, to the Legislature of Florida (Tallahassee, 1871).

Georgia

1. *Message* of Governor Charles J. Jenkins to the Georgia Legislature on November 1, 1866 (Macon, 1866).
2. *Message with Accompanying Documents* of His Excellency Rufus B. Bullock, Governor of Georgia to the General Assembly of the State, Read July 24, 1868 (Atlanta, 1868).
3. *Message* from His Excellency Governor Bullock Transmitting Reports of the Public Institutions on August 15, 1870 (Atlanta, 1870).
4. George N. Hester, C. Powell & W. D. Hill, *The Code of the State of Georgia* (Atlanta, 1868).
5. R. H. Clark, T. R. R. Cobb and D. Irwin, *The Code of the State of Georgia* (Atlanta, 1868).

Kentucky

1. *Report of the Railroad Commission of Kentucky* to November 30, 1883 (Property of the State of Kentucky, Frankfort, 1884).

Louisiana

1. *Message* of the Governor of Louisiana to the General Assembly held in the city of New Orleans, commencing January 28, 1867 (New Orleans, 1867).
2. *Message* of the Governor (J. Madison Wills) of Louisiana to the General Assembly held in New Orleans commencing June 28, 1867 (New Orleans, 1867).
3. *Governor's Message* (N. C. Wormoth), 1871, State of Louisiana.
4. *Annual Message* of His Excellency, Governor William Pitt Kellogg to the General Assembly of Louisiana, Session of 1874 (New Orleans, 1874).
5. *Special Message* of His Excellency Governor William Pitt Kellogg to the General Assembly of Louisiana, Extra Session of 1875 (New Orleans, 1875).
6. *Message* of His Excellency Governor S. D. McEnery to the General Assembly of the State of Louisiana, Regular Session of 1882 (Baton Rouge, 1882).
7. *Message* of His Excellency Governor S. D. McEnery to the General Assembly of the State of Louisiana, Regular Session of 1886 (Baton Rouge, 1886).

8. James O. Fuqua, ed. and comp., *Civil Code of the State of Louisiana* with Statutory Amendments from 1825 to 1866 inclusive and References to the Decisions of the Supreme Court of Louisiana to the 17th Volume of Annual Reports inclusive (New Orleans, 1867).

Maryland

Lewis Mayer, *Supplement to the Maryland Code:* Containing Acts of the General Assembly passed at the Session of 1868, (Baltimore, 1868).

Mississippi

1. *Inaugural Address* of Governor Adelbert Ames to the Mississippi Legislature, Thursday, January 22, 1874; printed by order of the Legislature (Jackson, 1874).
2. *Annual Message* and Inaugural Address of Governor J. M. Stone to the Legislature of Mississippi, Session of 1878 (Jackson, 1878).
3. *Biennial Message* of Governor Robert Lowry to the Legislature of Mississippi on January 9, 1884, printed by order of the House (Jackson, 1884).
4. Laws of the State of Mississippi passed at a call session of the Mississippi Legislature held in Jackson October 1866-February, 1867.
5. J. A. Campbell, *The Revised Code of the Statute Laws of the State of Mississippi*, Reported to and Amended, and adopted by the Legislature at its Biennial session in 1880 with Reference to the Decision of the High Court of Errors and Appeals and of the Supreme Court Applicable to the Statutes; published by authority of the Legislature (Jackson, 1880).

North Carolina

1. *Message* of Jonathan Worth, Governor of North Carolina, to the "Call Session" of the General Assembly 1866 (Raleigh, 1866).
2. *Annual Message* of Jonathan Worth, Governor of North Carolina to the General Assembly at its Session November 19, 1866 (Raleigh, 1866).

3. *Governor's* (Tod R. Caldwell) *Message,* November 20, 1871, Document No. 1, Session 1871-1872 (Raleigh, 1871).
4. *Annual Message* of Governor Tod R. Caldwell (Raleigh, 1873).
5. "Report of William H. Finch, Delegate to the National Insurance Convention", Document No. 13 of the Executive and Legislative Documents laid before the General Assembly of North Carolina, Session 1871-72.
6. William T. Dortch, John Manning, John S. Henderson, *The Code of North Carolina* enacted March 2, 1883, Prepared under Chapters 146* and 315 of the Laws of 1881 and under Chapter 171 of the Laws of 1883, 2 vols. (New York, 1883).

Ohio

1. *J. Bryant Walker, Solicitor, etc. Plaintiff, Against the City of Cincinnati, Trustee of the Cincinnati Southern Railroad, et al Defendants, Superior Court of Cincinnati 26007.*
2. *Report of the House Judiciary Committee on House Bill No. 254* (John M. Fleming, Chairman) November 30, 1869.

South Carolina

1. *Message No. 1* of His Excellency Governor J. L. Orr, with accompanying Documents, November, 1866 (Columbia, 1866).
2. *Message* of Robert K. Scott, Governor of South Carolina with accompanying Documents submitted to the General Assembly of South Carolina at the regular session, November, 1869 (Columbia, 1869).
3. *Annual Message* of His Excellency, Robert K. Scott, Governor of South Carolina to the General Assembly at the Regular Session commencing November 28, 1871 (Columbia, 1871).
4. *First Annual Message* of His Excellency Franklin J. Moses, Jr., Governor of South Carolina, to the General Assembly at the Regular Session of 1872-73 (Columbia, 1873).
5. *Inaugural Address* of Governor D. H. Chamberlain Delivered before the General Assembly of the South Carolina, December 1, 1874 (Columbia, 1874).

---

* Either 146 or 145

6. *Message* of Johnson Hagood, Governor of the State of South Carolina, to the General Assembly Delivered Wednesday, November 23, 1881 (Columbia, 1881).
7. Charles H. Simonton, William H. Parker, James F. Hart, *The General Statutes and the Code of Civil Procedure of the State of South Carolina,* adopted by the General Assembly of 1881-82 (Columbia, 1882).

Tennessee

1. Killebrew, J. B. Commissioner *Valuable Farms and Timbered Lands for Sale in the State of Tennessee,* Registered in the Office of Bureau of Immigration, (Nashville, 1880).
2. *Tennessee Commissioners on the Louisville and Nashville Railroads,* 1865, "Settlement with the Louisville and Nashville Railroad Company", Report of A. J. Fletcher, Secretary of State, S. W. Hatchett, Comptroller, Thomas A. Caldwell, Attorney General, and A. W. Hawkins, Commissioner of Roads.

Texas

1. *Message* of Governor J. W. Throckmorton to the Legislature of Texas (Austin, 1866).
2. *Message* of Governor Edmund J. Davis to the Twelfth Legislature on April 28, 1870 (Austin, 1870).
3. *General Message* of Governor Oran M. Roberts on the Judiciary, Education, the Department of Insurance, Statistics and History, Railroads, etc., to the Seventeenth Legislature of the State of Texas, convened at the city of Austin in Regular Session on January 11, 1881 (Galveston, 1881).
4. *Message* of J. S. Hogg, Governor of Texas, to the Twenty-second Legislature on January 21, 1891 (Austin, 1891).

Virginia

1. *Governor's* (F. H. Peirpont) *Message,* December, 1866 (Richmond, December 3, 1866).
2. *Annual Message* of the Governor of Virginia to the General Assembly, December 6, 1871 (Richmond, 1871).
3. *Inaugural Message* of James L. Kemper, Governor of Virginia to the General Assembly, January 1, 1874 (Richmond, 1874).

4. *Annual Message* and Accompanying Documents of the Governor of Virginia to the General Assembly, December 2, 1874 (Richmond, 1874).

5. *The Code of Virginia with the Declaration of Independence and the Constitution of the United States and the Constitution of Virginia:* Published pursuant to an Act of the General Assembly of Virginia, Approved May 21, 1887 (Richmond, 1887).

NEWSPAPERS

Texas

   Belton Journal

Virginia

   Spirit of the Valley (Harresonburg)
   The Southern Opinion (Richmond)
   The Abingdon Virginian (Abingdon)
   The Jeffersonian Republican (Charlottesville)
   The True Index (Warrenton)
   The Richmond Whig and Advertiser

Tennessee

   The Knoxville Weekly Tribune

North Carolina

   The Greenville Enterprise (Later called Enterprise and Mountaineer)

South Carolina

   The Daily South Carolinian (Charleston)
   Charleston Daily Courier

Georgia

   The National Republican (Augusta)
   The Daily Constitutionalist (Augusta)
   The Savannah Daily Republican

The Macon Daily Telegraph
The Georgia Enterprise (Covington)
The Southern Recorder (Milledgeville)
The Examiner (Savannah)

Alabama

The North Alabamian (Tuscumbia)

Louisiana

The Southwestern Advocate (New Orleans)

Ohio

The Cincinnati Enquirer
The Cincinnati Times Star
The Cincinnati Commercial Tribune
The Commercial Gazette
The Cincinnati Commercial

Massachusetts

Boston Daily Advertiser
Daily Evening Voice (Boston)
The Boston Journal
Boston Herald
Boston Transcript
Brookline Chronicle
The Boston Daily Advocate

New York

The Commercial and Financial Chronicle
The Nation (New York)
Journal of Commerce (New York)
The New York Daily Tribune
The New York Evening Herald
Evening Post (New York)
The World (New York)

Pennsylvania

The Philadelphia Press
The Railway World (Philadelphia)

The Philadelphia Inquirer
The Daily Evening Bulletin (Philadelphia)
The Daily Evening Telegraph (Philadelphia)

Washington

The Daily Morning Chronicle (Washington, D. C.)
National Intelligencer (Washington, D. C.)

Chicago

The Chicago Tribune

London

The Economist (London)

BIOGRAPHIES, MEMOIRS, AND THE WRITINGS OF PUBLIC MEN

Baker, George E., *The Work of William H. Seward,* 5 vols.
(Boston, 1885).

Biographical Directory of the American Congress

Brenson, Joseph F., ed., *Biographical Cyclopedia and Portrait
Gallery of Distinguished Men with an Historical Sketch of
the State of Ohio* (Cincinnati, 1879).
Briggs, Edward P., *Fifty Years on the Road, The Autobiography
of a Traveling Salesman* (Philadelphia, 1911).
*Catalogue of Portraits in the Chamber of Commerce of the State
of New York* (New York, 1924).
Clark, S. J. Publishing Co., *Cincinnati, the Queen City; Pictorial
and Biographical,* Deluxe Supplement (Cincinnati, n.d.).
Conard, Howard L., *Encyclopedia of the History of Missouri;
a Compendium of History and Biography* . . . 6 vols. (New
York, 1901).
Current, Richard N., *Old Thad Stevens* (Madison, 1942).
Dictionary of American Biography.
Dictionary of National Biography.
Ferguson, E. A., *Founding of the Cincinnati Southern Railway
with an Autobiographical Sketch* (Cincinnati, 1905).
Grave, Charles T., *Centennial History of Cincinnati and Repre-
sentative Citizens* (Chicago, 1864).

Hayes, George M., *Twenty Years on the Road* (Philadelphia, n.d. 1880?).

Hazard, Caroline, ed., *Rowland Gibson Hazard, Economics and Politics* (1846-1885) (Boston, 1889).

Herndon, Richard, *Boston of Today* . . . (Boston, 1892).

Herringshaw, Thomas W., *Herringshaw's Encyclopedia of American Biography of the Nineteenth Century* (Chicago).

Howard, Oliver Otis, *Autobiography of Oliver Otis Howard, Major General United States Army,* 2 vols. (New York, 1907).

Lloyd, Caroline A., *Henry Damerest Lloyd, 1847-1903,* 2 vols. (New York, 1912).

McCulloch, Hugh, *Men and Measures of a Half a Century* (New York, 1888).

Miller, Alphonse B., *Thaddeus Stevens* (New York, 1933).

National Cyclopedia of American Biography.

Nixon, Raymond B., *Henry W. Grady, Spokesman of the New South* (New York, 1943).

Pearson, Henry G., *The Life of John A. Andrew,* 2 vols. (Boston, 1904).

Pierce, Edward L., *Memoir and Letters of Charles Sumner IV, 1860-1874.* (Boston, 1894).

Strong, Alexander, *Mss. A. C. 3798 Division of Rolls and Manuscripts,* The Library of Congress.

The Biographical Encyclopedia of Pennsylvania in the Nineteenth Century (Philadelphia, 1874).

Williams, Charles Richard, *Diary and Letters of Rutherford Birchard Hayes,* 5 vols. (Columbus, 1924).

Williamson, Harold Francis, *Edward Atkinson, The Biography of An American Liberal, 1827-1905* (Boston, 1934).

Wilson, George, *Portrait Gallery of the Chamber of Commerce of the State of New York: Catalogue and Biographical Sketches* (New York, 1890).

Winslow, Stephen N., *Biographies of Successful Philadelphia Merchants* (Philadelphia, 1864).

Who Was Who in America, Vol. 1, 1897-1942 (Chicago, 1942).

Woodward, C. Vann, *Tom Watson, Agrarian Rebel* (New York, 1938).

GENERAL HISTORIES

Beard, Charles A. and Mary, *The Rise of American Civilization,* 2 vols. (New York, 1927).

SPECIAL HISTORIES

Albion, Robert G. and Jennie B. Pope, *The Rise of New York Port,* (New York, 1939).

Albion, Robert T., *Square Riggers on Schedule: The New York Sailing Packets to England, France and the Cotton Ports* (Princeton, 1938).

Allison, Young E., *The City of Louisville and a Glimpse of Kentucky* (Louisville, 1887).

Ambler, Charles Henry, *A History of Transportation in the Ohio Valley* (Glendale, 1932).

Beale, Howard K., *The Critical Year: A Study of Andrew Johnson and Reconstruction* (New York, 1930).

Bishop, Joseph B., *A Chronicle of One Hundred and Fifty Years: The Chamber of Commerce of the State of New York, 1768-1918* (New York, 1918).

Bowers, Claude G., *The Tragic Era* (New York, 1929).

Clark, S. J., Publishing Co., *History of Kentucky, the Blue Grass State* (Chicago and Louisville, 1928).

Clark, Thomas D., *Pills, Petticoats and Plows: The Southern Country Store, 1865-1915* (Indianapolis, 1944).

Clark, Thomas D., *The Beginning of the L & N: The Development of the Louisville and Nashville Railroad and its Memphis Branches from 1836 to 1860* (Louisville, 1933).

Collins, Lewis, *Collins' Historical Sketches of Kentucky:* History of Kentucky Revised by Richard H. Collins (Louisville, 1924).

Coulter, Ellis Merton, *The Civil War and Readjustment in Kentucky* (Chapel Hill, 1926).

Coulter, Ellis Merton, *The Cincinnati Southern Railroad and the Struggle for Southern Commerce, 1865-1872* (Chicago, 1922).

Cox, James, *Old and New St. Louis: A Concise History of the Metropolis of the West and Southwest, with a Review of its Present Greatness and Immediate Prospects,* with a Biographical Appendix (St. Louis, 1889).

Craven, Avery Odelle, *The Coming of the Civil War* (New York, 1942).

Derrick, Samuel M., *Centennial History of the South Carolina Railroad* (Columbia, 1930).

Flint, Henry M., *The Railroads of the United States; their History and Statistics* (Philadelphia, 1868).

Foner, Phillip S., *Business and Slavery: The New York Merchants and the Irrepressible Conflict* (Chapel Hill, 1941).

Ford, Henry A., *History of Hamilton County, Ohio* (Cleveland, 1881).

Frazier, E. Franklin, *The Negro Family in the United States* (Chicago, 1939).

French, George, ed., *New England* (Boston, 1911).

Halvey, Elie, *The World Crisis, 1914-1918* (New York, 1930).

Hall, Charles G., Ed., *The Cincinnati Southern Railroad, A History* (Cincinnati, 1902).

Harvey, T. Edgar, Ed., and comp., *Commercial History of the State of Ohio* (Columbus, 1916).

Harrison, Fairfax, *A History of the Legal Development of the System of the Southern Railroad Company* (Washington, D. C., 1901).

Herr, Kincaid A., *The Louisville and Nashville, 1850-1942* (Louisville, 1942).

Hesseltine, William Best, *The South in American History* (New York, 1943).

Jenks, Leland H., *The Migration of British Capital to 1875* (New York, 1938).

Joblin, M. and Co., comp., *Louisville Past and Present: Its Industrial History as Exhibited in the Life and Labors of Its Leading Men* (Louisville, 1875).

Johnson, E. Polk, *A History of Kentucky and Kentuckians: The Leaders and Representative Men in Commerce, Industry and Modern Activities* (Chicago, 1912).

Johnston, J. Stoddard, ed., *Memorial History of Louisville from its First Settlement to the Year 1896* (New York, 1896).

Kerr, John Leeds, *The Story of a Southern Carrier: The Louisville and Nashville* (New York, 1933).

Leighton, George R., *America's Growing Pains; the Romance, Comedy and Tragedy of Five Great Cities* (New York, 1939).

McPherson, Edward, *The Political History of the United States During the Period of Reconstruction* (Washington, 1880).

Milton, George Fort, *The Age of Hate: Andrew Johnson and the Radicals* (New York, 1930).

Mott, Frank Luther, *A History of American Magazines*, 3 vols. (Cambridge, 1938).

Myers, Margaret G., *The New York Money Market*, Vol. 1 *Origins and Developments* (New York, 1931).

Nelson, S. B. & Co., *History of Cincinnati and Hamilton County, Ohio* (Cincinnati, 1894).

Oberholtzer, Ellis Paxson, *Philadelphia, A History of a City and Its People* (Philadelphia, n.d.).

Ripley, William Z., *Railway Problems* (Boston, 1902).

Russel, Robert R., *Economic Aspects of Southern Sectionalism, 1840-1861* (Urbana, 1922).

Scholter, H. W., Asst. Treasurer, *The Growth and Development of the Pennsylvania Railroad Company: a Review of the Charter and Annual Reports, 1846-1926* (Philadelphia, 1927).

Somers, Robert, *The Southern States Since the War, 1870-1871* (London, 1871).

Taussig, Frank W., and H. D. White, *Some Aspects of the Tariff Question: An Examination of the Development of American Industries Under Protection* (Harvard Economic Studies, Vol. XII) (Cambridge, 1931).

Taylor, Frank H., *Philadelphia in the Civil War, 1861-1865* (Philadelphia, 1913).

Turner, Frederick J., *The United States, 1830-1850* (New York, 1935).

Wilson, William B., *History of the Pennsylvania Railroad Company,* 2 vols. (Philadelphia, 1895).

ARTICLES AND ESSAYS IN ANNUALS, PERIODICALS AND THE PUBLICATIONS OF LEARNED SOCIETIES

"Agricultural Department", *Debow's Review,* n.s. VIII (Jan.- Sept., 1870).

"American Land Company and Agency", *Debow's Review,* n.s. I (Jan.- June, 1866).

Biggs, R., "The Cincinnati Southern Railway: a Municipal Enterprise". East Tennessee Historical Society *Publications,* Vol. VII (1935).

Brown, C. K., "The Southern Railway Security Company, an Early Instance of the Holding Company", *The North Carolina Historical Review,* VI, No. 2 (April, 1929).

Callender, G. S., "The Early Transportation and Banking Enterprises of the States in Relation to the Growth of Corporations". *The Quarterly Journal of Economics,* XVI, No. 1 (Nov., 1902).

Canfield, James H., "What I think of Commercial Travellers". *The Sample Case,* Vol. 8, No. 3 (September, 1895).

Catterill, R. S., "The Louisville and Nashville Railroad, 1861-1865", *American Historical Review,* XXIX, No. 4 (July, 1924).

"Central Industrial Association of Mississippi", *Debow's Review,* n.s., V (January, 1869).

"Chinese Immigration", *Debow's Review,* n.s., VII (July-December, 1869).

Cole, Arthur C., "Lincoln's Election, an Immediate Menace to Slavery in the States?" *American Historical Review,* Vol. 36, no. 4 (July, 1931).

"Commercial Travelers and Taxes on Them". *Dunn and Bradstreets* (February 26, 1881).

Coulter, E. Merton, "The Effect of Secession upon the Commerce of the Mississippi Valley". *Mississippi Valley Historical Review,* Vol. III, No. 3 (December, 1916).

Crenshaw, Ollinger, "The Speakership Contest of 1859-1860". *Mississippi Valley Historical Review,* Vol. XXIX, No. 3 (December, 1942).

Dana, William B., "The Importance of the Reorganization of the South". *Hunt's Merchants Magazine and Commercial Review,* Vol. LIV, No. III (March, 1866).

Delmar, A., "Security for Capital". *Debow's Review,* n.s. I (January-June, 1866).

"Department of Miscellany". *Debow's Review,* n.s. III (January-June, 1867).

"Department of Miscellany". *Debow's Review,* n.s. VII (July-December, 1869).

Dodd, William E., "The Fight for the Northwest, 1860". *American Historical Review,* Vol. XVI, No. 4 (July, 1911).

Ellis, Lewis Ethan, "A History of the Chicago Delegation in Congress, 1853-1925". Illinois State Historical Society *Transactions,* Vol. 37 (1930).

"Emigration, A New Phase". *Hunts Merchant Magazine and Commercial Review,* Vol. LXII (January-June, 1870).

"Famine in the South". *Harper's Weekly* (March 23, 1867).

Fisher, Charles E., "The Early Railroads of Kentucky". *The Railway and Locomotive Historical Society Bulletin,* No. 5.

Fleischman, Charles F., "Our Exhausted Lands". *Debow's Review,* n.s., III (January-June, 1867).

Forest, Colonel J. W., "The Condition of the Poor Whites". *Putnams Magazine,* n.s., 1 (June, 1868).

Green, Evarts B., "Some Aspects of Politics in the Middle West, 1860-1872". *Proceedings* of the State Historical Society of Wisconsin at its Fifty-ninth Annual Meeting (Madison, 1912).

Haitheax, Frank, "Reminiscences of an Old Time Drummer". *The Sample Case,* Vol. 74, No. 8 (May, 1929).

Herrick, Samuel E., "Memoir of the Hon. Andrew Hill, LL. D." *Proceedings* of the Massachusetts Historical Society, 2nd Series, Vol. XI (November, 1896).

Hesseltine, William B., "Economic Factors in the Abandonment of Reconstruction". *Mississippi Valley Historical Review,* Vol. XXII, No. 2 (September, 1935).

Hofstader, Richard, "The Tariff Issue and the Civil War". *American Historical Review,* Vol. 44, No. 1 (October, 1938).

Hale, Edward E., "Memoir of the Hon. Lorenzo Sabine, A.M." *Proceedings of the Massachusetts Historical Society,* Vol. XVII, 1879-1880 (March, 1880).

Hubbart, Henry Clyde, "Pro Southern Influences in the Free West, 1840-1865". *Mississippi Valley Historical Review,* Vol. XX, No. 1 (June, 1933).

Johns, Alfred, "Report of the Committee of Agriculture of the Industrial Association of Mississippi". *Debow's Review,* n.s., V (January, 1868).

Levermore, Charles H., "Henry C. Carey and His Social System". *Political Science Quarterly,* Vol. 1, No. 4 (December, 1890).

Massey, George F., "Sixty-four Years on the Road—Uncle Charlie Terry Still a Live One at the Age of Eighty-seven". *The Sample Case,* Vol. 63, No. 2 (August, 1923).

"Miscellany". *The Banker's Magazine and Statistical Register,* n.s., XIV, No. 8 (February, 1865).

"National Cotton Convention". *The Banker's Magazine and Statistical Register,* n.s., XV, No. V (December, 1865).

"H. Victor Newcomb—The Great L & N Railroad Combination". *Graphic.* Clipping file No. 15213, Library of the Bureau of Railroad Economics, Washington, D. C.

Pitkin, Thomas M., "Western Republicans and the Tariff in 1860". *Mississippi Valley Historical Review,* Vol. XXVII, No. 3 (December, 1940).

Pritchett, John A., "On the Policy of the Usury Laws". *Debow's Review,* n.s., VII (July-December, 1869).

"Railroad Progress in the South". *Hunt's Merchants Magazine and Commercial Review,* Vol. 57 (September, 1867).

Schlesinger, Arthur M., "The City in American History". *Mississippi Valley Historical Review*, Vol. 27, No. I (June, 1940).

Smith, Charles H., "Introducing Another Grand Veteran of the Road—J. Aaron of Pittsburgh, one of the First in New York State in the Early 60's". *The Sample Case*, Vol. 63, No. I (July, 1923).

"Southern Immigration". *Littles Living Age.*

"The Chicago, Indianapolis, and Louisville Railroad Company". *The Monon Outlook*, Vol. I, No. 4 (October, 1939).

"The Cotton Tax". *Debow's Review*, n.s., III (January-June, 1867).

"The New Era of Southern Manufactures". *Debow's Review*, n.s., III (January-June, 1867).

"The Past and Future Cotton Supply". *Hunt's Merchant Magazine and Commercial Review*, XIV, No. VI (June, 1866).

"The Southern Cotton Trade and the Excise Laws". Department of Agriculture, *Debow's Review*, n.s., II (November, 1866).

Trenholm, W. L., Esq., "Portions of an Address Delivered at the Third Anniversary of the Charleston Board of Trade". *Hunt's Merchants Magazine and Commercial Review*, Vol. LXI (July-December, 1869).

Turner, Frederick J., "Greater New England in the Middle of the 19th Century". *Proceedings* of the American Antiquarian Society, Vol. XXX (October 15, 1919).

Wagner, Gen. Jno. A., "European Immigration". *Debow's Review*, n.s., III (January-June, 1867).

White, Edgar, "The Merchants of Yesterday". *The Sample Case*, Vol. 50, No. 5 (May, 1917).

Wilson, Charles R., "Cincinnati: A Southern Outpost in 1860-1861".
Mississippi Valley Historical Review, Vol. XXIV, No. IV (March, 1938).

Zerchner, Oscar, "The Transition from Slave to Free Agricultural Labor in the Southern States". *Agricultural History*, Vol. XII, No. 1 (January, 1939).

Zerchner, Oscar, "The Legal Status of the Agricultural Laborer in the South". *Political Science Quarterly*, Vol. LV, No. 3 (September, 1940).

MONOGRAPHS

Ferleger, Herbert Ronald, *David A. Wells and the American Revenue System, 1865-1870* (New York, 1942).

Fish, Carl Russell, *The Reconstruction of the Southern Railroads.* University of Wisconsin *Studies* in the Social Sciences and History, No. 2 (Madison, 1919).

Gavit, Bernard C., *The Commerce Clause of the United States Constitution* (Bloomington, 1932).

Henderson, Gerard C., *The Position of the Foreign Corporation in American Constitutional Law* (Cambridge, 1918).

Kendrick, Benjamin B., *The Journal of the Joint Committee on Reconstruction.* Columbia University Studies in History, Economics and Public Law, Vol. LXII (New York, 1914).

Peirce, Paul Skeels, *The Freedman's Bureau, a Chapter in the History of Reconstruction.* State University of Iowa *Studies* in Sociology, Economics, Politics and History, Vol. III, No. 1, *Bulletin* of the State University of Iowa, n.s., No. 74 (March, 1904).

Schoff, Wilfred H., *American Commercial Institutions.* Monograph no. 4 on American Social Economics, Department of Social Economy of the United States Commission for the Paris Exhibition of 1900 (Philadelphia, 1900).

Smith, George W., *Generative Forces of Union Propaganda,* MSS. thesis in the University of Wisconsin, 1939.

Sturges, Kenneth, *American Chambers of Commerce.* David A. Wells Prize Essay No. 4, Printed for the Department of Political Science of Williams College (New York, 1915).

Swanter, Eva, *Northern Control of Southern Railroads during the Civil War.* MSS. Thesis in the University of Wisconsin, January, 1939.

Tanner, James F., *The Louisville and Nashville Railroad to 1866.* MSS. Thesis in the University of Indiana, 1933.

Wright, Chester W., *Wool Growing and the Tariff* (Boston, 1910).

MISCELLANEOUS

Chamber of Commerce and Board of Trade Records

Boston Board of Trade

1. *Boston Board of Trade, 1856.* Second Annual Report of the Government. Presented to the Board at the Annual Meeting

on the 16th of January, 1856. Moore and Crosby, Printers, Boston. 1856.

2. *Boston Board of Trade, 1858*. Fourth Annual Report of the Government. Presented to the Board at the Annual Meeting on the 30th of January, 1858. Press of Geo. C. Rand and Avery. Boston. 1858.

3. *Boston Board of Trade, 1859*. Fifth Annual Report of the Government. Presented to the Board at the Annual Meeting on the 20th of January, 1859. Press of T. R. Marvin and Son. Boston, 1859.

4. *Boston Board of Trade, 1860*. Sixth Annual Report of the Government. Presented to the Board at the Annual Meeting on the 20th of January, 1860. Wright and Potter, Printers. Boston, 1860.

5. *Boston Board of Trade, 1861*. Seventh Annual Report of the Government. Presented to the Board at the Annual Meeting on the 16th of January, 1861. Press of T. R. Marvin and Son. Boston. 1861.

6. *Boston Board of Trade, 1862*. Eighth Annual Report of the Government. Presented to the Board at the Annual Meeting on the 15th of January, 1862. Printed by Alfred Mudge and Son. Boston, 1862.

7. *Boston Board of Trade, 1863*. Ninth Annual Report of the Government. Presented to the Board at the Annual Meeting on the 13th of January, 1863. Printed by Alfred Mudge and Son. Boston. 1863.

8. *Boston Board of Trade, 1864*. Tenth Annual Report of the Government. Presented to the Board at the Annual Meeting on the 13th of January, 1864. Press of T. R. Marvin and Son. Boston. 1864.

9. *Boston Board of Trade, 1865*. Eleventh Annual Report of the Government. Presented to the Board at the Annual Meeting on the 11th of January, 1865. Press of T. R. Marvin and Son. Boston. 1865.

10. *Boston Board of Trade, 1866*. Twelfth Annual Report of the Government. Presented to the Board at the Annual Meeting on the 10th of January, 1866. Geo. C. Rand and Avery, Printers. Boston. 1866.

11. *Boston Board of Trade, 1867*. Thirteenth Annual Report of the Government. Presented to the Board at the Annual Meeting on the 9th of January, 1867. John Wilson and Son. Boston. 1867.

12. *Fourteenth Annual Report* of the Boston Board of Trade, for the Year Ending January 6, 1868. J. H. Eastburn's Press. Boston. 1868.

13. *Fifteenth Annual Report* of the Boston Board of Trade for the Year Ending January 13, 1869. Press of Rand, Avery, Frye and Cornhill. Boston. 1869.

14. *Sixteenth Annual Report* of the Boston Board of Trade for the Year Ending January 12, 1870. Rockwell and Church, Printers. Boston. 1870.

15. *Seventeenth Annual Report* of the Boston Board of Trade for the Year Ending January 11, 1871. Barker, Cotter and Co., Printers. Boston. 1871.

16. *Eighteenth Annual Report* of the Boston Board of Trade for the Year Ending January 10, 1872. Barker, Cotter and Co., Printers. Boston. 1872.

17. *Nineteenth Annual Report* of the Boston Board of Trade for the Year Ending January 8, 1873. James F. Cotter and Co., Printers. Boston. 1873.

18. *Twenty-First Annual Report* of the Boston Board of Trade for the Year Ending January 8, 1873. James F. Cotter and Co., Boston. 1875.

19. *Twenty-Second Annual Report* of the Boston Board of Trade, January 1, 1876. James F. Cotter and Co., Printers. Boston. 1876.

20. *Twenty-Fourth Annual Report* of the Boston Board of Trade, January 1, 1878. James F. Cotter and Co., Boston. 1878.

21. *Twenty-Fifth Annual Report* of the Boston Board of Trade, January 1, 1879. James F. Cotter and Co., Boston. 1879.

The Chamber of Commerce of the State of New York

1. *Annual Report of the Chamber of Commerce of the State of New York for the year 1858.* Wheeler and Williams, Stationers. New York. 1859.

2. *Annual Report of the New York Chamber of Commerce. For the year 1859-60.* John W. Amerman, Printer. New York. 1860.

3. *Fourth Annual Report of the Chamber of Commerce. For the State of New York for the year 1861-62.* John W. Amerman, Printer. New York. 1862.

4. *Fifth Annual Report of the Chamber of Commerce. For the State of New York. For the year 1862-63.* John W. Amerman, Printer. New York. 1863.

5. *Sixth Annual Report of the Chamber of Commerce. For the State of New York. For the year of 1863-64.* (In two parts.) John W. Amerman, Printer. New York. 1864.

6. *Seventh Annual Report of the Chamber of Commerce. For the State of New York. For the year 1864-65.* John W. Amerman, Printer. New York. 1865.

7. *Eighth Annual Report of the Chamber of Commerce. For the State of New York. For the year 1865-66—in Two Parts.* John W. Amerman, Printer. New York. 1866.

8. *Ninth Annual Report of the Chamber of Commerce. For the State of New York. For the year 1866-67—in Two Parts.* John W. Amerman, Printer. New York. 1867.

9. *Tenth Annual Report of the Chamber of Commerce. For the State of New York. For the year 1867-68. In Two Parts.* John W. Amerman, Printer. New York. 1868.

10. *Eleventh Annual Report of the Chamber of Commerce. For the State of New York. For the year 1868-69. In Two Parts.* John W. Amerman, Printer. New York. 1869.

11. *Twelfth Annual Report of the Corporation of the Chamber of Commerce for the State of New York. For the year 1869-70. In Two Parts.* Press of the Chamber of Commerce. New York. 1870.

12. *Thirteenth Annual Report of the Corporation of the Chamber of Commerce for the State of New York. For the year 1870-71. In Two Parts.* Press of the Chamber of Commerce. New York. 1871.

13. *Fourteenth Annual Report of the Corporation of the Chamber of Commerce of the State of New York. For the year 1871-72. In Two Parts.* Press of the Chamber of Commerce. New York. 1872.

14. *Fifteenth Annual Report of the Corporation of the Chamber of Commerce of the State of New York. For the year 1872-73. In Two Parts.* Press of the Chamber of Commerce. New York. 1873.

15. *Sixteenth Annual Report of the Corporation of the Chamber of Commerce of the State of New York. For the year 1873-74. In Two Parts.* Press of the Chamber of Commerce. New York. 1874.

16. *Seventeenth Annual Report of the Corporation of the Chamber of Commerce of the State of New York. For the year 1874-75. In Two Parts.* Press of the Chamber of Commerce. New York. 1875.

17. *Eighteenth Annual Report of the Corporation of the Chamber of Commerce of the State of New York. For the year 1875-76. In Two Parts.* Press of the Chamber of Commerce. New York. 1876.

18. *Nineteenth Annual Report of the Corporation of the Chamber of Commerce of the State of New York. For the year 1876-77. In Two Parts.* Press of the Chamber of Commerce. New York. 1877.

19. *Twentieth Annual Report of the Corporation of the Chamber of Commerce of the State of New York. For the year 1877-78. In Two Parts.* Press of the Chamber of Commerce. New York. 1878.

20. *Twenty-First Annual Report of the Corporation of the Chamber of Commerce of the State of New York. For the year 1878-79. In Two Parts.* Press of the Chamber of Commerce. New York. 1879.

21. *Twenty-Second Annual Report of the Corporation of the Chamber of Commerce of the State of New York. For the year 1879-80. In Two Parts.* Press of the Chamber of Commerce. New York. 1880.

Philadelphia Board of Trade

1. *Twentieth Annual Report* of the Philadelphia Board of Trade to the Members of that Association, February 7, 1853. Printed by Deacon and Peterson. Philadelphia. 1853.

2. *Twenty-Second Annual Report* of the Directors of the Philadelphia Board to the Members of that Association, February 5, 1855. Printed by Deacon and Peterson. Philadelphia. 1855.

3. *Twenty-Sixth Annual Report* of the Philadelphia Board of Trade, Prepared by the Executive Council and presented to the Association. February 7, 1859. King and Baird, Printers. Philadelphia. 1859.

4. *Twenty-Eighth Annual Report* of the Philadelphia Board of Trade, Prepared for the Executive Council and Presented to the Association, February 5, 1861. Collins, Printer. Philadelphia. 1861.

5. *Twenty-Ninth Annual Report* of the Philadelphia Board of Trade, Prepared for the Executive Council and Presented to the Association, February 3, 1862. King and Baird, Printers. Philadelphia. 1862.

6. *Thirtieth Annual Report* of the Philadelphia Board of Trade, Prepared for the Executive Council and Presented to the Association, February 2, 1863. Collins, Printer. Philadelphia. 1863.

7. *Thirty-First Annual Report* of the Philadelphia Board of Trade, Prepared for the Executive Council and Presented to the Association, February 1, 1864. King and Baird, Printers. Philadelphia. 1864.

8. *Thirty-Second Annual Report* of the Philadelphia Board of Trade, Prepared for the Executive Council and Presented to the Association, February 6, 1865. J. B. Chandler, Printer. Philadelphia. 1866.

9. *Thirty-Third Annual Report* of the Philadelphia Board of Trade, Prepared for the Executive Council and Presented to the Association, February 5, 1866. J. B. Chandler, Printer. Philadelphia. 1866.

10. *Thirty-Fourth Annual Report* of the Philadelphia Board of Trade, Prepared by the Executive Council and Presented to the Association, February 4, 1867. J. B. Chandler, Printer. Philadelphia. 1867.

11. *Thirty-Fifth Annual Report* of the Philadelphia Board of Trade, Prepared for the Executive Council and Presented to the Association, February 5, 1868. J. B. Chandler, Printer. Philadelphia. 1868.

12. *Thirty-Sixth Annual Report* of the Philadelphia Board of Trade, Prepared for the Executive Council and Presented to the Association, February 1, 1869. J. B. Chandler, Printer. Philadelphia. 1869.

13. *Thirty-Seventh Annual Report* of the Philadelphia Board of Trade, Prepared for the Executive Council and Presented to the Association, February 7, 1870. J. B. Chandler, Printer. Philadelphia. 1870.

14. *Thirty-Eighth Annual Report* of the Philadelphia Board of Trade, Prepared for the Executive Council and Presented to the Association, February 6, 1871. J. B. Chandler, Printer. Philadelphia. 1871.

15. *Thirty-Ninth Annual Report* of the Philadelphia Board of Trade, Prepared for the Executive Council and Presented to

the Association, January 22, 1872. J. B. Chandler, Printer. Philadelphia. 1872.

16. *Fortieth Annual Report* of the Philadelphia Board of Trade, Prepared for the Executive Council and Presented to the Association, February 27, 1873. J. B. Chandler, Printer. Philadelphia. 1873.

17. *Forty-First Annual Report* of the Philadelphia Board of Trade, Presented to the Association February 26, 1874. J. B. Chandler, Printer. Philadelphia. 1874.

18. *Forty-Second Annual Report* of the Philadelphia Board of Trade Presented to the Association February 25, 1875. J. B. Chandler, Printer. Philadelphia. 1875.

19. *Forty-Third Annual Report* of the Philadelphia Board of Trade, Presented to the Association February 24, 1876. Philadelphia. 1876.

20. *Forty-Sixth Annual Report* of the Philadelphia Board of Trade Presented to the Association February 27, 1879. Philadelphia. 1879.

21. *Forty-Seventh Annual Report* of the Philadelphia Board of Trade Presented to the Association January 26, 1880. Philadelphia. 1880.

Cincinnati Chamber of Commerce

1. *Annual Review* of the Commerce of Cincinnati, for the Commercial Year Ending August 31, 1864 (Cincinnati, 1864).

2. *Annual Review* of the Commerce of Cincinnati, for the Commercial Year Ending August 31, 1865. Gazettee Steam Printing House. Cincinnati. 1865.

3. *Annual Report* of the Cincinnati Chamber of Commerce and Merchants' Exchange for the Commercial Year Ending August 31, 1866. Gazettee Steam Printing House. Cincinnati. 1866.

4. *Annual Report* of the Cincinnati Chamber of Commerce and Merchants' Exchange for the Commercial Year Ending August 31, 1867. Gazettee Steam Printing House. Cincinnati. 1867.

5. *Annual Report* of the Cincinnati Chamber of Commerce and Merchants' Exchange for the Commercial Year Ending August 31, 1868. Gazettee Steam Printing Establishment. 1868.

6. *Twenty-First Annual Report* of the Cincinnati Chamber of Commerce and Merchants' Exchange for the Fiscal Year

Ending August 31, 1869. Gazettee Steam Printing and Job Establishment. Cincinnati. 1869.

7. *Twenty-Second Annual Report* of the Cincinnati Chamber of Commerce and Merchants' Exchange for the Fiscal Year Ending August 31, 1870. Gazette Co. Printer, Cincinnatti, 1870.

8. *Twenty-Third Annual Report* of the Cincinnati Chamber of Commerce and Merchants' Exchange for the Fiscal Year Ending August 31, 1871. Gazettee Company, Printers. Cincinnati. 1871.

9. *Twenty-Fourth Annual Report* of the Cincinnati Chamber of Commerce and Merchants' Exchange for the Fiscal Year August 31, 1872. Cincinnati Steam Book and Job Printing Establishment. Cincinnati. 1872.

10. *Twenty-Fifth Annual Report* of the Cincinnati Chamber of Commerce and Merchants' Exchange for the Commercial Year Ending August 31, 1873. Times Steam Book and Job Printing Establishment. Cincinnati. 1873.

11. *Twenty-Sixth Annual Report* of the Cincinnati Chamber of Commerce and Merchants' Exchange for the Year Ending August 31, 1874. Cincinnati Gazettee Steam Book and Job Printing Company. Cincinnati. 1874.

12. *Twenty-Seventh Annual Report* of the Cincinnati Chamber of Commerce and Merchants' Exchange for the Commercial Year Ending August 31, 1875. Cincinnati Gazettee Steam Book and Job Printing Establishment. Cincinnati. 1875.

Union Merchants' Exchange (St. Louis)

1. *Annual Statement* of the Trade and Commerce of St. Louis for the Year 1865, Reported to the Union Merchants' Exchange. H. P. Studley and Co., St. Louis. 1866.

2. *Annual Statement* of the Trade and Commerce of St. Louis for the Year 1866, Reported to the Union Merchants' Exchange. H. P. Studley and Co., St. Louis. 1867.

3. *Annual Statement* of the Trade and Commerce of St. Louis for the Year 1867, Reported to the Union Merchants' Exchange. R. P. Studley and Co., Printers. St. Louis. 1868.

4. *Annual Statement* of the Trade and Commerce of St. Louis for the Year 1868, Reported to the Union Merchants' Exchange. R. P. Studley and Co., Printers. St. Louis. 1869.

5. *Annual Statement* of the Trade and Commerce of St. Louis for the Year 1870, Reported to the Union Merchants' Exchange. R. P. Studley and Co., Printers. St. Louis. 1871.

6. *Annual Statement* of the Trade and Commerce of St. Louis for the Year 1871, Reported to the Union Merchants' Exchange. R. P. Studley and Co., St. Louis. 1874.

7. *Annual Statement* of the Trade and Commerce of St. Louis for the Year 1872, Reported to the Union Merchants' Exchange. R. P. Studley and Co., Printers. St. Louis. 1873.

8. *Annual Statement* of the Trade and Commerce of St. Louis for the Year 1873, Reported to the Union Merchants' Exchange. R. P. Studley and Co. St. Louis. 1874.

9. *Annual Statement* of the Trade and Commerce of St. Louis for the Year 1874, Reported to the Union Merchants' Exchange. R. P. Studley and Co., Printers. St. Louis. 1875.

10. *Annual Statement* of the Trade and Commerce of St. Louis for the Year 1875, Reported to the Union Merchants' Exchange. R. P. Studley and Co., Printers. St. Louis. 1876.

11. *Annual Statement* of the Trade and Commerce of St. Louis for the Year 1876, Reported to the Union Merchants' Exchange. R. P. Studley and Co., Printers. St. Louis. 1877.

12. *Annual Statement* of the Trade and Commerce of St. Louis for the Year 1877, Reported to the Union Merchants' Exchange. R. P. Studley and Co., Printers. St. Louis. 1878.

13. *Annual Statement* of the Trade and Commerce of St. Louis for the Year 1878, Reported to the Union Merchants' Exchange. R. P. Studley and Co., Printers. St. Louis. 1879.

14. *Annual Statement* of the Trade and Commerce of St. Louis for the Year 1879, Reported to the Union Merchants' Exchange. R. P. Studley and Co., Printers. St. Louis. 1880.

15. *Annual Statement* of the Trade and Commerce of St. Louis for the Year 1880, Reported to the Union Merchants' Exchange. R. P. Studley and Co., Printers. St. Louis. 1881.

Louisville Board of Trade

1. *Annual Review* of the Trade and Commerce of Louisville for the Year Ending March 31, 1866. Supplement to the Louisville Letter Sheet Price-Current. Louisville. 1866.

2. *Annual Report* of the Board of Trade and Merchants' Exchange of the Commerce and Trade of Louisville for the

Year Ending March 31, 1867. Louisville Steam Printing
Establishment. Louisville. 1867.

3. *Annual Report* of the Board of Trade and Merchants' Exchange of the Commerce and Trade of Louisville for the
Year Ending March 31, 1869. Courier—Journal Job Department. Louisville. 1869.

4. *First Annual Report* of the Louisville Board of Trade for the
Year Ending December 31, 1879. Courier Book—Journal and
Jobs Room Print. Louisville, 1880.

5. *Second Annual Report* of the Louisville Board of Trade for
the Year Ending December 31, 1880. Courier Book—Journal
and Job Room Print. Louisville, 1881.

6. *Louisville Fifty Years Ago:* A Souvenir issued on the Occasion
of the Louisville Board of Trade Luncheon on March 9 in
Honor of Firms that have been in Business Fifty Years or
More, 1873-1923 (Louisville, 1923).

Chicago Board of Trade

1. *Eighth Annual Statement* of the Trade and Commerce of
Chicago for the Year Ending March 31, 1866. Reported to
the Chicago Board of Trade (Chicago, 1866).

2. *Tenth Annual Statement* of the Trade and Commerce of
Chicago for the Year Ending March 31, 1868. Reported to
the Chicago Board of Trade (Chicago, 1868).

Commercial Conventions

1. *Proceedings* of the National Commercial Convention Held in
Boston, February, 1868 (Boston, 1869).

2. *Minutes of the Proceedings* of the Commercial Convention
Held in the City of Memphis, Tennessee, May, 1869 (Memphis, 1869).

3. *Proceedings* of the Commercial Convention held in Detroit
July 11-14, 1865 (Detroit, 1865).

The National Board of Trade

1. *Proceedings* of the First Meeting of the National Board of
Trade Held in Philadelphia, 1868. J. H. Eastburn's Press.
Boston. 1868.

2. *Proceedings* of the First Annual Meeting of the National Board of Trade Held in Cincinnati, December, 1868. J.H. Eastburn's Press. Boston. 1869.

3. *Proceedings* of the Second Annual Meeting of the National Board of Trade Held in Richmond, December, 1869. Barker, Cotter, and Company, Printers. Boston. 1870.

4. *Proceedings* of the Third Annual Meeting of the National Board of Trade Held in Buffalo, December, 1870. Boston. 1871.

5. *Proceedings* of the Fourth Annual Meeting of the National Board of Trade Held in St. Louis 1871, December. Barker, Cotter and Company, Printers. Boston. 1872.

6. *Proceedings* of the Fifth Annual Meeting of the National Board of Trade Held in New York, October, 1872. James F. Cotter and Company, Printers. Boston. 1873.

7. *Proceedings* of the Adjourned Meeting of the National Board of Trade Held in Baltimore, January, 1874. Knight and Leonard, Printers. Chicago. 1874.

8. *Proceedings* of the Seventh Annual Meeting of the National Board of Trade Held in Philadelphia, June, 1875. Knight and Leonard, Printers. Chicago. 1875.

9. *Proceedings* of the Eighth Annual Meeting of the National Board of Trade Held in New York, June, 1876. Knight and Leonard, Printers. Chicago. 1876.

10. *Proceedings* of the Ninth Annual Meeting of the National Board of Trade Held in Milwaukee, August, 1877. Knight and Leonard, Printers. Chicago. 1877.

11. *Proceedings* of the Tenth Annual Meeting of the National Board of Trade Held in Washington, December, 1879. Tolman and White, Printers. (Boston, 1880).

12. *Proceedings* of the Eleventh Annual Meeting of the National Board of Trade Held in Washington, 1880. Tolman and White, Printers. Boston. 1881.

PAMPHLETS AND RECORDS

Railroads

1. Allen, Thomas, *To the Stock-holders and Bond-holders of the St. Louis, Iron Mountain and Southern Railway Company* (St. Louis, October 20, 1877).

2. *Annual Report* of the President and Directors of the Louisville and Nashville Railroad Company commencing on the 1st of July, 1865 and Ending on the 30th of June, 1866 (Louisville, 1866).

3. *Annual Report* of the President and Directors of the Louisville and Nashville Railroad Company commencing on the 1st of July, 1869 and Ending on the 30th of June, 1870 (Louisville, 1870).

4. Baxter, Jere. *Louisville and Nashville Monopoly, Its Method. and Purposes Exposed* (Probable date, 1893).

5. *Cincinnati Southern Railway:* Memorial of Trustees and Speech of the Hon. John C. Breckenridge to the General Assembly of Kentucky and the Proceedings of the Lexington Railroad (1871).

6. *Cincinnati Southern Railway, The Ferguson Railway Act, Views of the Press, Address of Committees, Action of the Board of Trade and Chamber of Commerce, Record of the Case and Opinion of the Superior Court of Cincinnati, and The Supreme Court of Ohio Thereon* (Cincinnati, 1872).

7. Cincinnati Southern Railroad Banquet Letters, March 18 1880, MSS. in the Ohio Philosophical and Historical Society Collection, Cincinnati, Ohio.

8. Cincinnati Trade List, *A Brief History of the Inaugura. Excursion and Banquet* (March 18, 1880).

9. *Charter of the Louisville and Nashville Railroad Company with Amendments to 1869,* Together with the General Railroad Laws of the State of Kentucky and Tennessee.

10. Goodin, Samuel H., *Plan for the Construction of the Direc. Railroad South, Connecting Cincinnati with the Southern System of Railroads* (1868).

11. Gunn, W. A. *Surveys of the Cincinnati Southern Railway. Preliminary Report of the Chief Engineer* (March, 1873).

12. *Inaugural Excursion and Banquet Celebrating the Opening o. the Cincinnati Southern Railway Connecting Cincinnati and Chattanooga, March 18, 1880* (Cincinnati, 1880).

13. Laws of Ohio, Kentucky and Tennessee authorizing the Construction of the Cincinnati Southern Railway (Cincinnati, 1881).

14. Mohn, Charles, *The Lands of the L. & N. Railroad in Alabama as Homesteads for the Settlers* (Roberts & Son, Printers, 1884).

15. *Organization and Charter of the Southern Railway Security Company* (December 4, 1871).
16. *The Case of the Union Trust Company Against the St. Louis, Iron Mountain and Southern Railway.* Important decision by Justice Miller, Concurred in by Justice Dillon (1878).

PAMPHLETS

General

1. Atkinson, Edward, *On the Collection of Revenue.* Read before the American Social Science Association in Boston, January, 1867 (Boston, 1867).
2. Baldwin, William H., *Traveling Salesmen:* An Address Delivered before the Boston Young Men's Christian Union, November 22, 1874.
3. Bigelow, Erastus B., *The Tariff Question Considered in Regard to the Policy of England and the Interest of the United States* (Boston, 1862).
4. Carey, Henry C., *Reconstruction, Industrial, Financial, and Political: Letters to the Honorable Henry Wilson, Senator from Massachusetts* (Philadelphia, 1867).
5. Colwell, Stephen, *The Five Cotton States and New York* (Philadelphia, 1861).
6. Elstner, J. M. & Company, *The Industries of St. Louis; Her Advantages, Resources, Facilities, and Commercial Relations as a Center of Trade and Manufacture, Together with a Delineation of Representative Industrial and Commercial Establishments* (St. Louis, 1885).
7. Kettle, Thomas P., *Southern Wealth and Northern Profits* (New York, 1860).
8. Lord, Daniel, *The Effect of Secession Upon the Commercial Relations Between the North and the South, and Upon Each Section* (London, 1861).
9. Powell, Samuel, *Notes on Southern Wealth and Northern Profits* (Philadelphia, 1861).
10. Reavis, L. U., *A Change of the National Empire: An Argument in Favor of the Removal of the National Capital From Washington City to the Mississippi Valley* (St. Louis, 1869).
11. Stille, Charles J., *Northern Interest and Southern Independence* (Philadelphia, 1863).
12. Trenholm, W. L., *The Centennial Address before the Charleston Chamber of Commerce,* 11th of February, 1884 (Charleston, 1884).

MISCELLANEOUS BOOKS

1. Andrews, Sidney, *The South Since the War as Shown by Fourteen Weeks of Travel and Observation in Georgia and the Carolinas 1865* (Boston, 1866).
2. Bently, Richard, *Two Months in the Confederate States* (London, 1863).
3. Brackett, L. P., *The Commercial Travelers' Guide Book* (New York, 1871).
4. Dodd, A. S., et al., *Descriptive Handbook and Abstract of the Advantages, Privileges and Franchises of the Commercial Travelers' National Association* (New York, 1872).
5. Ellison, Thomas, *A Handbook of the Cotton Trade* (London, 1863).
6. Fainsod, Merle & Lincoln Gordon, *Government and the American Economy* (New York, 1941).
7. Guthrie, Edwin, *The Cotton Trade: Its Condition and Prospects* (Manchester, 1883).
8. King, Edward, *The Southern States of North America: Journey Through Louisiana, Texas, Indian Territory, Missouri, Arkansas, Mississippi, Alabama, Georgia, Florida, South Carolina, North Carolina, Kentucky, Tennessee, Virginia, West Virginia, and Maryland* (London, 1875).
9. Marshall, George L., *O'er Rail and Crossties with Gripsack* (New York, 1891).
10. McHenry, George, *The Cotton Trade: Its Bearing Upon the Prosperity of Great Britain and the Commerce of the American Republics* (London, 1863).
11. McPherson, Edward, *A Political Manual for 1867* (Washington, D. C., 1867).
12. Parmele, George H., and M. B. Wiles, *Law Reports Annotated*. Vol. 60 (Rochester, N. W., 1929).
13. Peto, Sir Samuel M., Bart., M. P. for Bristol, *The Resources and Prospects of America Ascertained During a Visit to the States in Autumn 1866* (London, 1866).
14. Simons, M. L. ed., *Cyclopedia of American Literature*, Vol. II (Philadelphia, 1875).
15. *The Encyclopedia Britannica.*
16. *The New International Yearbook, 1910.*

Index

DATE DUE

9/2/94			
SEP 27 1999			
GAYLORD			PRINTED IN U.S.A.